Programming with Python
and its Applications to Physical Systems

Programming with Python
and its Applications to Physical Systems

Dr. M. Shubhakanta Singh
Department of Physics
Manipur University, Canchipur
Imphal, Manipur-795003

CRC Press
Taylor & Francis Group
Boca Raton London New York

CRC Press is an imprint of the
Taylor & Francis Group, an **informa** business

Manakin
PRESS

First published 2024
by CRC Press
4 Park Square, Milton Park, Abingdon, Oxon, OX14 4RN

and by CRC Press
2385 NW Executive Center Drive, Suite 320, Boca Raton FL 33431

© 2024 Manakin Press

CRC Press is an imprint of Informa UK Limited

The right of M. Shubhakanta Singh to be identified as author of this work has been asserted in accordance with sections 77 and 78 of the Copyright, Designs and Patents Act 1988.

Print edition not for sale in South Asia (India, Sri Lanka, Nepal, Bangladesh, Pakistan or Bhutan).

ISBN13: 9781032591667 (hbk)
ISBN13: 9781032591674 (pbk)
ISBN13: 9781003453307 (ebk)

DOI: 10.4324/9781003453307

Typeset in Times New Roman
by Manakin Press, Delhi

Manakin
PRESS

Dedicated

to

My Parents and Teachers

Brief Contents

Detailed Contents

Preface

This book is aimed at students with little or no prior knowledge of programming languages. However, several different audiences, including self-taught and hobbyist programmers, scientists, engineers, computing professionals and computer scientists and others who need to program part of their work, may use this book for understanding the basic concepts of Python. The fundamentals of programming and problem solving are the same regardless of which programming language is being used. Once programming in one language is mastered, it is easy to pick up other languages, because the basic techniques for writing programs are the same. The advantage of learning Python is that it is easy to learn, coding is simple, short, easily readable and very powerful. Thus, it is effective for introducing computing and problem solving to beginners.

Python is used to teach programming to complete beginners and at the same time widely used for system administration tasks. The US National Aeronautics and Space Administration (NASA) uses Python both for development and as a scripting language in several of its systems. Yahoo! uses it to manage its discussion groups. Google has used it to implement many components of its web crawler and search engine. It is also being used in such diverse areas such as computer games and bioinformatics.

The goal of this book is to help the learner become a skillful programmer well versed in making productive use of computational techniques. It covers the basic concepts of Python programming and Computational problem solving techniques with a wide variety of interesting examples and exercises. The best way to learn programming is by practicing the examples. Many objective and descriptive type questions with answers are given in Appendixes to test your knowledge of Python.

This book primarily focuses on Python 2.7, although the basic differences with Python 3.0 are highlighted and pointed out wherever it is needed.

Organization of this book:

The first part of the book is a preparation to embark on the journey of learning programming.

Chapter 1 presents the basics of programming languages, algorithms (the steps of sequences) and flowcharts (the pictorial representations of the algorithms) to understand the steps/concepts before starting to write programs with Python. It also explains how to install Python in different operating systems.

Chapter 2 introduces Python's programming features, including its reserve keywords, identifiers, basic data types and important usages of backslash character constants.

Chapter 3 presents the Python's operators, constants, assignments, and expressions. It also explains how to use comments in Python and difference between interactive mode and script mode in Python.

Chapter 4 shows how to read data from keyboard as input and display the processed data on the screen. The two powerful functions `raw_input()` and `input()` are explained with examples. Many functions for showing good appearance and clarity of the outputs are discussed with examples.

Chapter 5 introduces the concepts of decision making and branching, which enable changing of the order of execution of statements based on certain conditions.

Chapter 6 introduces the concepts of decision making and looping, also known as control structures, enabling to execute a program segment repeatedly based on certain conditions.

Chapter 7 presents the fundamental programming techniques with built-in-functions, user defined functions, Boolean functions, recursion functions and default arguments with examples.

Chapter 8 introduces Python's new concept of List which can handle large number of variables or arrays and subscripted variables. The basics of how to create a list and many common operations of list that are frequently used are explained in detail with examples.

Chapter 9 shows Python's Dictionary which enables fast retrieval, deletion and updating of the values by using the keys. The basics of how to create a dictionary, a set and common operations that are frequently used are explained with examples.

Chapter 10 presents Tuples including its important properties and common operations that are frequently used are explained in detail.

Chapter 11 introduces the concept of Files which is very necessary to have more flexible approach where data can be stored on the disks and read whenever necessary, without destroying the data. The important file operations which include naming, opening, reading, writing and closing a file are explained with examples.

Chapter 12 shows the applications of Python in physical systems. This chapter gives a brief introduction to Computational Physics and how it can be used in solving simple to complex physical systems with specific Python implementation.

Python's Graphical User Interfaces, Database, Interfacing the Web, Packaging Programs, Turtle graphics, Ktinkers, Mathplotlib, Numpy, Pylab and Scilab will be covered in the second volume of this book which will help all advance learners.

M. Shubhakanta Singh

Acknowledgement

It is with a deep sense of gratitude that I wish to express my indebtedness to Prof. Sumitra Phanjoubam, HOD, Department of Physics, Manipur University whose encouragement, guidance and support from the initial stage to the final level enabled me to complete this book. She managed her busy schedule to find the time to read almost the entire book with great care. She found out numerous errors and pointed out places where necessary explanations were missing.

My sincere thanks are due to Prof. Sanasam Brajamani Singh, Department of Physics, Manipur University who introduced me to Python Programming. The valuable discussions I had with him are gratefully acknowledged.

I am heartily thankful to Prof. Homendra Naorem, HOD, Department of Chemistry, Manipur University for his valuable suggestions.

Teaching M.Sc.(Physics) and MCA are the source of inspiration for this book. I would like to thank Department of Physics, Manipur University for enabling me to teach what I write and for supporting me in writing what I teach. I am grateful to my students who have offered comments, bug reports and suggestions.

I would like to thank Department of Computer Science, Manipur University for providing the necessary facilities to complete this book.

My deep sense of gratitude is also due to E. Balagurusamy, famous author of C, C++ and many such books, whose style of writing and presentation have always inspired me author a book someday.

It is a great pleasure, honor, and privilege to work with Manakin Press. I am grateful to K.L. Sharma for introducing me to Manakin Press and would like to thank Nishant Saini, Production Manager and his colleagues for organizing, producing, and promoting this book.

Last but not the least, my thanks and indeptedness goes to my family, especially my wife, R. K. Sanjeeta Devi, without their understanding and support this book would not have materialized. Further, I would like to offer my regards and well wishes to all those who supported me in any respect during the completion of this work.

M. Shubhakanta Singh

Introduction

This chapter presents the basics of programming languages, tools and procedures. Some worked out examples are given to enhance the understanding. The chapter then discusses the attraction of Python as an excellent programming language and how to install it in different operating systems. A brief idea about different Python distributions is also included.

1.1 WHAT IS A COMPUTER?

A computer is an electronic device that stores and processes data. Broadly it is classified into hardware and software. In general, hardware comprises the visible, physical elements of the computer, and software provides the invisible instructions that control the hardware and make it perform specific tasks.

A computer's storage capacity is measured in bytes, defined as follows:

One Byte = 8 bits

One kilobyte (KB) = 1024 bytes

One megabyte (MB) = 1024 kilobytes = 1024 × 1024 bytes

One gigabyte (GB) = 1024 megabytes = 1024 × 1024 × 1024 bytes

One terabyte (TB) = 1024 × 1024 × 1024 × 1024 bytes.

If a word document takes about 50 KB, imagine how many documents can be stored in a 1 GB memory space. Suppose a typical movie occupy about 700 MB, then we can store thousands of movies in 1TB space.

1.2 BASICS OF PROGRAMMING LANGUAGES

The programmer communicates with a machine using programming languages. There are many different classifications of programming languages and these programming languages differ in their closeness to the machine and in the way they are structured. Most of the programs have a highly structured set of rules. The primary classifications of programming languages are:

1. Machine Language

2. Assembly Language and

3. High level languages.

1.2.1 Machine Language

In machine language, instructions are coded as a series of ones and zeroes. Each computer has only one programming language which does not need a translating program – the machine language. Machine language programs, the first generation programs, are written at the most basic level of computer operations. Because their instructions are directed at this basic level of operation, machine language and assembly language are collectively called low-level language. The machine language programs are cumbersome and difficult to write. The machine language is native to that machine and understood directly by the machine. The machine language generally has two parts:

opcoded	operand

The **opcode** of the machine language tells what function to perform to the computer. The **operand** gives the data on which the operation has to be performed or the location where the data can be found. Machine language is a set of built-in primitive instructions. These instructions are in the form of binary code. For example the character **A** is equivalent to **01000001** in binary code.

Advantages and Disadvantages

As the machine inherently understands machine instructions, machine languages are very fast. However, they suffer major disadvantages

1. **Difficult to program.** Programming in machine language is the most difficult kind of programming. Instructions should be encoded as a sequence of incomprehensible 0's and 1's which is very difficult.

2. **Error-prone.** In machine language, the programmer has to look into all the activities like memory management, instruction cycle, etc., which diverts his attention from the actual logic of the program. This frequently leads to errors.

3. **Machine dependent.** Every computer is different from one another in its architecture. Hence, instructions of one machine will be different from the other.

1.2.2 Assembly Language

Programs written in machine language are very difficult to read and modify. A set of instructions for an assembly language is essentially one-to-one with those of machine language. Assembly language uses a short descriptive word, known as *mnemonic*, to represent each of the machine language instructions. Like machine language, assembly languages are unique to a computer, to represent instructions. For example, the mnemonic add typically means to add numbers and sub means to subtract numbers. To add the numbers **5** and **6** and get the result, we may write an instruction in assembly code like this:

```
add 5, 6, result
```

Machine language and assembly language are low-level languages which are dependent on particular machine architecture. Assembly languages were developed to make programming easier. However, because the computer cannot understand assembly language directly, another program—called an *assembler*—is used to translate assembly-language programs into machine code, as shown in Fig. 1.1.

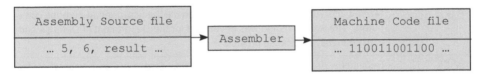

Fig. 1.1 An assembler translates assembly-language instructions into machine code.

Writing code in assembly language is easier than in machine language. However, it is still difficult to write code in assembly language. An instruction in assembly language essentially corresponds to an instruction in machine code.

1.2.3 High Level Languages

High-level languages are English-like language and easy to learn and use. The instructions in a high-level programming language are called *statements*. High level languages are more close to the programmer and ease the task of programming. Here, for example, is a high-level language statement that computes the area of a circle with a radius of **3**:

```
area = 3.1415 * 3 * 3
```

Some of the popular high-level programming languages are listed in Table 1.1.

Advantages of High Level Languages

The popularity of high-level languages is attributed to the following advantages:

Easier to program. The programmer can concentrate on the logic of the program rather than on the registers, ports and memory storage.

Machine-independent. Provided some other machine has the same compiler and libraries, the program can be ported across various platforms.

Easy maintenance. A program in a high-level language is easier to maintain than assembly language because it is easier to code and locate bugs in high-level languages.

Easy to learn. The learning curve for high-level languages is relatively smooth compared to low-level languages.

Other than this, high-level languages are more flexible and can be easily documented.

Table 1.1: Examples of High-level Programming Languages

Ada	Named after Ada Lovelace, who worked on mechanical general-purpose computers. The Ada language was developed for the Department of Defense and is used mainly in defense projects.
BASIC	Beginner's All-purpose Symbolic Instruction Code. It was designed to be learned and used easily by beginners.
C	Developed at Bell Laboratories. C combines the power of an assembly language with the ease of use and portability of a high-level language.
C++	C++ is an object-oriented language, based on C.
C#	Pronounced "C Sharp." It is a hybrid of Java and C++ and was developed by Microsoft.
COBOL	COmmon Business Oriented Language. Used for business applications.
FORTRAN	FORmula TRANslation. Popular for scientific and mathematical applications.
Java	Developed by Sun Microsystems, now part of Oracle. It is widely used for developing platform-independent Internet applications.
Pascal	Named after Blaise Pascal, who pioneered calculating machines in the seventeenth century. It is a simple, structured, general-purpose language primarily for teaching programming.
Python	A simple general-purpose scripting language good for writing short programs.
Visual Basic	Visual Basic was developed by Microsoft and it enables the programmers to rapidly develop Windows-based applications.

1.3 INTERPRETER AND COMPILER

A program written in a high-level language is called a *source code* or *source program*. Because a computer cannot understand a source program, a source program must be translated into machine code for execution. The translation can be done using another programming tool called an *interpreter* or a *compiler*.

- An interpreter reads one statement from the source code, translates it to the machine code or virtual machine code, and then executes it right away, as shown in Fig. 1.2. One statement from the source code may be translated into several machine instructions.

- A compiler translates the entire source code into a machine-code file, and the machine code file is then executed, as shown in Fig. 1.3.

Python code is executed using an interpreter. Other programming languages like C, C++ are processed using a compiler. Java used both interpreter and compiler.

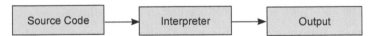

Fig. 1.2 An interpreter processes the program a line at a time.

Fig. 1.3 A compiler translates source code into object code at one go, which is run by a hardware executor.

Python is considered an interpreted language because Python programs are executed by an interpreter. There are two ways to use the interpreter: **interactive mode** and **script mode**.

In interactive mode, we type Python programs and the interpreter displays the result:

```
>>> 2 + 2
4
```

The chevron, >>>, is the **prompt** the interpreter uses to indicate that it is ready.

Alternatively, we can store code in a file and use the interpreter to execute the contents of the file, which is called a **script**. By convention, Python scripts have names that end with .py.

Working in interactive mode is convenient for testing small pieces of code because we can type and execute them immediately. But for anything more than a few lines, we should save our code as a script so that we can modify and execute it in the future.

Note: A **program** is a sequence of instructions that specifies how to perform a computation. The computation might be something mathematical, such as solving a system of equations or finding the roots of a polynomial, but it can also be a symbolic computation, such as searching and replacing text in a document.

1.4 ALGORITHMS AND FLOWCHARTS

An algorithm is a set of computational procedures which take some value or a set of values as input and produce some value or a set of values as output in a finite amount of time. An algorithm should have the following characteristics:

Finiteness: an algorithm must always terminate after a finite number of steps.

Definiteness : Each and every step of the algorithm should be rigorously and unambiguously defined.

Input : The algorithm should take zero or more inputs.

Output : The algorithm should produce one or more outputs.

Effectiveness: We should be able to calculate the values involved in the procedure of the algorithm manually.

1.4.1 Writing Algorithms

Writing algorithm is an art. Each and every step of the algorithm needs to be unambiguous and it should be able to explain to the point. The language used to write algorithms should be simple and precise. And the explanation should not convey two meanings to the reader.

1.4.2 Flowcharts

A flowchart is a pictorial representation of an algorithm. A flowchart is drawn using the following notations.

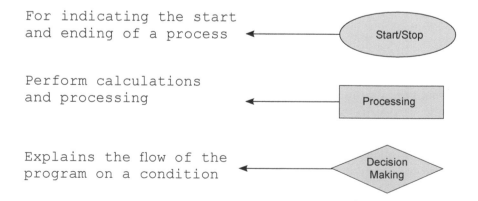

```
For indicating the start
and ending of a process          ◄────────────   Start/Stop

Perform calculations
and processing                   ◄────────────   Processing

Explains the flow of the                         Decision
program on a condition           ◄────────────   Making
```

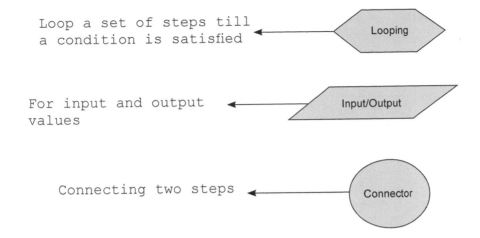

Loop a set of steps till a condition is satisfied — Looping

For input and output values — Input/Output

Connecting two steps — Connector

1.5 WRITING ALGORITHMS AND FLOWCHARTS FOR A FEW IMPORTANT PROBLEMS

1.5.1 Reversing the Digits of a Given Integer

In this problem, we are given a number, say 12345, the algorithm should convert this number to 54321. The algorithm and flowchart for solving this problem is shown in Fig. 1.4.

The reverse of an integer number is obtained by successively dividing the integer by 10 and accumulating the remainders till the quotient becomes less than 10.

Algorithm:

Step 1 : Start.

Step 2 : Read the integer n to be reversed.

Step 3 : Initialize "Reverse" to zero.

Step 4 : Write 'n' is greater than 0, do the following steps.

    (*a*) Divide the integer n by 10 to get the remainder

    (*b*) Store the quotient to n

    (*c*) Multiply 10 to the already existing value of "Reverse".

    (*d*) Add the remainder to the value of "Reverse".

Step 5 : Print the value of "Reverse".

Step 6 : Stop.

Flowchart:

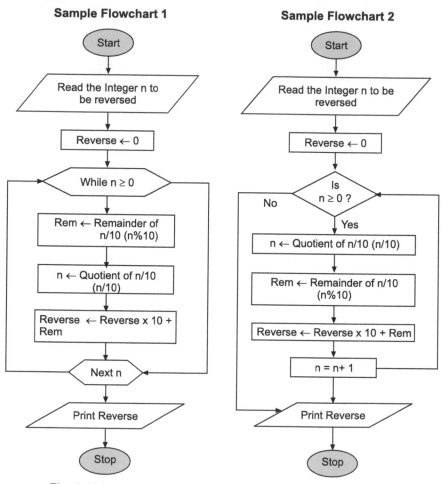

Fig. 1.4(a) Using loop.   Fig. 1.4(b) Without using loop.

1.5.2 To Verify Whether an Integer is a Prime Number or Not

Algorithm:

Step 1 : Start.

Step 2 : Read the number n which we want to verify the prime or not.

Step 3 : Check the number is negative or less than 2.

Step 4 : Initialize the value of the divisor i as 3.

Step 5 : Repeat the following steps till i less than or equal to square root of n, (or) the remainder of the divisor is zero.

(*i*) divide n by *i*

(*ii*) if remainder is zero, then print the no is not prime and exit the process.

Step 6 : If none of the remainder are zero, print n is a prime no.

Step 7 : Stop.

Flowchart:

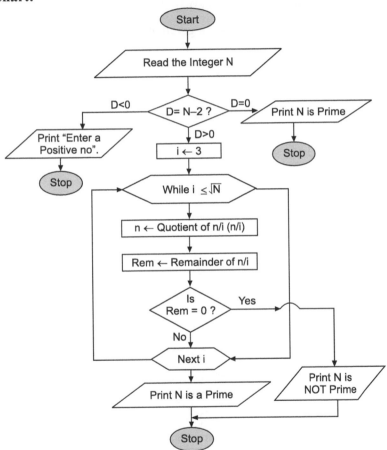

Analysis: Prime number is an integer which is exactly divisible by 1 and the number itself. For example, 37 is a prime number because 1 and 37 are the only two factors of 37.

To verify whether a number is prime or not, divide the number by 2 to $\sqrt{37} \approx 6$. If the remainder is zero in any of the cases, then the number is not prime. Now divide 37 by 2, 3, 4, 5 and 6. None of the division operation gives a remainder of zero. Hence, 37 is a prime number.

1.5.3 To Organize a given Set of Numbers in Ascending Order

Algorithm:

Step 1 : Start.

Step 2 : Read the array of the number 'n' of umbers.

Step 3 : Repeat the following steps till (*i*) is less than '*n*'

        (*i*) find the smallest no. (Swapping)

        (*ii*) increment for next number

Step 4 : Repeat the "step 3" until the given array is sorted.

Step 5 : Print the array.

Step 6 : Stop.

Flowchart:

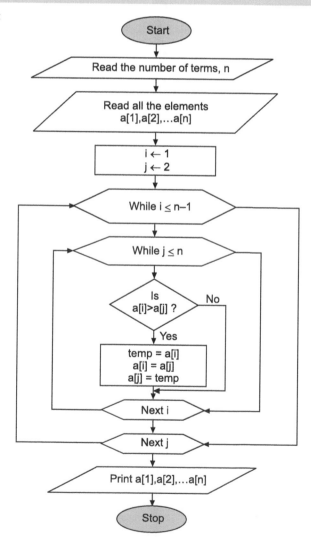

Analysis: The processing of organizing a given set of values in ascending/ descending order is called sorting. There are different methods for sorting algorithms; here we are using selection sort technique. This method involves identifying the smallest number in the array of numbers and placing it in the top of the list. Then the second smaller number is identified and placed second in the list. This process continues for the given array of numbers.

The algorithm shown above does not explain the detail of the sorting technique we used in the flowchart. In this flowchart we explained in detail the concept of selection sorting method.

1.5.4 To Find the Square Root of an Integer

Algorithm:

Step 1 :   Start.

Step 2 :   Read the integer n for which the square root has to be found.

Step 3 :   Pair the digits of *n* from the right side and group them using bars.

Step 4 :   Find the square root of the number which is less than or equal to the first pair.

Step 5 :   Place the square root in the divisor and the no. below the first pair. The divisor is put as quotient.

Step 6 :   Subtract the first pairs and bring down the next pair of digits.

Step 7 :   Double the quotient and put a blank digit to the right of the doubled quotient.

Step 8 :   Guess the digit such that multiplying the no. formed with the digit and the digit itself yields a product less than or equal to the formed divided.

Step 9 :   Repeat 6, 7 and 8 till there are no more digits to be brought down.

Step 10 : The quotient is the square root of *n*.

Step 11 : Stop.

Flowchart:

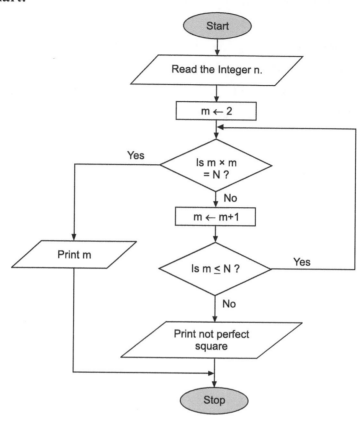

Analysis: If m is a square root of a number, n, then it can be derived as

$$m * m = n$$

and symbolically it can be denoted by:

$$\sqrt{n} = m$$

There are two ways of finding the square root of a number. The first one is the trial and error method where we can zero upon the square root by multiplying different numbers to itself and deciding on the number which produces the nearest number. It is shown in this flow chart.

1.5.5 To Find the Factorial for a Given Number

Algorithm:

Step 1 : Start.

Step 2 : Read the value 'n' for which factorial has to be evaluated.

Step 3 : Initialize i to 1.

Step 4 : Initialize fact to 1.

Step 5 : Repeat the following steps till '*i*' is less than or equal to '*n*'.

      (*a*) Calculate fact = fact * *i*

      (*b*) Increment *i* by 1.

Step 6 : Print the value of fact.

Step 7 : Stop.

Flowchart:

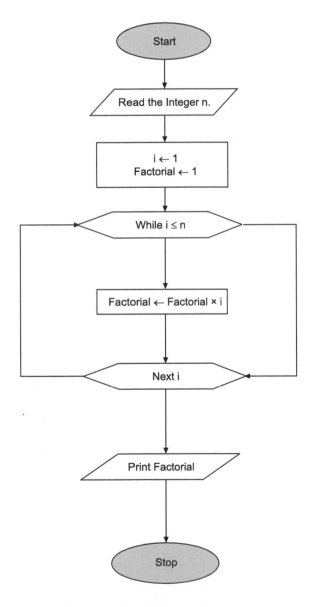

Analysis:

Factorial of a given number is the product of numbers from 1 to that number, say n. It can be found out by multiplying all the numbers from 1 to that number for which factorial has to be found out, *i.e*,

$$n! = 1 * 2 * 3 \ldots *(n-1) * n$$

where n is a positive integer.

Example: Consider $n = 5$

> Factorial of 1 = 1
>
> Factorial of 2 = 1 * 2 = 2
>
> Factorial of 3 = 1 * 2 * 3 = 6
>
> > = factorial of 2 *3
>
> Factorial of 5 = 1 * 2 * 3 * 4 * 5
>
> > = factorial of 4 * 5
>
> > = 120

Hence   5! = 120

1.5.6 To Generate the Fibonacci Series for n Terms

Algorithm :

Step 1 : Start.

Step 2 : Read the number of terms 'n'.

Step 3 : Initialized First_term to 0, Second_term to 1 and Third_term to 0.

Step 4 : Initialized i to 3.

Step 5 : Print First_term and Second_term as a part of the Fibonacci Series.

Step 5 : Repeat the following steps till 'i' is less than or equal to 'n'.

> (*a*) Calculate Third_term = First_term + Second_term
>
> (*b*) Print Third_term as a part of the Fibonacci Series.
>
> (*c*) Assign Second_term to First_term.
>
> (*d*) Assign Third_term to Second_term.
>
> (*e*) Increment i by 1.

Step 6 : Stop.

Flowchart:

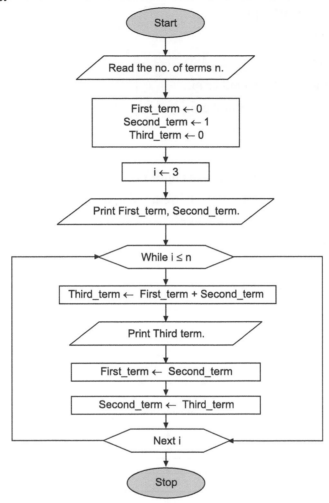

Analysis: In a Fibonacci sequence, the last two numbers are added to generate the sequence. The initial first two digited are taken as 0 and 1.

Let us generate a Fibonacci sequence for 8 terms:

First_term, $f_1 = 0$

Second_term, $f_2 = 1$

Third_term, $f_3 = f_1 + f_2 = 0 + 1 = 1$

Proceeding in this way:

$$f_4 = f_2 + f_3 = 1 + 1 = 2$$
$$f_5 = f_3 + f_4 = 1 + 2 = 3$$
$$f_6 = f_4 + f_5 = 2 + 3 = 5$$
$$f_7 = f_5 + f_6 = 3 + 5 = 8$$
$$f_8 = f_6 + f_7 = 5 + 8 = 13 \text{ so on.}$$

1.5.7 To Find the Value of the Power of a Number Raised by Another Integer

Algorithm 1:

Step 1 : Start.

Step 2 : Read the Base number m.

Step 3 : Read the Power number n.

Step 4 : Initialized power to 1.

Step 5 : Initialized i to 1.

Step 6 : Repeat the following steps until i is less than or equal to n.

   (*a*) Update/multiply the current value of power with m.

   (*b*) Increment i by 1.

Step 7 : Print the value of power.

Step 8 : Stop.

Flowchart 1:

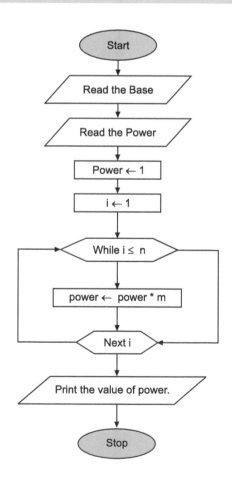

Analysis: Power of m raised by n (symbolically, m^n) means m is multiplied by itself n times.

For example: Let us consider a number: 10

$$10^4 = 10 * 10 * 10 * 10$$
$$= 10000$$

Another **Algorithm 2** which is given below with more options works for negative number and zero value also.

For example: $10^0 = 1$

$10^{-2} = 0.01$

Algorithm 2:

Step 1 : Start

Step 2 : Read the Base number m.

Step 3 : Read the Power number n.

Step 4 : Initialized power to 1.

Step 5 : Initialized i to 1.

Step 6 : Check the value of n.

    (*a*) If n is equal to zero :

        Go to Step 7.

    (*b*) If n is greater than zero :

        (*i*) Repeat the following steps until i is less than or equal to n.

        (*ii*) Update/multiply the current value of power with m.

        (*iii*) Increment i by 1.

        (*iv*) Go to Step 7.

    (*c*) If n is less than zero:

        (*i*) Repeat the following steps until i is less than or equal to n.

        (*ii*) Update/multiply the current value of power with $(1/m)$.

        (*iii*) Increment i by 1.

        (*iv*) Go to Step 7.

Step 7 : Print the value of power.

Step 8 : Stop.

Flowchart 2:

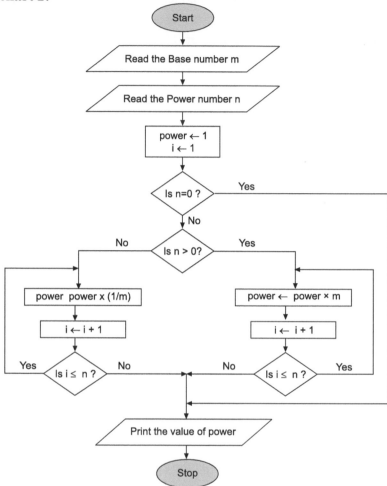

1.5.8 To Reverse the Order Elements of an Array
Algorithm:

Step 1 : Start.

Step 2 : Read the size of the array.

Step 3 : Read the array elements that has to be reversed a, e.g., $a_1, a_2, a_3,....$.

Step 4 : Initialized i to 1.

Step 5 : Repeat the following steps until i is less than $n/2$:

　　　　　(*i*) Swap $a[i]$ with $a[n-i+1]$.

　　　　　(*ii*) Increment i by 1.

Step 6 : Print the array.

Step 7 : Stop.

Analysis: Reversing an array is simply by swapping the first and the last element of the array. Swapping the second element and second last element of the array and so on.

For example: Let us consider an array of integers:

12	5	34	7	89

Reversing the elements, we get the new array (not sorting the elements),

89	7	34	5	12

Flowchart:

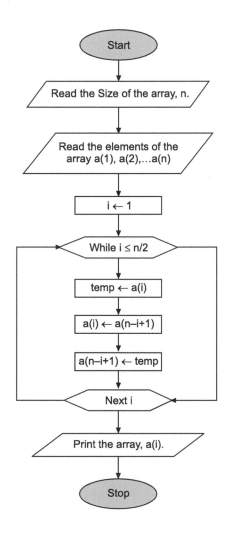

1.5.9 To Find the Largest Number in an Array

Algorithm:

Step 1 : Start.

Step 2 : Read the size of an array, *n*.

Step 3 : Read the elements of the array A.

Step 4 : Assign the value of A[1] to largest

(largest = A[1]).

Step 5 : Initialized *j* to 2.

Step 6 : Repeat the following steps until *j* is less than or equal to *n*.

(*i*) If A[*j*] is greater than the largest then assign the value of A[*j*] to largest.

(*ii*) Increment *j* by 1.

Step 7 : Print the value of largest.

Step 8 : Stop.

Flowchart:

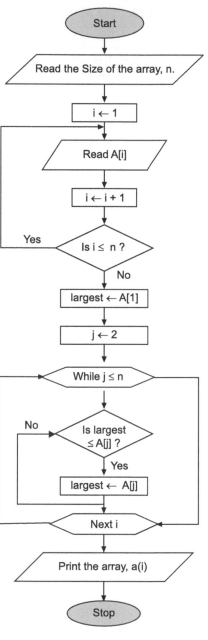

Analysis: To find the largest element in an array of *n* numbers can be done by comparing the elements of the array. Here we assume that the first element is the largest one. Compare it with the nest element. If it is greater than the next one, compare it with the next number. If it is not, make the next number as the largest number. Continue this process for the entire array.

For example:

25	6	7	78	99

Here we assign the largest element as = 25 (the first element). Compare it with the second element and so on. At last the largest element = 99.

1.5.10 To Solve a Quadratic Equation

Algorithm:

Step 1 : Start.

Step 2 : Read the values of a, b and c in the Equation $ax^2 + bx + c = 0$;

Step 3 : If $a = 0$ and $b = 0$, print No Root Exists and stop.

Step 4 : If $a = 0$ and $b \neq 0$ then calculate root as $-c/b$ and print it as a Linear Equation.

Step 5 : Compute Dino = square root of $(b^2 - 4ac)$

Step 6 : If D < 0, print the Roots are Imaginary and stop.

Step 7 : If D = 0, print the Roots are Real and Equal.

Step 8 : Calculate Root 1 (= Root 2) $\leftarrow (-b)/(2*a)$.

Step 9 : Print Root 1 and Root 2 and Stop.

Step 10 : If D > 0, print the Roots are Unequal.

Step 11 : Calculate Root 1 $\leftarrow (-b + \sqrt{\text{Dino}})/(2*a)$.

Step 12 : Calculate Root 2 $\leftarrow (-b - \sqrt{\text{Dino}})/(2*a)$.

Step 13 : Print Root 1 and Root 2 as roots of the Equation.

Step 14 : Stop.

Analysis: The roots of a quadratic equation can be found out using the formula:

$$x = \frac{-b \pm \sqrt{b^2 - 4ac}}{2a} \qquad \text{... (1)}$$

If $a = 0$ and $b = 0$, then there will be no root of the equation. And if $a = 0$ and $b \neq 0$, then $-c/b$ will be the root of the linear equation.

If $a \neq 0$ and $b \neq 0$, then we have to check the value of the $\sqrt{b^2 - 4ac} = $ D(say).

If D < 0, then the roots are imaginary

If D = 0, then the roots are equal roots and given by $\dfrac{-b}{2a}$

If D > = 0, then we can compute the roots using equation (1)

$$x_1 = \frac{-b + \sqrt{b^2 - 4ac}}{2a} \qquad x_2 = \frac{-b - \sqrt{b^2 - 4ac}}{2a}$$

The complete flowchart is shown below.

Flowchart:

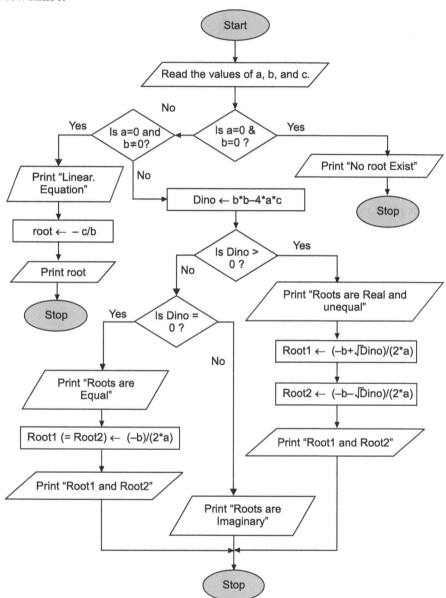

1.6 WHY PYTHON?

The first reason why Python is an excellent programming language is that it is **easy to learn**. If a language cannot help one become productive quite quickly, the attraction of that language is strongly reduced. It is not worth spending weeks or months studying a language before we are able to write a program that does something useful. However, a language that is easy to learn but does not allow us to do fairly complex tasks is not worth much either. With Python, we can start writing useful scripts that can accomplish complex tasks almost immediately.

The second reason we consider Python to be an excellent language is its **readability**. Python relies on whitespace (tabs) to determine where code blocks begin and end. The indentation helps the eyes quickly follow the flow of a program. Python also tends to be "word-based," meaning that while Python uses its share of special characters, features are often implemented as keywords or with libraries. The emphasis on words rather than special characters helps the reading and comprehension of code.

Another element of Python's excellence comes not from the language itself, but from the **python community**. In the Python community, there is much consensus about the way to accomplish certain tasks and the idioms that one should (and should not) use. While the language itself may support certain phrasings for accomplishing something, the consensus of the community may steer one away from that phrasing. For example, `from module import*` at the top of a module is valid Python statement. However, the community frowns upon this and recommends that we use either: `import module or:` `from module import resource`. Importing all the contents of a module into another module's namespace can cause serious annoyance when one try to figure out how a module works, what functions it is calling, and where those functions come from. This particular convention will help us writing code that is clearer and will allow people to have a more pleasant maintenance experience. Following common conventions for writing a code is considered the best practice.

Easy access to numerous **third-party packages** is another real advantage of Python. In addition to the many libraries in the Python Standard Library, there are a number of libraries and utilities that are easily accessible on the internet that one can install with a single shell command. The Python Package Index, PyPI (*http://pypi.python.org*), is a place where anyone who has written a Python package can upload it for others to use. At present, there are over 4,000 packages available for download and use.

1.7 INSTALLING PYTHON

Before starting with the programming, some new softwares are needed. What follows is a short description of how to download and install Python. Simply visit `http://www.python.org/download` to get the most recent version of Python. The correct version of Python for the operating system and follow the install instructions for the particular Python distribution — instructions can vary significantly depending on what operating system you are installing to.

1.7.1 Windows

To install Python on a Windows machine, follow these steps:

1. Open a web browser and go to `http://www.python.org`.

2. Click the Download link.

3. You should see several links here, with names such as Python 2.7.*x* and Python 3.0.*x* Windows installer. Click the Windows installer link to download the installer file. (If you're running on an Itanium or AMD machine, you need to choose the appropriate installer.)

4. Store the Windows Installer file somewhere on your computer, such as C:\download\python-2.5.x.msi. (Just create a directory where you can find it later.)

5. Run the downloaded file by double-clicking it. This brings up the Python install wizard, which is really easy to use. Just accept the default settings, wait until the installation is finished, and the program is ready for use.

Assuming that the installation went well, we now have a new program in our Windows Start menu. Run the Python Integrated Development Environment (IDLE) by selecting Start ➤ Programs ➤ Python2.7 ➤ IDLE (Python GUI). We should now see a window that looks like the one shown in Fig. 1.5.

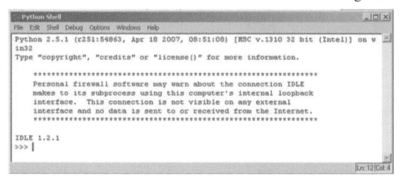

Fig. 1.5

For more documentation on IDLE, The website `http://www.python.org/idle` provides more information on running IDLE on platforms other than Windows. On pressing F1, or selecting Help ➤ Python Docs from the menu, we will get the full Python documentation.

(The document there of most use to us will probably be the Library Reference.) All the documentation is searchable.

1.7.2 **Linux and UNIX**

In most Linux and UNIX installations (including Mac OS X), a Python interpreter will already be present. We can check the Python version by running the python command at the prompt, as follows:

```
$ python
```

Running this command should start the interactive Python interpreter, with output similar to the following:

```
Python 2.7.6 (r251:54869, June 4 2014, 16:28:07)
[GCC 4.0.1 (Apple Computer, Inc. build 5367)] on darwin
Type "help", "copyright", "credits" or "license" for more information.
>>>
```

If the version is other than the desired by us (Python 2.7.x), it can be updated from the command prompt to get the desired version.

Note : To exit the interactive interpreter, use Ctrl + D (press the Ctrl key and press D).

If there is no Python interpreter installed, you will probably get an error message similar to the following:

```
bash: python: command not found
```

For example, if you're running Debian Linux, you should be able to install Python with the following command:

```
$ apt-get install python
```

If you're running Gentoo Linux, you should be able to use Portage, like this:

```
$ emerge python
```

In both cases, $ is, of course, the bash prompt.

Note: Many other package managers out there have automatic download capabilities, including Yum (Fedora OS), Synaptic (specific to Ubuntu Linux), and other Debian-style managers. You should probably be able to get the latest versions of Python through these.

1.7.3 **Macintosh**

If you're using a Macintosh with a recent version of Mac OS X, you'll have a version of Python installed already. Just open the Terminal application and enter the command python to start it. Even if you would like to install a newer version of Python, you should leave this one alone, as it is used in several parts of the operating system. You could use either MacPorts (http://macports.org) or Fink (http://finkproject.org), or you could use the distribution from the Python web site, by following these steps:

1. Go to the standard download page (see Steps 1 and 2 from the Windows instructions earlier in this chapter).

2. Follow the link for the Mac OS X installer. There should also be a link to the MacPython download page, which has more information. The MacPython page also has versions of Python for older versions of the Mac OS.

3. Once you've downloaded the installer .dmg file, it will probably mount automatically. If not, simply double-click it. In the mounted disk image, you'll find an installer package (.mpkg) file. If you double-click this, the installation wizard will open, which will take you through the necessary steps.

1.8 OTHER PYTHON DISTRIBUTIONS

You now have the standard Python distribution installed. Unless you have a particular interest in alternative solutions, that should be all you need. If you are curious (and, perhaps, feeling a bit courageous), read on.

Several Python distributions are available in addition to the official one. The most well-known of these is probably ActivePython, which is available for Linux, Windows, Mac OS X, and several UNIX varieties. A slightly less well-known but quite interesting distribution is Stackless Python. These distributions are based on the standard implementation of Python, written in the C programming language. Two distributions that take a different approach are Jython and IronPython. If you're interested in development environments other than IDLE, Table 1.2 lists some options.

Table 1.2: Some Integrated Development Environments (IDEs) for Python

Environment	Variable	Web Site
IDLE	The standard Python environment	http://www.python.org/idle
Pythonwin	Windows-oriented environment	http://www.python.org/download/windows
ActivePython	Feature-packed; contains Pythonwin IDE	http://www.activestate.com
Komodo	Commercial IDE	http://www.activestate.com3
Wingware	Commercial IDE	http://www.wingware.com
BlackAdder	Commercial IDE and (Qt) GUI Builder	http://www.thekompany.com

(Contd...)

Boa Constructor	Free IDE and GUI builder	http://boa-constructor.sf.net
Anjuta	Versatile IDE for Linux/UNIX	http://anjuta.sf.net
Arachno Python	Commercial IDE	http://www.python-ide.com
Code Crusader	Commercial IDE	http://www.newplanetsoftware.com
Code Forge	Commercial IDE	http://www.codeforge.com
Eclipse	Popular, flexible, open source IDE	http://www.eclipse.org
eric	Free IDE using Qt	http://eric-ide.sf.net
KDevelop	Cross-language IDE for KDE	http://www.kdevelop.org
VisualWx	Free GUI builder	http://visualwx.altervista.org
wxDesigner	Commercial GUI builder	http://www.roebling.de
wxGlade	Free GUI builder	http://wxglade.sf.net
Enthought Canopy	Free GUI Builder with 250 pre-built and tested packages.	https://www.enthought.com

ActivePython is a Python distribution from ActiveState (`http://www.activestate.com`). At its core, it's the same as the standard Python distribution for Windows. The main difference is that it includes a lot of extra goodies (modules) that are available separately. It's definitely worth a look if you are running Windows.

Stackless Python is a reimplementation of Python, based on the original code, but with some important internal changes. To a beginning user, these differences won't matter much, and one of the more standard distributions would probably be more useful. The main advantages of Stackless Python are that it allows deeper levels of recursion and more efficient multithreading. As mentioned, both of these are rather advanced features, not needed by the average user. You can get Stackless Python from `http://www.stackless.com`.

Enthought Canopy provides python with easy installation and updates of 250 pre-built and tested scientific and analytic packages such as NumPy, Pandas, SciPy, Matplotlib and IPython. It also includes graphical debugger, online Python Essentials and Python Development Tools training courses. All versions are available for Windows, Mac and Linux users.

Jython(`http://www.jython.org`) and **IronPython** (`http://www.code plex.com/IronPython`) are different—they're versions of Python implemented in other languages. Jython is implemented in Java, targeting the Java Virtual Machine, and IronPython is implemented in C#, targeting the .NET and MONO implementations of the common language runtime (CLR). At the time of writing, Jython is quite stable, but lagging behind Python—the current Jython version is 2.7.02, while Python is at 3.5.1. There are significant differences in these two versions of the language. IronPython is still rather young, but it is quite usable, and it is reported to be faster than standard Python on some benchmarks.

1.9 KEEPING IN TOUCH AND UP-TO-DATE

The Python language evolves continuously. To find out more about recent releases and relevant tools, the python.org web site is an invaluable asset. To find out what's new in a given release, go to the page for the given release, such as http://python.org/2.7 for release 2.7. There you will also find a link to Andrew Kuchling's in-depth description of what's new for the release, with a URL such as http://python.org/doc/2.7/whatsnew for release 2.7. If there have been new releases since this book went to press, you can use these web pages to check out any new features.

For a summary of what's changed in the more radically new release 3.0, see http://docs.python.org/dev/3.0/whatsnew/3.0.html.

If we want to keep up with newly released third-party modules or software for Python, we can check out the Python email list python-announce-list; for general discussions about Python, try python-list, but be warned: this list gets a *lot* of traffic. Both of these lists are available at http://mail.python.org. If you're a Usenet user, these two lists are also available as the newsgroups comp.lang. python.announce and comp.lang.python, respectively. If you're totally lost, you could try the python-help list (available from the same place as the two other lists) or simply email help@python.org. Before you do, you really ought to see if your question is a frequently asked one, by consulting the Python FAQ, at http://python.org/doc/faq, or by performing a quick Web search.

EXERCISES

1.1 State **True** or **False:**

(*i*)   Machine language is close to the programmer.

(*ii*)   Machine language is difficult to write.

(*iii*)   High level language is more close to the machine.

(*iv*)   Assembler translates high level language to machine language.

(*v*)   Machine languages are composed of 0's and 1's.

(*vi*)   Assembly and machine languages are known as low level languages.

(*vii*)   Compilers occupy more memory than interpreters.

(*viii*)   Interpreter is faster than compiler.

(*ix*)   Python is an example of high level languages.

(*x*)   Python use both Interpreter and Compiler.

(*xi*)   High level languages are easy to write programs.

1.2. What is an assembler?

1.3. What language does the CPU understand?

1.4. What is a source program?

1.5. What is an interpreter?

1.6. What is a compiler?

1.7. What is the difference between interpreter and compiler?

1.8. What is a high-level programming language?

1.9. What is the difference between an interpreted language and a compiled language?

1.10. What is an algorithm?

1.11. What is a flowchart?

1.12. What is an assembly language?

1.13. Write algorithms and draw flowcharts for the following problems:

    (*i*) Exchanging of two values of two variables

        (*a*) using a third variable

        (*b*) without using a third variable.

    (*ii*) To find the sum of a set of integer numbers

    (*iii*) To convert a given decimal number to Binary number

    (*iv*) To find the Greatest Common Divisor (GCD) of two numbers

    (*v*) To generate prime numbers from 1 to 1000

    (*vi*) Adding of two matrices

    (*vii*) To check a given number is in Fibonacci series or not.

Identifiers and Data Types

2.1 KEYWORDS

In Python, every word is classified as either a *keyword* or an *identifier*. All keywords have fixed meanings and these meanings cannot be changed. Keywords are the basic building blocks for program statements and must be written in lowercase. They are reserved words that cannot be used as variable names. The lists of all keywords are listed in Table 2.1.

Table 2.1: Python Keywords

and	assert	break	class	continue
def	del	elif	else	except
exec	False	finally	for	from
global	if	import	in	is
lambda	None	not	or	pass
print	raise	return	True	try
while	yield	as		

Note: For different versions of Python (2.*x*, 3.*y*, etc.), the number of keywords may vary slightly. We can check the keywords with the following commands:

```
>>> import keyword
>>> print keyword.kwlist
['and', 'as', 'assert', 'break', 'class', 'continue',
'def', 'del', 'elif', 'else', 'except', 'exec',
'finally', 'for', 'from', 'global', 'if', 'import',
'in', 'is', 'lambda', 'not', 'or', 'pass', 'print',
'raise', 'return', 'try', 'while', 'with', 'yield']
```

In Python 3.0, exec is no longer a keyword.

To check the version of Python, try the following commands:

```
>>> import sys
>>> print sys.version_info
(2, 5, 1, 'final', 0)
```

2.2 IDENTIFIERS

Identifiers refer to the names of variables, functions and lists. These are user defined names and consist of a sequence of letters and digits, with a letter as a first character. Both uppercase and lowercase are permitted, although lowercase letters are commonly used. The underscore character is also permitted in identifiers. It is usually as a link between two words in long identifiers (*e.g.* average_weight etc.).

2.2.1 Rules for Identifiers

The following rules must be followed when we define an identifier:

1. First character must be an alphabet or underscore
2. Must consist of only letters, digits and underscore
3. Keywords cannot use as an identifier
4. Must not contain whitespace.

Some examples of valid identifiers are:

Value	value	avg_ht	sum1	product

Some of the invalid identifiers are:

1sum	(distance)	3rd	%per	avg val
def	lambda	rs$		

More advanced conventions for Python identifiers:

1. Class name start with an uppercase letter. All other identifiers start with a lowercase letter.
2. Starting an identifier with a single leading underscore (_) indicates that the identifier is private.
3. Staring an identifier with two leading underscore (__) indicates that the identifier is a strongly private identifier.
4. If the identifier also ends with two trailing underscores, the identifier is a language defined special name.

2.3 DATA TYPES

Python provides a rich collection of data types to enable programmers to perform virtually any programming task they desire in another language. One nice thing about Python is that it provides many useful and unique data types (such as lists, tuples and dictionaries), and stays away from data types such as the pointers used in C, which have their use but can also make programming much more confusing and difficult for the nonprofessional programmer.

Python is known as a *dynamically typed* language, which means that we do not have to explicitly identify the data type when initializing a variable. The following table shows the most commonly used available data types and their attributes:

Data Type	Attribute	Example
Numeric Types		
Integer	Implemented with C longs	1234 987243
Float	Implemented with C doubles	2378.67543 18922.8765
Long integer	Size is limited with the system resources	7653897654L
Complex	It has real and imaginary parts, where each can also be floating point numbers.	12.0 + 45.78 j 12.0 + 45.78 J
Sequence Types		
String	A sequence of characters. Immutable (not changeable in-place). It can be represented by single quotes or double quotes.	'This is a string' "This is also a string"
List	Mutable (changeable) sequence of data types. List elements may be of same or different data types.	[1, 2, 3] [1.2, 4, 'c'] [4.5, 6.7, 7.8]
Tuple	An immutable sequence of data types. It works just like a list.	(1, 2, 3) (1.2, 4, 'c') (4.5, 6.7, 7.8)
Dictionary	A list of items indexed by keys. It has a value corresponding to its key.	{ 1: 3, 2 : 8, 3 :10} {'a' : 11, 'b' : 22} {2 : 'd', 5 :'k', 6 : 't'}

2.4 VALUES AND TYPES

A **value** is one of the basic things a program works with, like a letter or a number. The values we have seen so far are 1, 2, and 'Hello!'. These values belong to different **types**: 2 is an integer, and 'Hello!' is a string, so-called because it contains a "string" of letters. We can identify strings because they are enclosed in quotation marks. If we are not sure what type a value has, the interpreter can tell us. Let us try some simple examples with Python interpreter. The interpreter acts as a simple calculator: we can type an expression at it and it will write the value.

```
>>> type(123)
<type 'int'>
>>> type(123.456)
<type 'float'>
>>> type(1234L)
<type 'long'>
>>> type(12.45 + 67.89 j)
<type 'complex'>
>>> type("Hello")
<type 'str'>
```

Not surprisingly, strings belong to the type str and integers belong to the type int. Numbers with a decimal point belong to a type called float, because these numbers are represented in a format called **floating-point**. Complex numbers are also supported; imaginary numbers are written with a suffix of "j" or "J". Complex numbers with a nonzero real component are written as "(*real* + *imag***j**)", or can be created with the "complex(*real*, *imag*)" function.

2.5 BACKSLASH CHARACTER CONSTANTS

Python supports some special backslash character constants that are used in output functions. For example, the symbol '\n' stands for newline character. A list of backslash character constants is given in Table 2.2. Note that each character represents a single character, although it consist of two characters. These character combinations are known as escape sequence.

Table 2.2: Backslash Character Constants

Constant	Meaning
'\a'	audible alert (bell)
'\b'	back space
'\n'	new line
'\r'	carriage return
'\t'	horizontal tab
'\' '	single quote
'\" '	double quote
'\?'	question mark
'\\'	backslash
'\0'	null

Let us see how it works in python. Using the python interpreter, let us start with a string

```
>>> print '\aHello world'
Hello world
```

Here you will hear a beep sound with the output.

```
>>> print 'Hello\b world'
Hell world
>>> print 'Hello\n world'
Hello
 World
>>> print 'Hello\r world'
 World
>>> print 'Hello\t world'
 Hello    World
>>> print '\'Hello world'
 'Hello World
>>> print '\Hello world'
 \Hello World
>>> print '\\Hello world'
 \Hello World
```

Note: Here \H is not a backslash character constant, so we get the same output in the last two examples. If H were one of the escape sequences, then the output will be different.

For example:

```
>>> print '\new world'
ew World
>>> print '\\new world'
 \new World
```

2.6 VARIABLES

A variable is a data name that may be used to store a data value. Unlike constants that remain unchanged during the execution of a program, a variable may take different values at different times during execution.

A variable name can be chosen by the programmer in a meaningful way so as to reflect its function or nature in the program. Some examples are:

```
Average
total
Total
sl_no
```

As mentioned earlier in identifiers, variable names may consists of letters, digits and the underscore character, subject to the conditions mentioned in Table 2.1.

Now let us write a program using the concept of the variable. To calculate the area of a circle, we require two variables, radius and area.

```
>>> radius = 5
>>> area   =   3.1415 * radius * radius
>>> print area
78.537500
```

In this example the statement `radius = 5` assigns **5** to the variable `radius`. So now `radius` references the value **5**. The next statement

```
area   =   3.1415 * radius * radius
```

uses the value in `radius` to compute the expression and assigns the result into the variable `area`. Again, let us calculate the second area with the same variable names:

```
>>> radius = 10
>>> area   =   3.1415 * radius * radius
>>> print area
314.150000
```

Can we see any difference between Identifiers and variables? They look like same. The difference is that variables are used to reference values that may be *changed* in the program whereas Identifier simply stored their values in the memory and does not changed. Variables may reference different values also. For example, in the above code, radius is initialized to 5.0 and then changed to 10.0, and area is computed as 378.537500 and then reset to 314.150000.

EXERCISES

2.1. State True or False:

    (*a*) Any valid printable ASCII character can be used in an identifier.

    (*b*) Declaration of variables can appear anywhere in a program.

    (*c*) Python treats the variables **total** and **Total** to be same.

    (*d*) The underscore can be used anywhere in an identifier.

(*e*) Initialization is the process of assigning a value to a variable at the time of declaration.

(*f*) Python is a case-sensitive language.

(*g*) Variables can't be initialized at the time of declaration.

(*h*) The precision of a data type increases when the space occupied by the variable is more.

2.2. What will be output of the following code:

```
width = 7.5
height = 3
print "Area = ", width * height
```

2.3. Translate the following algorithm into Python code:

Step 1: Use a variable named **miles** with initial value **75**.

Step 2: Multiply miles by **1.609** and assign it to a variable named **kilometers**.

Step 3: Display the value of **kilometers**.

What is the value of **kilometers** after Step 3?

2.4. Find errors, if any, in the following declaration statements.

```
(a) 5 = radius
(b) x + y = z
(c) class = "Python"
(d) number1 = 23.46
(e) 2number = 34.56
(f) number@3 = 78
(g) Row Total = 123
(h) _variable = 12.89
(i) _number_ = 123
(j) First.name = "Singh"
```

2.5. After corrections, what output would you expect when you execute it?

number1 = 123

number2 = 456

number3 = 789

Compute average

average = (number1 + number2 + number3) / **3**

Display result

print **"The average of"**, number1, number2, number3, **"is"**, average

2.6. What is the difference between an identifier and a variable?

2.7. Identify variables and identifiers in the following program segment.

```
PI = 3.14.152
radius = 7
area   =   PI * radius * radius
print area
circumference = 2 * PI * radius
print circumference
radius = 12
area   =   PI * radius * radius
print area
```

3

Operators and Expressions

INTRODUCTION

Python supports a rich set of built-in-operators. An Operator is a special symbol that tells the computer to perform certain mathematical and logical operations like addition and multiplication. Operators form a part of the mathematical and logical expressions. An expression is a sequence of operands and operators that reduces to a single value.

Python operators can be classified into a number of categories. They include:

1. Arithmetic operators
2. Relational operators
3. Logical operators
4. Assignment operators

3.1 ARITHMETIC OPERATORS

Python provides all the basic arithmetic operators. They are listed in Table 3.1. The operators *, /, + and – work the same way as they do in other languages.

Table 3.1: Arithmetic Operators

Operator	Meaning
*	Multiplication
**	Exponentiation
/	Division
//	Pure integer division
%	Modulo Division
+	Addition or unary plus
-	Subtraction or unary minus
^	Bitwise operator(XOR)

Integer division truncates the fractional part. The modulo division operation produces the remainder of an integer as well as float divisions.

3.1.1 Integer Arithmetic

When both the operands in a single arithmetic expression such as a + b are integers, the expression is called an integer expression, and the operation is called integer arithmetic.

For example: $2+2$, $3**5$, $8\%3$ are valid integer arithmetic. We can start with the interactive python interpreter for these operations.

```
>>> 2 + 4
6
>>>6 % 4
2
>>> 3 ** 5
243
>>> -3 ** 2
-9
>>> (-3) ** 2
9
>>> 10 / 4
2
>>> 10 // 4
2
>>> -8 / -2
4
>>> -8 / 2
-4
>>> 1 + 2 + 3
6
>>> 1 / 2
0
```

What happened here in the last integer division? One integer (a non-fractional number) was divided by another, and the result was rounded down to give an integer result. This behavior can be useful at times, but often (if not most of the time), we need ordinary division. By using real numbers (numbers with decimal points) representations rather than integers, Python change to ordinary division.

```
>>> 1/2.0
0.5
```

or

```
>>> 1.0 / 2
0.5
```

But

```
>>> 1/2
0
```

> **Note:** Try these examples for better understanding and explain why the output looks like that?
>   (*i*) − 7/3
>   (*ii*) − 14/3
>   (*iii*) 14/ −3

3.1.2 Large Integers

Python can handle really large integers:

```
>>> 10000000000000000000
10000000000000000000L
```

The number suddenly got an L tacked onto the end. L stands for long integers.

Note: Python older than 2.2, you get the following behaviour:

```
>>> 1000000000000000000
OverflowError: integer literal too large
```

The newer versions of Python are more flexible when dealing with big numbers.

Ordinary integers cannot be larger than 2147483647 (or smaller than −2147483648). For really big numbers, we must use longs. A *long* (or *long integer*) is written just like an ordinary integer but with an L at the end. (lowercase l also can be used but that looks all too much like the digit 1, so we would advise against lower case l.)

In the previous example, Python converted the integer to a long, but we can do it, too. Let's try that big number again:

```
>>> 1987163987163981639186L * 198763981726391826L + 23
39497662643200556761300014378479169365 9L
```

3.1.3 Hexadecimals and Octals

In python, hexadecimal numbers are preceded by 0x or 0X. They may also include alphabets A through F or a through f. Letter A represents 10, B represents 11 and so on. Following are the valid hexadecimal integers.

0xA, 0Xb, 0x8B, 0XABC

An octal integer constant consists of any combination of digits from the set 0 through 7, with a leading 0. Some of the valid octal integers are:

036, 034, 0553

Let us try some examples by using the python interpreter

```
>>> 0xAF
175
```

and octal numbers like this:

```
>>> 010
8
```

The first digit in both of octal and hexadecimal is zero. We rarely use octal and hexadecimal numbers in programming.

3.1.4 Real Arithmetic

An arithmetic operation involving real operands is called real arithmetic. A real operand may assume either decimal or exponential notation. Real numbers are called *floats* (or *floating-point numbers*) in Python. If either one of the number in a division is a float, the result will be also a float.

Some of the examples are:

```
>>> 1.0/2.0
0.5
>>> 1. / 2.0
0.5
>>> 1 / 2.0
0.5
>>> 6.0 / 7.0
0.8571428571428571
```

Python provides up to 16 decimal points (Python 2.7). This feature of python can be used in many scientific simulations where fractional part takes a major role.

Note: We will be using a concept of " __future__ " (two underscore on both sides of future) in Python. This will make it easier in proper arithmetic operations. This concept is explained in 3.8.

3.1.5 Mixed Mode Operations

Python fully supports mixed arithmetic: when a binary arithmetic operator has operands of different numeric types, the operand with the lower size type is converted to that of the higher size type. Plain integer is smaller than long integer; Long integer is smaller than floating point and floating point is smaller than complex. Let us start with a few examples

>>> x = 12 + 34

>>> type (x)

<type 'int'>

>>> y = 12 + 34.45

>>> type(y)

<type 'float'>

>>> z = 12 + 34L

>>>type(z)

<type 'long'>

>>> z1 = 12.45 + 34L

>>>type(z1)

<type 'float'>

>>> c = (12 + 34j) + 34L

>>> type(c)

<type 'complex'>

From the above examples we see that, if the operands are of different types, the 'lower' type is automatically converted to the 'higher' type before the operation proceeds. The result is of the higher type.

3.1.6 Rules for Conversion

1. If one of the operands is float, and the other is int, the result will be converted to float.
2. If one of the operands is int, and the other is long int, the result will be converted to long int.
3. If one of the operands is float, and the other is long int, the result will be converted to float.
4. If one of the operands is float, and the other is complex, the result will be converted to complex.

3.1.7 Explicit Conversions

We have just discussed how Python performs type conversion automatically. However there are instances when we want to force a type conversion in a way that is different from the automatic conversion. The constructors **int()**, **long()**, **float()**, and **complex()** can be used to produce numbers of a specific type.

```
>>> int (12.43 + 45)
57
```

57.43 is converted to integer by truncation.

```
>>> int(12.34)/int(4.67)
3
```

Evaluated as 12/4 and the result is 3

```
>>> long(123.456 * 100)
12345L
```

The result is converted to long int.

```
>>> float (12.456 + 100L)
112.456
```

The result is converted to float. However this explicit conversion is not required because it will do automatically. Let us try for complex numbers

```
>>> 1j * 1J
(-1+0j)
>>> 1j * complex(0,1)
(-1+0j)
>>> 3+1j*3
(3+3j)
>>> (3+1j)*3
(9+3j)
>>> (1+2j)/(1+1j)
(1.5+0.5j)
```

Complex numbers are always represented as two floating point numbers, the real and imaginary part. To extract these parts from a complex number z, use z.real and z.imag.

```
>>> a=1.5+0.5j
>>> a.real
1.5
>>> a.imag
0.5
```

3.2 RELATIONAL OPERATORS

Comparisons can be done with the help of relational operators. An expression such as a > b containing a relational operator is termed as relational expression. The value of a relational expression may be either TRUE or FALSE .

For example 12 > 10 is TRUE.

Some of the frequently used relational operators and their meaning are shown in Table 3.2

Table 3.2: Relational Operators

Operator	Meaning
>	is greater than
>=	is greater than or equal to
<	is less than
<=	is less than or equal to
==	is equal to
!=	is not equal to

Let us try to use some of the relational examples using python interpreter.

```
>>> 6 > 5
True
>>> 6 > 8
False
>>> 5 >= 5
True
>>> 8 == 8
True
>>> 9 != 8
True
```

Note: There should not be any blank or space in between the operators. For example 7 >= 5 is valid whereas 7 > = 5 is not a valid expression. The operators <, <=, > and >= operators will raise a **Type Error** exception when any operand is a complex number.

3.2.1 More Relational Operators

Expression	Meaning
x **is** y	is x and y are the same object ?
x **is not** y	is x and y are different objects ?
x **in** y	is x is a member of the sequence (*e.g.*, lists, tuples or dictionaries) y ?
x **not in** y	is not x a member of the sequence y ?

Some of these operators deserve some special attention and will be described in the following sections. Let us try to use some of these operators with strings and lists.

We can use the equality operator (==) for comparing two strings:

```
>>> "abc" == "abc"
True
>>> "abc" == "abd"
False
```

What will happen if we use a *single* equality sign, as they do in mathematics? let's try it:

```
>>> "abc" = "abc"
SyntaxError: can't assign to literal
```

The single equality sign is the assignment operator, which is used to *change* things, which is *not* what we want to do when comparing things.

3.2.2 is : The Identity Operator

The **is** operator is interesting. It seems to work just like ==, but it doesn't:

```
>>> x = y = [1, 2, 3] # these are lists
>>> z = [1, 2, 3]
>>> x == y
True
>>> x == z
True
>>> x is y
True
>>> x is z
False
```

We will learn more about lists in the following sections.

3.3 LOGICAL/BOOLEAN OPERATORS

In addition to relational operators, python has the following three logical operators, shown in Table 3.3 along with this meaning.

Table 3.3: Logical Operators

Operator	Meaning
or	logical OR
and	logical AND
not	logical NOT

The logical operators **and** and **or** are used when we want to test more than one condition and make decisions. For example,

`x > y and y > z` is a valid expression.

Note: not has a lower priority than non-Boolean operators, so not a `==` b is interpreted as not (a `==` b), and a `==` not b is a syntax error.

3.4 ASSIGNMENT OPERATORS

Assignment operators are used to assign the result of an expression to a variable. Python has a set of shorthand assignment operators of the form

$$V \text{ op= expr}$$

Where V is a variable, `expr` is an expression and `op` is a python arithmetic operator. The operator `op=` is known as shorthand assignment operator.

The assignment statement

$$V \text{ op= expr}$$

is equivalent to

$$V = V \text{ op (expr)}$$

Let us consider an example

$$x \mathrel{*}= y + 5 \text{ is equivalent to } x = x * (y + 5)$$

Some of the commonly used shorthand assignment operators are illustrated in Table 3.4.

Table 3.4: Shorthand Assignment Operators

Statement with shorthand operators	Meaning
a += (n+1)	a = a + (n+1)
a −= (n+1)	a = a - (n+1)
a *= (n+1)	a = a * (n+1)
a /= (n+1)	a = a / (n+1)
a //= (n+1)	a = a // (n+1)
a %= b	a = a % b

Let us consider a and n are integers with a = 12 and n = 4. Using python interpreter, we can check the output as follows.

```
>>> a =14
```

```
>>> n = 4
>>> a += (n+1)
>>>print a
19
```

Now the new value of a is 19 not 14. However the value of n remains 4. If we want to change the value of a to 14, we can assign it again, as follows:

```
>>> a= 14
>>> a -= (n+1)
>>>print a
9
```

The result of the expression of a /= (n+1) will be same as a //= (n+1) because we are using only integer data types. But we can see the difference when we use the floating point numbers. Consider a = 14.5 n = 4.3, then

```
>>> a = 14.5
>>> n = 4.3
>>> a /= (n+1)
>>> print a
2.7538490566
>>> a = 14.5
>>> a //= (n+1)
>>> print a
2.0
```

The advantages for using shorthand assignment operators are:

1. What appears on the left hand side need not be repeated on the right hand side and therefore easier to write.
2. The statement is more concise and easier to read.
3. The statement is more efficient.

Note: Expressions and statements

An **expression** is a combination of values, variables, and operators. So x + 8 is a legal expression (assuming that the variable x has been assigned a value).

A **statement** is a unit of code that the Python interpreter can execute. We have seen two kinds of statement: print and assignment.

Technically an expression is also a statement, but it is probably simpler to think of them as different things. The important difference is that an expression has a value; a statement does not.

3.5 INTERACTIVE MODE AND SCRIPT MODE

We can rewrite bits of code in python interactive mode (python command prompt) before we put them in a script (using an Editor, as we mentioned in Table 1.1). But there are differences between interactive mode and script mode that can be confusing.

For example, using Python as a calculator, we can write

```
>>> m = 20
>>> m * 5
100
```

The first line assigns a value to m, but it has no visible effect. The second line is an expression, so the interpreter evaluates it and displays the result.

But if we type the same code into a script and run it, we cannot get output at all. In script mode an expression, all by itself, has no visible effect. Python actually evaluates the expression, but it doesn't display the value unless you tell it to:

```
m = 20
print m * 5
```

A script usually contains a sequence of statements. If there is more than one statement, the results appear one at a time as the statements execute.

The following pictures show the interactive mode and script mode.

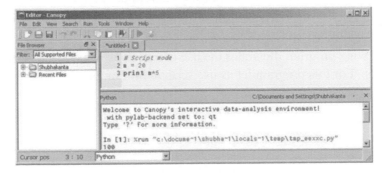

Fig. 3.1 Interactive mode.

Fig. 3.2 Python Script mode.

For example, when we write the following code segment in the script mode

```
print 1
x = 2
print x
```

produces the output

```
1
2
```

The assignment statement does not produce output in the script mode.

3.6 ORDER OF OPERATIONS

When more than one operator appears in an expression, the order of evaluation depends on the **rules of precedence**. For mathematical operators, Python follows mathematical convention. An arithmetic expression without parentheses will be evaluated from *left to right*. The acronym **PEMDAS** is a useful way to remember the rules:

- **P**arentheses have the highest precedence and can be used to force an expression to evaluate in the order you want. Since expressions in parentheses are evaluated first, 5 * (3–1) is 10 and 5 * 3–1 is 14. And parenthesized sub expressions are evaluated from left to right. If the parentheses are nested, the evaluation begins with the innermost sub expression.

- **E**xponentiation has the next highest precedence, so 3**2+1 is 10, not 27, and 3*1**3 is 3, not 27.

- **M**ultiplication and **D**ivision have the same precedence, which is higher than **A**ddition and **S**ubtraction, which also have the same precedence. So 3*3–2 is 7, not 3, and 6+6/3 is 8, not 4.

- Operators with the same precedence are evaluated from left to right (except exponentiation). So in the expression 12 / 2 * x, the division happens first and the result is multiplied by x. To divide by 2x, we can use parentheses or write 12 / 2 / x.

The following program illustrates the use of variables in expressions and their evaluation. For this program let us use script/editor mode.

```
# Evaluation of expressions
a = 12
b = 16
c = 4
x = a - b / 3 + c * 2 - 1
```

```
y = a - b / (3 + c) * (2 - 1)
z = a - (b / (3 + c) * 2) - 1
print 'x = ', x
print 'y = ', y
print 'z = ', z
```

```
Output of the above program:
x =   14
y =   10
z =   7
```

3.7 COMMENTS IN PYTHON

The hash sign (#) is used for comments in Python. As programs get bigger and more complicated, they get more difficult to read and also difficult to figure out what it is doing. For this reason, it is a good idea to add notes to our programs to explain in natural language what the program is doing. These notes are called **comments**. When we put the hash sign in our code, everything to the right of it is ignored.

Here is an example:

```
# Interchange of two numbers
a = 123
b = 456
temp = a   # temp is a variable
a = b
b = temp
```

In this case, the comment appears on a line by itself. We can also put comments at the end of a line:

```
temp = a   # temp is a variable
```

Everything from the # to the end of the line is ignored—it has no effect on the program. Comments are most useful when they document non-obvious features of the code. It is reasonable to assume that the reader can figure out what the code does; it is much more useful to explain why.

Again if we want to use multiple comments in our program, instead of using # for every line, we can use Strings with, (Single quote) or" (double quote). In both cases, we have to start with 3(three) single quotes or 3(three) double quotes and ended with the same. For example, if we want to add 3 lines of comment, we can write in three different ways as follows:

1. Option One (using hash)

   # This is a first line of comment

   # This is a second line of comment

   # This is a third line of comment

2. Option Two (using single quote)

   '''

   This is a first line of comment

   This is a second line of comment

   This is a third line of comment

   '''

3. Option Three (using double quote)

   """"""

   This is a first line of comment

   This is a second line of comment

   This is a third line of comment

   """"""

3.8 __FUTURE__ IN PYTHON

When the module future is imported in the instruction, it is surrounded by two underscores on both sides: __future__. From it, we can import features that will be standard in Python in the future but that aren't part of the language yet. Let us try the feature of this module.

Let us start with integer division

```
>>> 1 / 2
0
```

Sometimes, if we would rather have Python do proper division, we could add the following statement to the beginning of our program (we can use in script mode also for writing full programs) or simply execute it in the interactive interpreter:

```
>>> from __future__ import division
>>> 1 / 2
0.5
```

Here the division will suddenly make a bit more sense. Of course, the single slash can no longer be used for the kind of integer division shown earlier. The double slash operator will do this:

```
>>> 1 // 2
0
```

The double slash consistently performs integer division, even with floats:

```
>>> 1.0 // 2.0
0.0
```

This problem is solved in Python 3. In this updated version, the division operator performs floating point division even with integer operands. So 1/2 or 1.0/2.0 is 0.5.

3.9 HOW TO TRACK ERRORS?

Python displays lot of information when an error occurs, but it can be overwhelming, especially when there are many frames on the stack. The most useful parts are usually:

- What kind of error it was, and
- Where it occurred.

Syntax errors are usually easy to find. Whitespace errors can be tricky because spaces and tabs are invisible and we are used to ignoring them. For example

```
>>> y = 6
File "<stdin>", line 1
y = 6
^
```

IndentationError: unexpected indent

In this example, the error is that the line is indented by one space. But the error message points to y, which is misleading. In general, error messages indicate where the problem was discovered, but the actual error might be earlier in the code, sometimes on a previous line.

Again, when we try to use some built-in-functions, like

```
>>> sqrt(5)
Traceback (most recent call last):
    File "<stdin>", line 1, in <module>
NameError: name 'sqrt' is not defined
```

In this example, it mentioned that the function sqrt() can't be imported.

```
Traceback (most recent call last):
File "snr.py", line 5, in ?
decibels = 10 * math.log10(ratio)
ValueError: math domain error
```

3.10 COMMON ERRORS

Mostly we encounter three kinds of errors in a program. They are:

1. syntax errors
2. runtime errors and
3. semantic errors.

It is useful to distinguish between them in order to track them down more quickly.

3.10.1 Syntax Errors

Python can only execute a program if the syntax is correct; otherwise, the interpreter displays an error message. **Syntax** refers to the structure of a program and the rules about that structure. For example, parentheses have to come in matching pairs, so 10 + 20) is legal, but 8) is a **syntax error**.

If there is a single syntax error anywhere in the program, Python will display an error message and quit, and we will not be able to run the program.

3.10.2 Runtime Errors

The second type of error is a runtime error, because the error does not appear until the program has started running. These errors are also called **exceptions** because they usually indicate that something exceptional has happened.

A simple example of runtime error is shown below:

>>> no = 0

>>> no2 = 1/no

```
Traceback (most recent call last):
   File "<pyshell#16>", line 1, in <module>
     no2 = 1/no1
ZeroDivisionError: integer division or modulo by zero
```

3.10.3 Semantic Errors

The third type of error is the **semantic error**. If there is a semantic error in the program, it will run successfully in the sense that the computer will not generate any error messages, but it will not do the right answer. It will do something else. Specifically, it will do what we told it to do. The problem is that the program we wrote is not the program we wanted to write. The meaning of the program (its semantics) is wrong. Identifying semantic errors can be tricky because it requires you to work backward by looking at the output of the program and trying to figure out what it is doing. **For example:**

```
>>> radius = 5
>>> area = 3.1415 + radius + radius
>>> print area
13.1415
```

The result is not what we want. However there is no syntax or runtime errors.

EXERCISES

3.1. State whether the following statements are **true** or **false**:

    (*i*) Arithmetic operators do not have the same level of precedence.

    (*ii*) The modulo operator (%) can be used only with integers.

    (*iii*) The operators >=, !=, = and <= all enjoy the same level of priority.

    (*iv*) In Python, if a data item is zero, it is considered as *False*.

    (*v*) A unary expression consists of only one operand with no operators.

    (*vi*) In Python, an expression statement can be terminated by a period.

    (*vii*) When evaluation of mixed expressions, an implicit cast is generated automatically.

    (*viii*) An explicit cast can be used to change the expression.

    (*ix*) Parentheses can be used to change the order of evaluation expressions.

    (*x*) Python supports 6 relational operators.

3.2. State whether the following statements are **true** or **false**:

    (*i*) The statement b = + 20 is valid.

    (*ii*) The expression 10 + 6/5 * 5/6 evaluates to 10.

    (*iii*) The expression (10 + 6/5) * 5/6 evaluates to 10.

    (*iv*) The statement a = 1/3 + 1/3 + 1/3 assigns 1 to a.

    (*v*) The statement b = 1.0/3 + 1/3.0 + 1.0/3.0 assigns 1.0 to b.

    (*vi*) The statement c = 1.0/3.0 * 3.0 gives 1.0 to c.

3.3. Which of the expressions are **true**?

    (*i*) !(10+10) <= 10   (*ii*) !(10+10 <= 10)

    (*iii*) 6 + 9 == 16 or 2 + 7 == 9   (*iv*) 6 + 9 == 16 and 2 + 7 == 9

    4 != 6 and !(7+8+9 == 24 or 7 == 9–2)

3.4. Which of the following arithmetic expressions are valid? If valid, give the value of the expression; otherwise give reason.

    (*i*) 45/4%3   (*ii*) +12/4 + 12

    (*iii*) 12.5 % 4   (*iv*) 45 / int(6.89)

    (*v*) 14 % 4 + 4 % 14   (*vi*) float(56/6) + –5

    (*vii*) 45 + –8

3.5. Write a Python assignment statements to evaluate the following equations:

(*i*)   Area $= \pi r^2 + 2\pi r h$

(*ii*)   Force $= \dfrac{2m_1 m_2}{m_1 + m_2} \cdot g$

(*iii*)   Length of a side $= \sqrt{a^2 + b^2 - 2ab\cos(x)}$

(*iv*)   Energy $= \text{mass}\left[\text{acceleration} * \text{height} + \dfrac{(\text{velocity})^2}{2}\right]$.

3.6. Write a Python program to exchange the values of *x*, *y* and *z* such that *x* has the value of *y*, *y* has the value of *z*, and *z* has the value of *x*.

[**Hints:** $x = 12$. $y = 34$, $z = 56$

Output: $x = 34$, $y = 56$ and $z = 12$]

3.7. Write a Python program that reads a floating point number(real number) and then displays the rightmost digit of the integral part of the number.

[**Hints:** Input 1234.56, Output = 4]

3.8. Write a Python program that will obtain the length and width from the user and compute its area and perimeter.

3.9. Write a Python program to evaluate the distance travelled by a vehicle in regular intervals of time, *t* which is given by the following equation:

$$\text{distance} = ut + \frac{(at^2)}{2}$$

where *u* is the initial velocity (metres per second), *a* is the acceleration (metres per second^2).

3.10. Write a Python program to read a five digit integer and print the sum of its digits.

4

Managing Input and Output Operations

INTRODUCTION

Reading, processing and writing of data are the three essential functions of a computer program. Most programs take some input and display the processed data, known as results on a suitable medium (may be on the screen or in a file).

In the previous chapters, we have used a method of providing data to the program variables through the assignment statements such as $a = 123$, $x =$ 'c'; and so on.

4.1 MANAGING INPUTS

Another method is to use the input functions **input()** or **raw_input()** which can read data from the keyboard. The basic difference between the two input functions is that `raw_input()` is provided by Python 2 and `input()` from Python 3.

4.1.1 `raw_input()` and `input()` functions

A. `raw_input()` functions

When this function is called, the program stops and waits for the user to type something. When the user presses Return or Enter, the program resumes and raw_input returns what the user typed as a string. Let us start with an example without using any argument, as below:

```
>>> x = raw_input()
123
>>> print x
123
```

What happens here is that the first line (raw_input()) is executed in the interactive interpreter. It waits an input from the user. When we type 123 and press Enter, the value is stored in *x*. We can see this value using the print statement.

Again let us try this function in some meaningful way.

```
>>> name = raw_input(" Enter your Name: ")
 Enter your Name: Shubha
>>> print name
Shubha
```

Here, it prints out the string " Enter your Name: " as a new prompt. When we enter a string of characters and press Enter, the resulting value of input is stored in name variable. In both examples, we used variables like *x* and name.

This function can also be used without assigning a variable. The basic difference is that in this case the value we enter will be printed out automatically.

```
>>> raw_input(" Enter your Name: ")
 Enter your Name: Shubha
'Shubha'
```

When we work with script mode, it is better to assign to a variable. Otherwise we cannot see the output. Let us try these examples in script mode.

```
# Without using argument
no = raw_input()
print no
# using arguments
name = raw_input("Enter your name:")
print name
raw_input("Enter your Age:")
```

Output of this program:

123

123

Enter your name: xyz

xyz

Enter your Age: 40

B. input() functions

Let us use this input function in a meaningful way:

```
>>> x = input ("x = ")
x = 30
>>> y = input ("y = ")
y = 40
>>> print x * y
1200
```

The advantage of using input function is that we can supply the values at run time.

> **Note:** We can use the input function raw_input() in the same way
> ```
> >>> x = raw_input ("x = ")
> x = 30
> >>> y = raw_input ("y = ")
> y = 40
> >>> print x * y
> 1200
> ```

But the best option is that for strings it is better to use raw_input() and for numbers input() works well. For example:

```
a=raw_input ("Enter the value of a :")
b=raw_input ("Enter the value of b :")
if a-b !=0 :
    print 'a and b are not same'
```

when you run this program, you will get the following error message:

```
      1 a=raw_input ("Enter the value of a :")
      2 b=raw_input ("Enter the value of b :")
----> 3 if a-b !=0 :
      4     print 'a and b are not same'
```

`TypeError: unsupported operand type(s) for -: 'str' and 'str'`

The problem is that the values of *a* and *b* are treated as strings. So subtraction of strings are not possible. If you change the sign with positive, you will not get the error but the result may not be what you expect.

To solve this problem, we have many options. The simplest options are either change the values to integers or simply use the input() function as follows:

```
a=raw_input("Enter the value of a :")
b=raw_input("Enter the value of b :")
if (int(a)-int(b) !=0 ) :
    print 'a and b are not same'
a=input("Enter the value of a :")
b=input("Enter the value of b :")
if a-b !=0 :
    print 'a and b are not same'
```

Note: the following is also valid

```
a=int(raw_input("Enter the value of a :"))
b=int(raw_input("Enter the value of b :"))
if a - b !=0 :
    print 'a and b are not same'
```

4.2 MANAGING OUTPUTS

We have seen how **print** can be used to print an expression, which is either a string or automatically converted to one. But we can actually print more than one expression, as long as they are separated with commas:

```
>>> print 'Age:', 42
Age: 42
```

Note: In Python 3.0, print is no longer a statement at all—it's a function (with essentially the same functionality).

As we can see, a space character is inserted between each argument. This behavior can be very useful if we want to combine *text* and *variable* values without using the full power of string formatting:

```
>>> name = 'Shubha'
>>> salutation = 'Dr.'
>>> greeting = 'Hello,'
>>> print greeting, salutation, name
Hello, Dr. Shubha
```

If the greeting string had no comma, how would we get the comma in the result? We **couldn't** just use print greeting, ',', salutation, name because that would introduce a space before the comma. For example:

```
>>> name = 'Shubha'
>>> salutation = 'Dr.'
>>> greeting = 'Hello'
```

```
>>> print greeting, ',', salutation, name
Hello , Dr. Shubha # See space after Hello
```

One solution would be the following, using the plus operator:

```
>>> print greeting + ',', salutation, name
Hello, Dr. Shubha   # No space after greeting 'Hello'
```

which simply adds the comma to the greeting.

One more important application of comma is that, if we add a comma at the end of the statement, our next print statement will continue printing on the same line. For example, the statements

```
print 'Hello,',
print 'world!'
print "Hello, world!"*
```

* This will work only in a script, *and not in an interactive Python session*. In the interactive session, each statement will be executed (and print its contents) separately.

We often want more control over the formatting of our output than simply printing space separated values. There are two ways to format the output; the first way is to do all the **string handling** ourselves; using string slicing and concatenation operations. The string type has some methods that perform useful operations for padding strings to a given column width; these will be discussed shortly. The second way is to use the **str.format()** method.

4.2.1 `repr()` or `str()` Functions

Python can convert any value to a string by passing it to the repr() or str() functions. The `str()` function is meant to return representations of values which are fairly human readable, while `repr()` is meant to generate representations which can be read by the interpreter (or will force a SyntaxError if there is no equivalent syntax). For example:

```
>>> str1 = "Hello World!\n"
>>> str2 = str(str1) #In str()- '\n' is equivalent
to a new line
>>> print str2
Hello World!

>>> str3 = repr(str1)#In repr()-'\n' is NOT a new
line
>>> print str3
'Hello World!\n'
```

```
        OR
>>> str1 = "Hello World!\n"
>>> str2 = str(str1) #In str()- '\n' is equivalent
>>> print str2        #to a new line
Hello World!

>>> str3 = repr(str1)#In repr()-'\n' is NOT a new
>>> print str3        #line
'Hello World!\n'
```

The repr() of a string adds string quotes and backslashes whereas str() does not.

Strings, in particular, have two distinct representations. Some examples are:

```
>>> s = 'Programming in Python'
>>> print str(s)
Programming in Python
>>> print repr(s)
'Programming in Python'
```

However, in numeric values, as shown in the following example, we may use either str() or repr() functions.

```
>>> a = 10.25
>>> b = 5000
>>> s1 = 'The value of a is ' + repr(a) + ', and b is
' + repr(b) + '.'
>>> print s1
The value of a is 10.25, and b is 5000.
>>> s2 = 'The value of a is ' + str(a) + ', and b is
' + str(b) + '.'
>>> print s2
The value of a is 10.25, and b is 5000.
```

Again, The argument to repr() may be any Python object, for example:

```
>>> print repr((a, b, ('Tuple', 'Example')))# Tuple
as argument
(10.25, 5000, ('Tuple', 'Example'))
>>> print repr([a, b, ['List', 'Example']])# List as
argument
```

```
[10.25, 5000, ['List', 'Example']]
>>> print repr({1:123, 2:'Dictionary'}) # Dictionary
as argument
{1: 123, 2: 'Dictionary'}
```

4.2.2 `rjust()` and `format()` Functions

We have seen that the print function can be used for printing captions and numerical results. However, it is desirable that the outputs are produced in such a way that they are understandable and are in easy to use form. For showing good appearance and clarity of the outputs, Python also provides many functions. Most frequently used functions **rjust()** and **format()** are explained below.

To demonstrate with an example, let us try to write table of squares and cubes. Here let us use rjust() and format() functions, as follows:

A. rjust() function :

It is possible to force the printing to be left justified centered or right justified.

With **rjust()** function, we can align the output as right justified.

For example:

```
for x in range(1, 11):
    print repr(x).rjust(2), repr(x*x).rjust(3), \
repr(x*x*x).rjust(4)
```

The output of the above program segment is:

```
 1    1     1
 2    4     8
 3    9    27
 4   16    64
 5   25   125
 6   36   216
 7   49   343
 8   64   512
 9   81   729
10  100  1000
```

rjust (2)   rjust (3)   rjust (4)

On the other hand, if we used ljust() function, output can be align as left justified.

```
for x in range(1, 11):
    print   repr(x).ljust(2),   repr(x*x).ljust(3),\
repr(x*x*x).ljust(4)
```

```
 1    1    1
 2    4    8
 3    9    27
 4   16    64
 5   25    125
 6   36    216
 7   49    343
 8  64  512
 9  81  729
10 100 1000
```

ljust (2) ljust (3)   ljust (4)

The above examples demonstrate the repr.rjust() and repr.rjust() (same as str.rjust() and str.ljust()) methods of string objects, which right-justifies a string in a field of a given width by padding it with spaces on the left and left justifies a string on the right respectively.

However, one space between each column was added by the print() statement. It always adds spaces between its arguments.

Another method str.center() also works in the same way. These methods just return a new string. If the input string is too long, they don't truncate it, but return it unchanged. If we really want truncation we can always add a slice operation, as in x.ljust(n) [:m]. The following example explains about the usages of this slice notation.

```
for x in range(1, 11):
    x=x+0.24
    print repr(x).rjust(2), repr(x*x).rjust(3)[:4], \
    repr(x*x*x).rjust(4)[:5]
```

The output of the above program:

```
1.24    1.53    1.906
2.24    5.01    11.23
3.24    10.4    34.01
4.24    17.9    76.22
```

```
 5.24    27.4    143.8
 6.24    38.9    242.9
 7.24    52.4    379.5
 8.24    67.8    559.4
 9.24    85.3    788.8
10.24   104.    1073.
```

In this example the second column is restricted to four places and the third column to 5 places.

B. format() function

In Python format() function can be used in different ways. Here we want to print the output in tabular form. This can be achieved using the curly bracket.

For example:

```
for x in range(1, 11):
    print('{0:2d} {1:3d} {2:4d}'.format(x, x*x, x*x*x))
```

The output of this program is:

```
 1    1      1
 2    4      8
 3    9     27
 4   16     64
 5   25    125
 6   36    216
 7   49    343
 8   64    512
 9   81    729
10  100   1000
```

Thus a positional parameter of the format method can be accessed by placing the index of the parameter after the opening brace, *e.g.* {0} accesses the first parameter, {1} the second one and so on. In the above example the index inside of the curly braces is followed by a colon and a format string which tells us the width of the argument/values, *e.g.* {0:5*d*}.

If the positional parameters are used in the order in which they are written, the positional argument specifiers inside of the braces can be omitted, so '{} {} {}' corresponds to '{0} {1} {2}'. But they are needed, if we want to access them in different orders: '{2} {1} {0}'.

Again in the following example we demonstrate how keyword parameters can be used with the format method:

```
>>> print " a={a:5d}".format(a = 123)
a=  123
```

We can use the `str.format()` method for printing strings also.

```
>>> print 'We {} learning {}'.format('are','Python')
```

The brackets and characters within them (called format fields) are replaced with the objects passed into the `str.format()` method. A number in the brackets can be used to refer to the position of the object passed into the `str.format()` method.

```
>>> print "{0} and {1} ".format("Position1","Position2")
Position1 and Position2
>>> print "{1} and {0} ".format("Position1","Position2")
Position2 and Position1
```

If keyword arguments are used in the `str.format()` method, their values are referred to by using the name of the argument. For example:

```
>>> print 'We {var1} learning{var2}.'.format(var1='
are', var2='Python')
We are learning Python.
```

C. Important conversions:

'**!a**' (apply ascii()), '**!s**' (apply str()) and '**!r**' (apply repr()) can be used to convert the value before it is formatted:

```
>>> import math
>>> print 'The value of PI is approx.= {}.'.format(math.pi)
The value of PI is approx.= 3.14159265359.
>>> print 'The value of PI is approx.= {!r}.'.format(math.pi)
The value of PI is approx.= 3.141592653589793.
```

An optional ':' and format specifier can follow the field name. This allows greater control over how the value is formatted. The following example rounds Pi to three places after the decimal.

```
>>> print 'The value of PI is approx.=
{0:.3f}.'.format(math.pi)
The value of PI is approx.= 3.142.
```

Note: zfill methods:

There is another method, `str.zfill()`, which pads a numeric string on the left with zeros. It also understands about plus and minus signs:

```
>>> print '123'.zfill(6)
000123
>>> print '-3.141'.zfill(8)
-003.141
>>> print '3.14159265359'.zfill(5)
3.14159265359
```

4.3 FREQUENTLY USED FORMATTING SPECIFIERS

A. Formatting Floating Point Numbers:

The syntax to invoke `format ()` function in floating point numbers can be used as follows:

```
format(item, format-specifier)
```

If the item is a float value, we can use the specifier to give the width and precision of the format in the form of **width.precisionf**. Here, **width** specifies the width of the resulting string, **precision** specifies the number of digits after the decimal point, and **f** is called the conversion code, which sets the formatting for floating point numbers. For example:

```
print format(12.345678, "10.2f")
print format(12345678.9876, "10.2f")
print format(12.3, "10.2f")
print format(89, "10.2f")
```

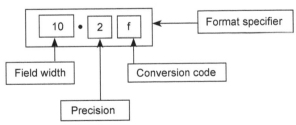

```
The formatted output is:
        12.35
 12345678.99
        12.30
        89.00
```

The following table illustrate the output of the above different format specifications.

$\longleftarrow$————————— 10 —————$\longrightarrow$

					1	2	.	3	5
1	2	3	4	5	6	7	8	.	9
					1	2	.	3	0
					8	9	.	0	0

Here a square box denotes a blank space. Note that the decimal point is counted as one space. The `format("10.2f")` function formats the number into a string whose width is 10, including a decimal point and two digits after the point. The number is rounded to two decimal places. Thus there are seven digits allocated before the decimal point. If there are fewer than seven digits before the decimal point, spaces are inserted before the number. If there are more than seven digits before the decimal point, the number's width is automatically increased. For example, `format(12345678.923, "10.2f")` returns 12345678.92, which has a width of 11.

We can omit the width specifier. If so, it defaults to 0. In this case, the width is automatically set to the size needed for formatting the number. For example:

```
print format(57.467657, "10.2f")
print format(57.467657, ".2f")
will give output as
      57.47
57.47
```

The following table shows the detail of the output.

					5	7	.	4	7
5	7	.	4	7					

B. Formatting in Scientific Notation

If we change the conversion code from **f** to **e**, the number will be formatted in scientific notation. For example:

```
print format(12.345678, "10.2e")
print format(12345678.9876, "10.2e")
print format(12.3, "10.2e")
print format(89, "10.2e")
The formatted output is:
   1.23e+01
   1.23e+07
   1.23e+01
   8.90e+01
```

The following table illustrates the output of the above different format specifications.

		1	.	2	3	e	+	0	1
		1	.	2	3	e	+	0	7
		1	.	2	3	e	+	0	1
		8	.	9	0	e	+	0	1

The + , – and . signs are counted as places in the width limit.

C. Formatting as a Percentage

We can use the conversion code **%** to format a number as a percentage. For example,

```
print format(0.56789, "10.2%")
print format(0.008765, "10.2%")
print format(4.9, "10.2%")
print format(89, "10.2%")
will display as:
```

```
    56.79%
     0.88%
   490.00%
  8900.00%
```

The following table illustrates the output of the above different format specifications.

				5	6	.	7	9	%
					0	.	8	8	%
			4	9	0	.	0	0	%
		8	9	0	0	.	0	0	%

The format **10.2%** causes the number to be multiplied by 100 and displayed with a % sign following it. The total width includes the % sign counted as one space.

D. Justifying Format

By default, the format of a number is right justified. We have shown earlier that by using `rjust()` and `ljust()` methods, we can adjust right and left justification of the outputs. On the other hand, we can put the symbol < in the format specifier to specify that the item be left-justified in the resulting format within the specified width. For example,

```
print format(12.345678, "10.2f")   # RIGHT Justified
print format(12.345678, "<10.2f")  # LEFT Justified
        12.35
12.35
```

The following table illustrates the output of the above format specifications.

					1	2	.	3	5
1	2	.	3	5					

E. Formatting Integers

The conversion codes **d**, **x**, **o**, and **b** can be used to format an integer in decimal, hexadecimal, octal, or binary numbers respectively. We can also specify a width for the conversion. For example,

```
print format(12345, "10d")
print format(12345, "<10d")
print format(12345, "10x")
print format(12345, "<10x")
```

```
The outputs of the above codes are as follows:
        12345
12345
        3039
3039
```

The format specifier **10d** specifies that the integer is formatted into a decimal with a width of ten spaces. The format specifier **10x** specifies that the integer is formatted into a hexadecimal integer with a width of ten spaces.

F. Formatting Strings

We can use the conversion code **s** to format a string with a specified width. For example,

```
print format("Learning Python", "20s")
print format("Learning Python", "<20s")
print format("Learning Python", ">20s")
print format("Welcome to Python Programming", ">20s")
```

The output is as follows:

Learning Python

Learning Python

    Learning Python

Welcome to Python Programming

The following table illustrates the output of the above string format specifications:

|←———————————— 10 ————————————→|

L	e	a	r	n	i	n	g		P	y	t	h	o	n				'	
L	e	a	r	n	i	n	g		P	y	t	h	o	n					
					L	e	a	r	n	i	n	g		P	y	t	h	o	n
W	e	l	c	o	m	e		t	o		P	y	t	h	o	n		P	r

The format specifier **20s** specifies that the string is formatted within a width of 20. By default, a string is left justified. So, the symbol < has no meaning in string formatting. To right-justify it, we can put the symbol > in the format specifier. If the string is longer than the specified width, the width is automatically increased to fit the string.

On the other hand, we can use the formatting operator of a tuple or a mapping (like a dictionary) with special treatment. We haven't looked at mappings (such as dictionaries) yet, so let's focus on tuples here. We'll use mappings in forthcoming Chapters, where they're discussed in greater detail.

If the right operand is a tuple, each of its elements is formatted separately, and we need a conversion specifier for each of the values. For example:

```
>>> print '%s plus %s equals %s' ↑ (5, 5, 10)
5 plus 5 equals 10
```

The % character marks the beginning of the conversion specifier. And if we don't enclose the values in Parentheses, the following error will come up.

```
>>> print '%s plus %s equals %s' % 5, 5, 10
TypeError: not enough arguments for format string
```

The most commonly used conversion types are summarized in Table 4.1.

Table 4.1: String Formatting Conversion Types

Conversion Type	Meaning
i or d	Signed integer decimal
o	Unsigned octal
u	Unsigned decimal
x	Unsigned hexadecimal (lowercase)

(Contd...)

X	Unsigned hexadecimal (uppercase)
e	Floating-point exponential format (lowercase)
E	Floating-point exponential format (uppercase)
f or F	Floating-point decimal format
g	Same as e if exponent is greater than –4 or less than precision; f otherwise
G	Same as E if exponent is greater than –4 or less than precision; F otherwise
c	Single character (accepts an integer or a single character string)
r	String (converts any Python object using repr)
s	String (converts any Python object using str)

G. Formatting Strings (without using methods)

1. Simple Conversions

We have discussed many important methods that frequently used in formatting *e.g.*, `rjust()`, `zfill()` and `format()` methods. The following sections discuss the various elements of the conversion specifiers in more detail.

```
>>> print 'Price of Apples = ₹ %d' % 50

Price of Apples = ₹ 50
```

The number 50 will be printed at the place of %d. Also check carefully the role of modulo operator (%).

```
>>> print 'Hexadecimal price of Apples = %x' % 50
Hexadecimal price of Apples = 32
>>> from math import pi
>>> print 'Value of Pi = %f' % pi
Value of Pi = 3.141593
>>> print 'Estimate of pi = %i' % pi #Same with %d
Estimate of pi = 3
>>> print 'Using str = %s' % 50
Using str = 50
>>> print 'Using str = %s' % 'Python'
Using str = Python
>>> print 'Using repr: %r' % 50L
Using repr: 50L
>>> print 'Using repr: %r' % 'Python'
Using repr: 'Python'
```

2. Width and Precision

As we have seen that most of the output formatting had done with the help of `format()` methods. In a very simple way, we can specify a field width and a precision. The width is the minimum number of characters reserved for a formatted value. The precision is (for a numeric conversion) the number of decimals that will be included in the result or (for a string conversion) the maximum number of characters the formatted value may have.

These two parameters are supplied as two integer numbers (width first, then precision), separated by a . (dot). Both are optional, but if we want to supply only the precision, the dot is a must. Let us see some examples:

```
>>> from math import pi
>>> print '%10f' % pi
   3.141593
```

| | | 3 | . | 1 | 4 | 1 | 5 | 9 | 3 |

```
>>> print '%10.2f' % pi # Field width 10, precision 2
      3.14
>>> print '%.2f' % pi # Precision 2
3.14
>>> print '%.5s' % 'Programming' # with dot
Progr # prints only 5 characters
>>> print '%5s' % 'Programming'  # without dot
Programming # prints all the characters
```

Note: We can use an * (asterisk) as the width or precision (or both). In that case, the number will be read from the tuple argument:

```
>>> print '%.*s' % (7, 'Programming')
Program
```

3. Zero-Padding, Signs, and Alignments

We discussed about `zfills()`, `ljust()`, `rjust()` and `center()` methods for zero padding and different alignments. Without using these methods we also can get formatted outputs in a simple way.

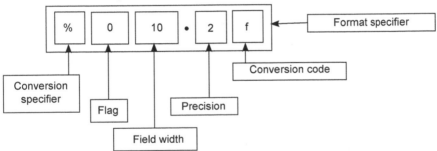

Let us see with some examples. Before the field width and precision numbers, we may put a "flag," which may be either zero, blank, plus or minus. A zero means that the number will be zero-padded:

```
>>> print '%010.2f' % 123.456
0000123.46
```

Here the leading zero in 010 in the preceding code does not mean that the width specifier is an octal number, as it would in a normal Python number. From the conversion specifier, Python knows that it is not an Octal number, just as the width specifier. However, if you write as follows:

```
>>> print 010
8
```

Here it is an octal number. The basic difference is that it is not enclosed within the string quotes and here is no conversion specifier(%).

Again by using a minus sign (−) in the value of flag will left-aligns the value:

```
>>> print '%-10.2f' % 123.456
123.46
```

By defining these width values, we can align positive and negative numbers:

```
>>> print ('%d' % 123) + '\n' + ('%d' % −123) # No values of
123                                           # field width
−123
>>> print ('% 5d' % 123) + '\n' + ('% 5d' % −123)# With field
  123                                              # width 5
 −123
```

Example 4.1: Formatting Example

```
#The following example prints out  a formatted price list with a given width
width = input('Please enter width: ')
item_width = width - 10
format = '%-*s%10.2f'
print '_' * width
print '%-*s%10s' % (item_width, 'Item', 'Price')
print '-' * width
print '%-*s%10.2f' % (item_width, 'Tomato', 56.75)
print format % (item_width, 'Potato', 40.00)
print format % (item_width, 'Waterlemon', 25.50)
print format % (item_width, 'Cucumber', 7.75)
print format % (item_width, 'Garlic(per Kg)', 120)
print '=' * width
```

The output of the above program is:

```
Please enter width: 30
```

```
Item                    Price
```

```
Tomato                  56.75
Potato                  40.00
Waterlemon              25.50
Cucumber                 7.75
Garlic(per Kg)         120.00
```

==============================

In this example, the width of the **Item** is 'width – 10' because 10 is reserved for the Price column. By default, the strings are right aligned, so using minus(–) sign we can right aligned for the Item column.

Note: However, if we used format() method, then the strings are left aligned, so we used < and > operators for left and right alignments respectively.

From the above examples, we can conclude that the orders of these format specifier items are crucial.

- **The % character**: This marks the beginning of the conversion specifier.
- **Conversion flags**: These are optional and may be -, indicating left alignment; +, indicating that a sign should precede the converted value; " " (a space character), indicating that a space should precede positive numbers; or 0, indicating that the conversion should be zero-padded.
- **The minimum field width**: This is also optional and specifies that the converted string will be at least this wide. If this is an * (asterisk), the width will be read from the tuple value.
- **A · (dot) followed by the precision**: This is also optional. If a real number is converted, this many decimals should be shown. If a string is converted, this number is the *maximum field width*. If this is an * (asterisk), the precision will be read from the tuple value.
- **The conversion type**: This can be any of the types listed in Table 4.1.

EXERCISES

4.1. State whether the following statements are *true* or *false*.

(*i*) The input list in a input () function may contain one or more variables.

(*ii*) The input () function can't be use for reading a single character from the keyboard.

(*iii*) The format specification %+-6d prints an integer left justified in a field width of 6 with a sign, if the number is positive.

(*iv*) If the field width of a format specifier is larger than the actual width of the value, the value is printed right justified in the field.

(*v*) The print list in a `input()` function can contain function calls.

(*vi*) The `input()` function is used for reading integer values only.

(*vii*) The `input()` function cab be used for reading both integer and numeric values.

(*viii*) The format specification `%5s` will print only the first 5 characters of a given string to be printed.

4.2. Show the printout of the following statements:

```
print(format(57.467657, "9.3f"))
print(format(12345678.923, "9.1f"))
print(format(57.4, ".2f"))
print(format(57.4, "10.2f"))
```

4.3. Show the output of the following statements:

```
print(format(57.467657, "9.3e"))
print(format(12345678.923, "9.1e"))
print(format(57.4, ".2e"))
print(format(57.4, "10.2e"))
```

4.4. Show the printout of the following statements:

```
print(format(5789.467657, "9.3f"))
print(format(5789.467657, "<9.3f"))
print(format(5789.4, ".2f"))
print(format(5789.4, "<.2f"))
print(format(5789.4, ">9.2f"))
```

4.5. Show the printout of the following statements:

```
print(format(0.457467657, "9.3%"))
print(format(0.457467657, "<9.3%"))
```

4.6. Show the printout of the following statements:

```
print(format(45, "5d"))
print(format(45, "<5d"))
print(format(45, "5x"))
print(format(45, "<5x"))
```

4.7. Show the printout of the following statements:

```
print(format("Programming is fun", "25s"))
print(format("Programming is fun", "<25s"))
print(format("Programming is fun", ">25s"))
```

4.8. What is the return value from invoking the **format** function?

4.9. What happens if the size of the actual item is greater than the width in the format specifier?

4.10. What is the difference between input () and raw_input() functions? Explain with an example.

4.11. Write a Python program to read the following numbers, round them off to the nearest integers and print out the results in integer form:

67.7   65.11   −12.89   −23.56   89.90   89.10

4.12. Write a Python program that prints the value 12.345678 in exponential format with the following specifications:

(*i*)   correct to three decimal places.

(*ii*) correct to five decimal places.

(*iii*) correct to seven decimal places.

4.13. Write a Python program that prints the value 12.345678 in fixed point format with the following specifications:

(*i*)   correct to two decimal places.

(*ii*) correct to four decimal places.

(*iii*) correct to zero decimal places.

5

Decision Making and Branching

INTRODUCTION

Most of the programs we executed in the previous chapters are a set of statements which are normally executed sequentially in the order in which they appear. However, in practice, we have a number of situations where they may have to change the order of execution of statements based on certain conditions. This involves a kind of decision making to see whether a particular condition has occurred or not leading to what is known as Branching.

5.1 IF STATEMENT

The **if** statement is used to control the flow of execution of statements. It is a two way decision making statement and is used in conjunction with an expression. It takes the following form:

`if (test condition):`

In the above syntax, colon is a must. It allows the computer to evaluate the expression first and then, depending on whether the value of the expression (relation or condition) is TRUE or FALSE, it transfers the control of the statement. This point of program has two paths to follow, known as branching, one for the true condition and the other for the false condition as shown in Fig. 5.1.

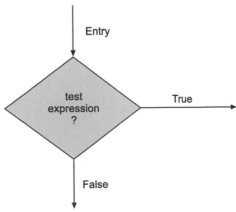

Fig. 5.1. Two way branching.

Some examples of if statements are:

(*a*) If (code is M)

Person is male

(*b*) If (age is more than 60)

Person is retired.

The **if** statement may be implemented in different forms depending on the complexity of conditions to be tested. Some of the different forms are:

1. Simple if statement

2. if else statement

3. nested if else statement

4. else if ladder.

They are explained In the following subsections

5.1.1 Simple if Statement

The general form of a simple if statement is as follows:

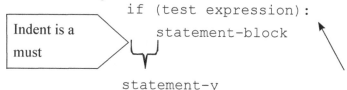

```
                               if (test expression):
                                   statement-block


                           statement-y
```

In Python, indent plays an important role. After the `test-expression`, colon is mandatory and the `statement-block` will be written after an indent (means 4 blank spaces). The `statement-block` may be a single statement or a block of statements. If the `test  expression` is true, the `statement-block` will be executed, otherwise the `statement-block` will be skipped and the execution will jump to the `statement-y`. Here python knows that `statement-y` is outside the if statement because it comes out of the `statement-block` by an indent. If the condition is true, both the `statement-block` and `statement-y` are executed in sequence. This is illustrated in Fig. 5.2.

As an example, we can consider the following segment of program for processing marks in a final examination.

....

....

```
if (marks >= 75 and marks<=100)  :
    print '\n Distinction.\n'
```

....

....

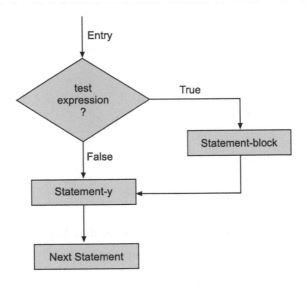

Fig. 5.2 Flowchart of simple if statement.

Example 5.1: Write a python program to read four values *a*, *b*, *c* and *d* from the terminal and evaluate the ratio of (*a+b*) to (*c–d*) and print the result if *c–d* is not equal to zero.

Solution: When we write more than one statement inside the statement-block, proper indent must be maintained. No other brackets are required.

```
a=input("Enter the value of a :")
b=input("Enter the value of b :")
c=input("Enter the value of c :")
d=input("Enter the value of d :")
if ((c-d) != 0) :
      ratio = float(a+b)/float(c-d)    # Statement-block
      print 'Ratio =', ratio          # Statement-block
print 'Program Ends' # Statement-y
```

```
OUTPUT of this program:
(First Run)
Enter the value of a :12
Enter the value of b :7
Enter the value of c :15
```

```
Enter the value of d :17
Ratio = -9.5
Program Ends
(Second Run)
Enter the value of a :12
Enter the value of b :7
Enter the value of c :15
Enter the value of d :15
Program Ends
```

The above program has been run for two set of data to check the paths of the statement blocks. The result of the first run is printed as

```
                  Ratio = -9.5

                  Program Ends
```

During the first run the statements contained in the 'Statement-block' are executed and again the 'Statement-y' is executed. The condition is true, so both are executed in sequence. However, in the second run, it executes the 'Statement-y' only because the value of (c − d) is equal to zero and therefore, the statements contained in the 'Statement-block' are skipped.

5.1.2 if else Statement

The 'if else' statement is an extension of the simple if statement. The general form is:

```
if (test expression) :
     true-block statement(s)
else :
     false-block statement(s)
statement-y
```

If the test expression is TRUE, then the true-block statement(s) are executed; otherwise the false-block statement(s) are executed. In either case, either true-block or false block will be executed, not both. This is illustrated in Fig 5.3. In both the cases, the control is transferred subsequently to the statement-y. Note that the colons are required in both statements of if and else lines.

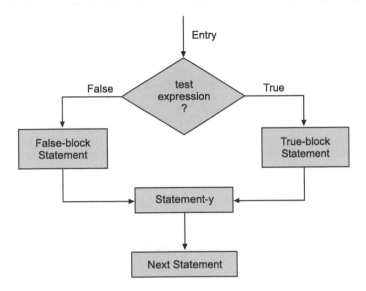

Fig. 5.3 Flowchart of 'if else' control.

Let us consider an example of counting the number of boys and girls in a class. We use code 1 for girls and code 2 for boys. The program segment may be written as:

```
.........
.........
if code == 1 :
     girls = girls + 1
     print '\n Distinction.\n'
else :
     boys = boys + 1
.........
.........
```

The first test determines whether the student is a girl or not. It yes, the number of girls is increased by one and the program continues to the second test. Once a student is identified as a girl, there is no need to test again for a boy. A student can be either a girl or a boy, not both.

Let us consider the example discussed in Example 5.1. When the denominator $(c–d)$ is zero, the ratio is not calculated. In such cases, we can improve this by adding an else clause as follows:

```
a=input("Enter the value of a :")
b=input("Enter the value of b :")
```

```
c=input("Enter the value of c :")
d=input("Enter the value of d :")
if ((c-d) != 0) :
    ratio = float(a+b)/float(c-d) # True-block Statement 1
    print 'Ratio =', ratio # True-block Statement 2
else:
    print 'c-d is zero.',   #False-block Statement 1
    print "Ratio can't be calculated." #False-block
                                           Statement 2
print 'Program Ends' # Statement-y
```

If the values of c and d are same, then we will get the two messages "c-d is zero. Ratio can't be calculated." After executing one of the block statement(s) the control is transferred subsequently to the statement-y (print 'Program Ends'). Another important point to be noted here is that you may be thinking why we are using single quote and double quote in False-block Statements. In False-block Statement 1 we can use either single quote or double quote, it does not make any difference. However in False-block Statement 2, we have to use double quote only because single quote will not work here. Why? The single quote in 'can't' will create confusion in string terminating condition.

Example 5.2: Write a Python program to check a given number is even or odd.

Solution:

```
no=input("Enter a Number :")
rem= no % 2
if rem == 0 :
    print 'The number is Even.'
else:
    print 'The number is Odd.'
```

Output of this Program:

First Run:

Enter a Number :123

The number is Odd.

Second Run:

Enter a Number :234

The number is Even.

5.1.3 Nested if else Statement

When a series of decisions are involved, we may have to use more than one if else statement in nested form as shown below:

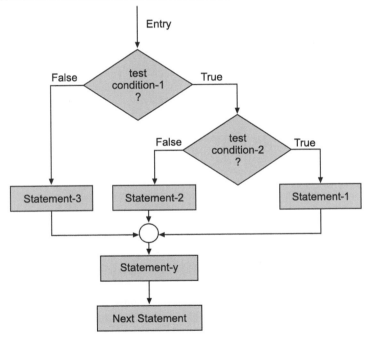

Fig. 5.4 Flowchart of 'nested if else' control statement.

The logic of execution is that, if condition-1 is false, the statement-3 will be executed; otherwise it continues to perform the second test. If the condition-2 is true, the statement-1 will be evaluated; otherwise statement-2 will be executed and then the control is transferred to the statement-y.

Example 5.3: Write a python program to print the largest of the three numbers using nested if else statements.

Solution: To make sure that this program works properly, we should try with different options. Input '*a*' as largest value than '*b*' and '*c*' and so on.

```
a=input("Enter the value of a :")
b=input("Enter the value of b :")
c=input("Enter the value of c :")
print 'Largest Number is :'
if a>b :
    if a > c:
        print a
    else :
        print c
else :
    if b>c :
        print b
    else :
        print c
```

Output of the above program: (with different options)

```
Enter the value of a :12        Enter the value of a :12
Enter the value of b :34        Enter the value of b :45
Enter the value of c :56        Enter the value of c :32
Largest Number is :
56
Enter the value of a :34        Enter the value of a :22.6
Enter the value of b :12        Enter the value of b :65.8
Enter the value of c :22        Enter the value of c :32.5
Largest Number is :             Largest Number is :
34                                   65.8
```

Note: In Python, as we mentioned earlier that indent takes an important role. In the following example, the else clause belongs to inner if statement.

```
if a>b :
    if a > c:
        print a
    else :
        print c
```

But if we write as,

```
if a>b :
    if a > c:
        print a
else :
    print c
```

the `else` clause belongs to the outer `if` statement. Interpreter will not give error in such logical error.

5.1.4   else if (elif) ladder Statement

There is another way of putting **if**s together when multipath decisions are involved. A multipath decision is a chain of **if**s in which the statement associated with each **else** is an **if**. The general form is:

```
if(condition-1)  :
     statement-1
elif (condition-2):
     statement-2
elif (condition-3):
     statement-3
...

...

elif (condition-n):
     statement-n
else :
     default-statement
statement-y
```

This construct is known as the else if (represented by `elif` in Python) ladder. The conditions are evaluated from the top to downwards. As soon as the true condition is found, the statement associated with it is executed and the control is transferred to the `statement-y`, skipping the rest of the ladder. When all the **n** conditions are false, then the final else containing the `default statement` will be executed. Figure 5.5 shows the logic of the execution of **else if ladder** statements.

Let us consider a simple example:

```
num = input('Enter a number:')
if num > 0:
     print 'The number is positive'
elif num < 0:
     print 'The number is negative'
else:
     print 'The number is zero'
```

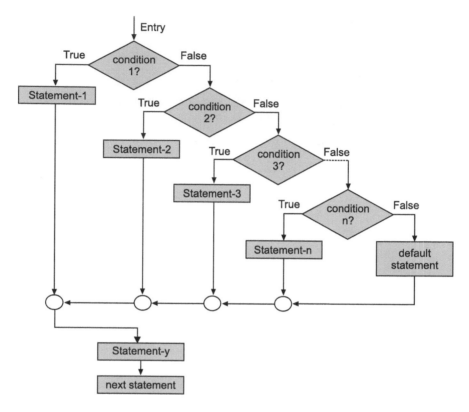

Fig. 5.5 Flowchart of 'else if(elif)' ladder.

This is how we can use else if statement.

Example 5.4: Write a python program to show the grading the students in an academic institution. The grading is done according to the following rules:

Average marks	Grade
75 to 100	Distinction
60 to 74	First Division
50 to 59	Second Division
40 to 49	Third Division
0 to 39	Fail

Solution:

```
marks=input("Enter the average marks of the student:")
if marks >=75 and marks<=100 :
    print '\n Distinction.'
elif marks >=60 and marks<75 :
    print '\n First Division.'
```

```
elif marks >=50 and marks<60 :
    print '\n Second Division.'
elif marks >=40 and marks<50 :
    print '\n Third Division.'
elif marks >=0 and marks<40 :
    print '\n Fail.'
else : # for negative numbers and greater than 100
    print '\n Out of Range\n'
```

Output of the above program: (with multiple runs)

Enter the average marks of the student: 100

Distinction.

Enter the average marks of the student: 98

Distinction.

Enter the average marks of the student: 74

First Division.

Enter the average marks of the student: 65

First Division.

Enter the average marks of the student: 56

Second Division.

Enter the average marks of the student: 43

Third Division.

Enter the average marks of the student: 23

Fail.

Enter the average marks of the student: 20

Out of Range

Example 5.5: Suppose we want to develop a program to practice subtraction. The program randomly generates two single-digit integers, *number1* and *number2*, with *number1* >= *number2* and asks the student a question such as "*What is 10 – 7?* " After the student enters the answer, the program displays a message indicating whether the answer is correct or not.

Solution:

The algorithm of the program is as follows:

Step 1 : Generate two single-digit integers for *number1* and *number2*.

Step 2 : If *number1* < *number2*, interchange *number1* with *number2*.

Step 3 : Prompt the student to answer, "What is number1 – number2?"

Step 4 : Check the student's answer and display whether the answer is correct. The complete program is shown below.

```
import random
#Generate two random integers
number1 = random.randint(0, 99)
number2 = random.randint(0, 99)
# Interchange number1 with number2, if number1 <
number2
if number1 < number2:
    number1, number2 = number2, number1
#Prompt the student to answer "What is number1 -
number2?"
answer = input("What is "+ str(number1) + " - " + \
                str(number2) + "? "))
#Check the answer and display the result
if number1 - number2 == answer:
    print "You are Right!!!"
else:
    print "Your answer is wrong.\n", number1, '-', \
    number2, "is", number1 - number2, '.'
```

Output of the above program:
```
First Run:
What is 90 - 12? 78
You are Right!!!
Second Run:
What is 50 - 27? 6
Your answer is wrong.
50 - 27 is 23 .
```

5.2 BOOLEAN VALUES (TRUE OR FALSE)

The following values are considered by the interpreter to mean *false* when evaluated as a Boolean expression (for example, as the condition of an if statement):

False None 0 " "   () [] {}

Note: Representation of the some of these sequences are:

1. " " represents empty string

2. ( ) represents empty tuples

3. [ ] represents empty lists

4. { } represents empty dictionaries.

We will discuss in details about these in next chapters.

In other words, the standard values False and None, numeric zero of all types (including float, long, and so on), empty sequences (such as empty strings, tuples, and lists), and empty dictionaries are all considered to be false. *Everything else* is interpreted as *true*, including the special value True.

This means that every value in Python can be interpreted as a truth value, which is extremely useful. And the standard truth values are **True** and **False**. In some languages (such as C and Python prior to version 2.3), the standard truth values are 0 (for *false*) and 1 (for *true*). In fact, True and False aren't that different—they're just glorified versions of 0 and 1 that *look* different but act the same: Let us see some examples:

```
>>> True
True
>>> False
False
>>> True == 1
True
>>> False == 0
True
>>> True + False + 50
51
```

So now, a logical expression returning 1 or 0 (probably in an older version of Python), is *really* meant is True or False. One point to be noted here is that Python is also case sensitive. If we type TRUE or true, we will the following error message.

```
>>>TRUE
Traceback(most recent call last):
    File "<stdin>" line 1, in <module>
NameError: name 'TRUE' is not defined
>>>false
```

```
Traceback(most recent call last):
    File "<stdin>" line 1, in <module>
NameError: name 'false' is not defined
```

The Boolean values True and False belong to the type bool, which can be used to convert other values, as follows:

>>> bool('Anything')

True

>>> bool(42)

True

>>> bool('')

False

>>> bool(0)

False

EXERCISES

5.1. State whether the following are *false* or *true*:

(*i*) When **if** statements are nested, the last **else** get associated with the nearest **if** without an **else**.

(*ii*) One **if** statement can have more than one **else** clause.

(*iii*) Program stops its execution when a **break** statement is encountered.

(*iv*) Any expression can be used for the **if** expression.

(*v*) Each expression in the **elif** clause must test the same variable.

(*vi*) The or operator is true only when both the operands are true.

(*vii*) Multi-way selection can be accomplished using an **elif** statement.

(*viii*) The expression !(a != b) is equivalent to the expression ($a == b$).

5.2. Find errors, if any in each of the following segments:

```
(a)  if (a + b = c and d > 0):
            print "Greater than Zero."
(b)  if (a > 0) ;
            print "a + b =c"
(c)  if (a > 0 or b > 0 ):
            print " Both are positive."
```

5.3. The following is a segment of a program:

```
            a = 1
            b = 1
        if n > 0 :
```

```
                    a += 1
                    b -= 1
          print "a =", a
          print "b =", b
```

What will be the values of a and b when (*i*) *n* = 1 and (*ii*) *n* = 0 ?

5.4. Rewrite each of the following without using compound relations:

```
     (a) if (marks >= 60 and marks <75):
              print 'First Division.'
     (b) if (number < 0 or number > 100):
              print "Out of Range"
         else:
              print " The number lies between 0
              and 100."
     (c) if ((marks > 75 and marks <=100) or
         Total = 560):
              print "Distinction."
         else:
              print "Try Again!"
```

5.5. Assuming *a* = 1, state whether the following logical expressions are true or false.

```
     (i) a == 1 and a > 1 and !a
     (ii) a == 1 or a > 1 and !a
     (iii) a == 1 and a > 1 or !a
     (iv) a == 1 or a > 1 or !a
```

5.6. Assuming that *x* = 2, *y* = 0 and *z* = 1, what will be their values after executing the following code segments?

```
     (a) if (x or y or z):
              y = 5
         else:
              z = 0
     (b) if (x and y):
              x = 12
         else:
              y = 20
     (c) if (x):
              if(y):
```

```
            z = 100
    else:
        z = 10
(d) if (x == 0 or x and y):
        if(!y):
            z = 123
    else:
        z = 80
(e) if (x == 0 or x and y):
        if(!y):
        z = 123
    else:
        z = 80
```

5.7. What will be the output of the following code segments? Assume $x = 6$, $y = 5$ and $z = 12$

```
1. if x%2 == 0:
       if x%3 == 0:
       print 'Divisible by 2 and 3'
   else:
       print 'Divisible by 2 and not by 3'
   elif x%3 == 0:
       print 'Divisible by 3 and not by 2'
2. if x < y and x < z:
       print 'x is least'
   elif y < z:
       print 'y is least'
   else:
       print 'z is least'
3. if x == 6 :
       print " Python "
       if x == 12:
           print " Anaconda "
       else:
           print " Spyder "
   else :
       print "Program Ends."
```

5.8. What is the output of the following code segment if $n = 10$ and $n = 11$ respectively?

(*a*)
```
if n % 2 == 0:
    print n, "is even."
print n, "is odd."
```

(*b*)
```
if n % 2 == 0:
    print n, "is even."
else
    print n, "is odd."
```

5.9. Suppose $x = 10$ and $y = 9$; show the output, if any, of the following code. What is the output if $x = 30$ and $y = 40$? What is the output if $x = 10$ and $y = 20$? Draw a corresponding flowchart for the code.

```
if x >= 10:
    if y > 9:
        z = x + y
        print("z is", z)
else:
    print("x is", x)
```

5.10. Suppose $x = 2$ and $y = 4$. Show the output, if any, of the following code. What is the output if $x = 3$ and $y = 2$? What is the output if $x = 3$ and $y = 3$?

```
if x > 2:
    if y > 2:
        z = x + y
    print("z is",)
else:
    print("x is", x)
```

5.11. What is wrong in the following code segment?

```
if score >= 60.0:
    grade = 'D'
elif score >= 70.0:
    grade = 'C'
elif score >= 80.0:
    grade = 'B'
elif score >= 90.0:
    grade = 'A'
else:
    grade = 'F'
```

5.12. Rewrite the following statement using a Boolean expression:

```
if count % 10 == 0:
    flag = False
else:
    flag = True
```

5.13. Write a Python program that accepts three variables x, y, and z and prints the largest odd number among them. If none of them are odd, it should print a message "No Odd Numbers are entered".

5.14. Fermat's Last Theorem says that there are no positive integers a, b and c such that

$$a^n + b^n = c^n$$

for any values of n greater than 2. Write a Python program to explain this theorem.

5.15. Write a Python program to check a given year is a leap year or not.

6

Decision Making and Looping

INTRODUCTION

If we want to execute a program segment repeatedly, then we can use the concept of *loops*. The looping capabilities enable us to develop concise programs containing repetitive process (for both known and unknown number of repetitions). In looping, sequences of statements are executed until some conditions of termination of the loop are satisfied.

A *program loop* therefore consists of two segments, one known as the *control statement* and the other one is known as the *body of the loop*. The control statement tests certain conditions and then directs the repeated execution of the statements contained in the body of the loop. The flow chart in Fig. 6.1 illustrate this.

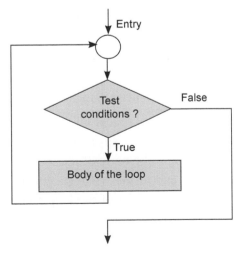

Fig. 6.1 Loop control structure.

The test conditions should be carefully stated to perform the desired number of loop executions. The test condition will transfer the control out of the loop. In case, due to some reason it does not do so, the control sets up an infinite loop and the body is executed again and again.

In general, a looping process consists of the following four steps:

1. Setting and initialization of the condition variable.

2. Execution of the statements in the body of the loop.

3. Test for a specified value of the condition variable for execution of the loop.

4. Updating the condition variable.

Python provides two ways for performing loop operations. They are:

1. The **while loop** statement

2. The **for loop** statement.

6.1 THE WHILE LOOP STATEMENT

The syntax for using while loop is:

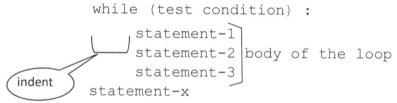

```
            while (test condition) :
                    statement-1
                    statement-2  body of the loop
                    statement-3
    indent      statement-x
```

The `test condition` is evaluated first and if it is *true*, then the body of the loop is executed. After execution of the body, the test condition is once again evaluated and if it is true, the body is executed once again. This process is repeated again and again until the test condition becomes *false*. When the condition becomes false the control is transferred out of the loop. On exit, the program continues with the statement immediately after the body of the loop.

In Python, as we mentioned earlier, indent takes an important role. After the while statement, an indent (four blank spaces) is a must and it represents the starting of the body of the loop. The body of the loop may have one or more statements. The colon at the end of the while statement is mandatory. In the above loop, the `statement-x` is out of the loop and it represents the next statement after the loop. So, this `statement-x` will execute only when the condition becomes false.

Few examples are given to make clear these concepts of loops

Example 6.1: To find the sum of 1 to 100 using while loop.

Solution:
```
sum = 0                # initialization
i = 1
while i<=100 :         # Condition testing (See the Colon here)
    sum = sum + i      # Body of the loop begins here
    i = i + 1          # incrementing
print "Sum = ",sum     # Printing the value of the sum (this
                       # statement is out of the loop)
```

The body of the loop is executed 100 times for $i = 1, 2, 3,...,100$, each time adding the sum of the value i, which is incremented inside the loop. The test condition may also be written as $i<101$; the result would be the same. The local variable i is also known as *counter* or *control variable*.

Note: Initialize $i = 0$, check the value of sum and number of iterations. Did you see any difference? Why? And, the statement `while i<=100:` can be written as, `while (i<=100) :` (using bracket also). Here bracket is not mandatory but we can use it for better understanding.

Example 6.2: A program to evaluate the equation
$$y = x^n$$
when n is a non negative integer.

Solution:
```
x = input("Enter the value of x:")
n = input("Enter the value of n:")
y=1.0
count = 1
while count <=n :
    y = y * x
    count = count + 1
print "\nx = ", x,
print "\tn = ", n,
print "\t x to power n = ", y
```

```
Output of the above program:
Enter the value of x: 2.5
Enter the value of n: 4
x =   2.5         n =   4    x to power n =   39.0625
Enter the value of x:3
Enter the value of n:5
x =   3  n =   5    x to power n =   243.0
```

Here the variable *y* is initialized to 1 and then multiplied by *x*, *n* times using the while loop. The loop control variable **count** is initialized outside the loop and incremented inside the loop. When the value of **count** is greater than *n*, the control exists the loop.

Examples 6.3: Read a string from the keyboard and print it. If you don't enter any string, it should ask again and again until you enter a valid string.

Solution: Using a while statement, we can wait for a string. If we don't enter any valid string, it will not come out of the loop.

```
name = ''           #An empty string
while not name: #while not empty => not false => true
    name = raw_input('Please enter your name: ')
print 'Hello, %s!' % name # with formatted output way.
```
OR
```
name = ''           #An empty string
while not name:
    name = raw_input('Please enter your name: ')
print 'Hello, %s!' % name   # with formatted output way.
```

```
Output of the program:
Please enter your name: shubha
Hello, shubha!
Please enter your name: ↵
Please enter your name: ↵
Please enter your name: abcde
Hello, abcde!
```

Here, if we do not enter a valid string, we can't come out of the loop. So we will get the message 'Please enter your name:' again. When we enter a valid one, it will come out of the loop and show the string.

Note: Just run this program and pressing the Enter key when asked to enter your name. You'll see that the question appears again, because name is still an empty string, which evaluates to *false*. But, What would happen if you entered just a space character as your name? It is accepted because a string with one space character is not empty, and therefore not false. This is definitely a flaw in our little program, but easily corrected: just change `while not name` to `while not name or name.isspace()`, or perhaps, `while not name.strip()`. We will learn more about built-in-functions in next chapters.

Example 6.4: Write a Python program to generate the Fibonacci series (0, 1, 1, 2, 3, 5, 8,...) using a while loop.

Solution: We can write an initial sub-sequence of the *Fibonacci* series as follows:

```
# Fibonacci series:
a, b = 0, 1 # multiple assignment here a = 0 and b =1.
while b < 1000:
     print b,
     a, b = b, a+b
```

Output of the above program:

```
The Fibonacci series :

1 1 2 3 5 8 13 21 34 55 89 144 233 377 610 987
```

In this example we introduce a new feature. The first line contains a *multiple assignment*: the variables *a* and *b* simultaneously get the new values 0 and 1. On the last line this is used again, demonstrating that the expressions on the right-hand side are all evaluated first before any of the assignments take place. The right-hand side expressions are evaluated from the left to the right. This is exactly same as a = b, b = a + b.

The while loop executes as long as the condition (here: *b* < 1000) remains true. In Python, any non-zero integer value is true; zero is false. The condition may also be a string or list value, in fact any sequence; anything with a non-zero length is true, empty sequences are false, as we explained in the above Example 6.3.

6.2 THE FOR LOOP STATEMENT

The **for** statement in Python differs a bit from other programming languages. Pythons for statement iterates over the items of any sequence (*e.g.*, a list or a string), in the order that they appear in the sequence.

The general form of for loop is :

```
          for var_name in sequence/functions
                  statement-1
                  statement-2  body of the loop
                  statement-3
      indent    statement-x
```

The *var_name* is any valid variable name and *sequence* may be either list, strings, tuples or dictionaries. *Functions* are provided by python and mainly we use the `range()` or `xrange()` functions. The body of the `for` loop may have a single statement or more statements. The `statement-x` represents the statement after the for loop.

Let us start with a few examples.

Example 6.5: Printing each word in a list of strings using for loop.

```
words = ['this', 'is', 'an', 'example'] # A sequence (list)
for word in words:
    print word,
```

The `word` is a variable name of our choice and `words` is the list we defined. Here `for` and `in` are reserve keywords and we can't change them. To understand this concept clearly, we can write the above segment of program as follows:

```
xyz = ['this', 'is', 'an', 'example'] # A sequence (list)
for a in xyz:
    print a,
```

See the difference in the above two program segments and we can differentiate between the reserve keywords and variable names.

```
The output of the above program is :
this is an example
Note 1: if we omit the comma at the end of the print
statement, the words will be printing vertically,
as follows:
this
is
an
example
Note 2:Modify the above list as follows and see the
difference
(i) words = ['this is an example']
    for word in words:
        print word,
(ii)words = 'this is an example'
    for word in words:
        print word,
Now analyze why you get two different outputs
```

Example 6.6: Printing numbers in a list using for loop.

Again we can use the `for` loop in numbers as follows:

```
numbers = [0, 1, 2, 3, 4, 5, 6, 7, 8, 9] # a list of numbers
for number in numbers:
    print number,
```

The output of the above program segment is:
0 1 2 3 4 5 6 7 8 9

A lot of computations involve processing a string one character at a time. Often they start at the beginning, select each character in turn, do something to it, and continue until the end. This pattern of processing is called a **traversal**. One way to write a traversal is with a for loop is as follows:

```
fruit = 'orange'
for char in fruit:
    print char,
```

Each time through the loop, the next character in the string is assigned to the variable char. The loop continues until no characters are left. The output of the above program segment will look like this:

o r a n g e

Example 6.7: The following example shows how to use concatenation (string addition) and a for loop to generate an abecedarian series (that is, in alphabetical order).

```
prefixes = 'JKLMNOPQ'
suffix = 'ack'
for letter in prefixes:
    print letter + suffix
```

The output of the above program is:
```
Jack
Kack
Lack
Mack
Nack
Oack
Pack
Qack
```

However, the word "Qack" is misspelled. We can fix this error by using an if-else statement as follows:

```
prefixes = 'JKLMNOPQ'
suffix = 'ack'
for letter in prefixes:
    if letter == 'Q' :
    print letter + 'u' + suffix
    else :
        print letter + suffix
```

Now we can get "Quack" instead of "Qack".

Example 6.8: The following example counts the number of times the letter a appears in a string:

```
word = 'banana'
count = 0
for letter in word:
    if letter == 'a':
        count = count + 1
print count
```

The variable count is initialized to 0 and then incremented each time an *a* is found. When the loop exits, count contains the result—the total number of *a*'s.

Example 6.9: Encapsulate this code in a function named count, and generalize it so that it accepts the string and the letter as arguments.

```
def count(string, letter):
    count = 0
    for character in string:
        if character == letter:
            count = count + 1
    return count
str1='banana'
letter ='a'
counter = count(str1, letter)
print 'No of the character','"',letter,'"',' present
=', counter
```

In the above program, we directly initialized the two strings str1 and letter as 'banana' and 'a' respectively. However we can generalize it again by using raw_input() function.

Output of the Program:

No of the character " a " present = 3

Example 6.10: Measure the length of the words in a list of strings using for loop.

```
s = ['capture', 'python', 'Programming']
    for x in s:
        print x, len(x)
```

Output of this program:

capture 7

python 6

Programming 11

Note: The len() is a built-in-function in Python which gives the length of a string. If we write the above program as below:

```
s = ['capture', 'python', 'Programming']
    for x in s[:] : # See the changes here (slicing)
        print x, len(x)
```

The output of the program will be exactly same. The basic difference is that in the second program where we are using slice options, it can create a copy of the list, s.

Suppose, If we need to modify the list we are iterating over, *e.g.*, duplicate selected items, it is better to iterate over a copy. The slice notation makes this particularly convenient. For example:

```
s = ['capture', 'python', 'Programming']
for x in s[:]:
    if len(x) > 7 :
        s.insert(0, x)
print s
```

The insert() function will add a new string in the list. The first argument represents the location of the list and the second argument is the string. We will discuss more functions in Chapter 7.

The output of the above program is:

['Programming', 'capture', 'python', 'Programming']

If we write as below in the 4th line of the above program,

```
s.insert(1, x), the output will look like:
```
['capture', 'Programming', 'python', 'Programming']
```
And,
```
```
s.insert(2, x)
```
['capture', 'python', 'Programming', 'Programming']

6.3 THE `range()` FUNCTION

To iterate over a sequence of numbers, Python provides the built-in function `range()` which can generates lists containing arithmetic progression. This function can take different arguments. The general syntax for the `range()` function is as follows:

```
range(argument1)
```
```
range(argument1, argument2)
```
```
range(argument1, argument2, argument3)
```

6.3.1 `range(argument1)` function

In this case, the `range` returns a list of indices from 0 to **argument1** - 1, where **argument1** is the length of the list. For example let **argument1** be 10, then

```
>>> # range (End_value) with one argument
>>> range(10) # range(argument1)
[0, 1, 2, 3, 4, 5, 6, 7, 8, 9]
```

The given end point is never part of the generated list; `range(10)` generates a list of 10 values, exactly the legal indices for items of a sequence of length 10 starting from 0 to 9.

6.3.2 `range(argument1, argument2)` function

In this case, the range function can take two arguments. And the `argument1` represents the starting value and `argument2` represents the end value (excluding itself). For example let be **argument1** be 5 and **argument2** be 15. Then,

```
>>> # range (starting_value, End_value)
>>> range(5, 15) # range() function with two arguments
[5, 6, 7, 8, 9, 10, 11, 12, 13, 14]
```

The starting value may be either negative or positive value. For example, if we enter negative value as starting value, then,

```
>>> range(-1,5) # starting value may be negative.
[-1, 0, 1, 2, 3, 4]
```

6.3.3 range(argument1, argument2, argument3) function

As above, the first two arguments represent the first and final values respectively. And argument3 represents the 'step size' of the list to be generated. For example,

```
>>> # range(starting_value, End_value, step_size)
>>> range(0, 10, 3)
[0, 3, 6, 9]
```

This will generate the list starting from 0 and incrementing by 3 till the final value 10. And again,

```
>>> range(0, 15, 3)
[0, 3, 6, 9, 12] # 15 will NOT be in the list.
```

Step size may be either negative or positive value. For example, let us consider an example with negative value of step size as:

```
>>> range(-10, -100, -30)
[-10, -40, -70]
```

Note: Suppose if you write the step size in the range() function as fractional value rather than integer value, you will get an error message.

```
>>> range(0, 15, 3.1)
TypeError: range() integer step argument expected, got float.
The question is: how to use fractional value in step size?
```

Example 6.11: Implementing float value in step size in for loop

The easiest way is that we can write our own program using a user defined function called drange() as follows:

```
def drange(start, stop, step) :
    while start < stop :
        yield start
        start += step
min_val = 1.0
max_val = 2.0
step_size = 0.1
```

```
for i in drange(min_val,max_val,step_size):
    print i,
```

The output of the above program is:

1.0 1.1 1.2 1.3 1.4 1.5 1.6 1.7 1.8 1.9

The function drange() can be used as range() function. The basic difference is that the drange() function is not a built-in-function.

6.4 THE xrange() FUNCTION

In Python 3.0, range() will be turned into an xrange-style function.

```
>>> zip(range(5), xrange(100))
[(0, 0), (1, 1), (2, 2), (3, 3), (4, 4)]
```

Here, the built-in function zip() which "zips" together the sequences, returning a list of tuples, we will learn tuples in Chapter 10. The zip() function works with as many sequences . It's important to note what zip() does when the sequences are of different lengths: it stops when the shortest sequence is used up. So in the above example, range(5) function will give you from 0 to 4 whereas xrange(100) will not give you from 0 to 99. Instead, it calculates only those numbers needed.

Note: Parallel iterations

We can iterate over two sequences at the same time. Let's say that we have the following two lists:

```
names = ['Tomba', 'Smith', 'Tom', 'Singh', 'John']
ages = [22, 55, 39, 65, 43]
for i in range(len(names)):
    print names[i], 'is', ages[i], 'years old'
```

Output of the program:

```
Tomba is 22 years old
Smith is 55 years old
Tom is 39 years old
SIngh is 65 years old
John is 43 years old
```

We can use the built-in function zip() for parallel iteration as follows:

```
names =['Tomba', 'Smith', 'Tom','Singh','John']
ages = [22, 55, 39, 65, 43]
names = zip(names, ages)
print names
```

Output of the above program:

```
[('Tomba',    22),    ('Smith',    55),    ('Tom',    39),
('Singh',65),  ('John',  43)]
```

6.5 JUMPS IN LOOPS

Loops perform a set of operations repeatedly when the condition becomes true. The number of times a loop is repeated is decided in advance and the test condition is written to achieve this. Sometimes, when executing a loop it becomes desirable to skip a part of the loop or to leave the loop as soon as a certain condition occurs. For example, let us consider the case of searching for a particular name in a list containing, say, 100 names. A program loop written for reading and testing the names 100 times must be terminated as soon as the desired name is found. Python permits a jump from one statement to another within a loop as well as a jump out of a loop.

The break Statement

The break statement breaks out of the smallest enclosing for or while loop. An early exit from a loop can be made by using the break statement. They are illustrated in Figs. 6.2 and 6.3.

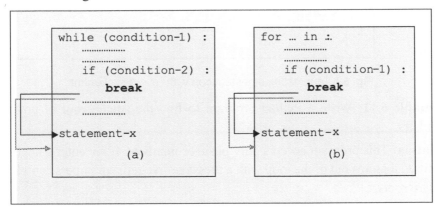

Fig. 6.2 Exiting a loop with break statement.

When a break statement is encountered inside a loop, the loop is immediately jumped out and the program continues with the statement immediately following the loop. In the above Fig. 6.2(*a*), if the given condition, condition-2, is true, then instead of executing other statements inside the loop, it will jump out of the loop and will execute the statement-x. Similarly in Fig. 6.2(*b*), if the given condition, condition-1, is true, it will execute the statement, statement-x, outside the loop.

When the loops are nested, the `break` would only exit from the loop containing it. That is, the `break` will exit only a single loop.

In Fig. 6.3, if the given condition, `condition-1` is true, the `break` will exit only from the inner loop and will execute the statement, `statement-y` not `statement-z`.

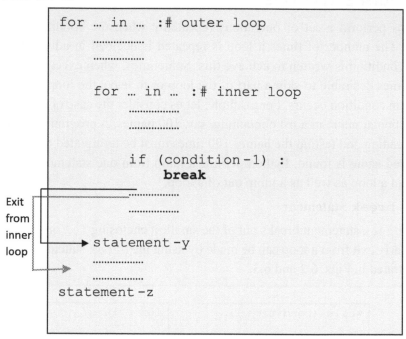

Fig. 6.3 Terminating a nested loop with `break` statement.

Example 6.12: Write a Python program to find the square root of positive numbers.

Solution: This program accepts only positive numbers. If we enter a negative number, it jumps out of the loop with a message "Negative numbers can't have square roots....!".

```
from math import sqrt
no = input("Enter a number :")
while True :
    sqr_rt = sqrt(no)
    print "The square root of the number",
    no, "is",sqr_rt
    no = input("Enter a number :")
    if no < 0 :
        print " Negative numbers can't have square
        roots....!" break
```

```
Output of the program:
Enter a number :23
The square root of the number  23  is  4.79583152331
Enter a number :33
The square root of the number  33  is  5.74456264654
Enter a number :36
The square root of the number  36  is  6.0
Enter a number :-34
 Negative numbers can't have square roots....!
```

6.6 SKIPPING A PART OF A LOOP

A loop simply executes a block until its condition becomes false, or until it has used up all sequence elements. But sometimes we may want to interrupt the loop to start a new iteration by skipping the part of the loop.

The Continue Statement

Like the break statement, Python supports another similar statement called the continue statement. However, unlike the break statement which causes the loop to be terminated, the continue statement causes the loop to be continued with the next iteration after skipping any statements in between. The continue statement tells the interpreter *"Skip the rest of the body and continue with the next iteration"*.

The use of the continue statement in loops is illustrated in Fig. 6.4.

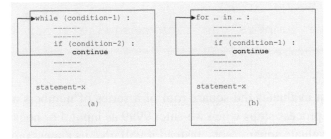

Fig. 6.4 Continuing in loops with continue statement.

The use of continue statement in while loop causes the control to go directly to the test condition, condition-1, and then to continue the iterative process. In case of **for loop**, if the condition, condition-1, is true, it will not execute the remaining statements, instead it will start the next iteration.

Example 6.13: Rewrite **Example 6.12** using the continue statement.

Solution: In this case let us slightly modify the above **example 6.12** using the continue statement.

```
from math import sqrt
print"Enter 99999 to stop."
while True :
    no = input("Enter a number :")
    if no == 99999 :
        break
    if no < 0 :
        print "Negative numbers can't have square
roots....!"
        continue
    sqr_rt = sqrt(no)
    print "The square root of the number" ,no, " is
",sqr_rt
print "End of Program."
```

Output of the above program:
```
Enter 99999 to stop.
Enter a number :123
The square root of the number  123  is  11.0905365064
Enter a number :234
The square root of the number  234  is  15.2970585408
Enter a number :-12
 Negative numbers can't have square roots....!
Enter a number :99999
End of Program.
```

The program evaluates the square root of a series of numbers and prints the results. The process stops when we enter 9999 as input. For negative numbers it will not evaluate square roots, instead it will give us a message.

Note: The continue statement is used less often than break. Even though continue can be a useful tool, it is not essential in Python. Because in Python, we have one more logical operator called 'not' which is more flexible than continue statement. To understand this, let us modify the above program as follows:

```
from math import sqrt
print"Enter 99999 to stop."
```

```
while True :
    no = input("Enter a number :")
    if no == 99999 :
        break
if not (no < 0) :
        sqr_rt = sqrt(no)
        print "The square root of the number " ,no,"
is ",sqr_rt
print "End of Program."
```

6.7 THE else CLAUSES ON LOOPS

Loop statements may have an else clause; it is executed when the loop terminates through exhaustion of the list (with for) or when the condition becomes false (with while), but not when the loop is terminated by a break statement.

One of the most commonly use format of the else clause is shown in Fig. 6.5.

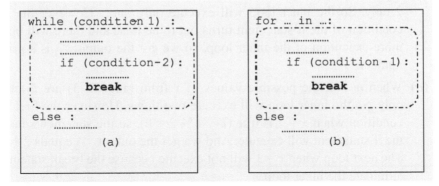

Fig. 6.5 else clause with while and for loops

In case of while loop, suppose the given condition, condition-1 is *true*, then the body of the loop represented by the dotted area will be executed and if the condition is *false*, then the else part will be executed.

We can use continue, break, and else clauses with both for loops and while loops. Let us start with an example.

Example 6.14: Write a Python program for searching Prime numbers in a given range.

Solution: Let us give the range between 2 to 9.

```
for n in range(2,10) :
    for x in range(2,n) :
```

```
        if n % x == 0 :
            print n, 'equals', x, '*', n/x
            break
    else :
        print n, ' is a prime number.'
```

Output of this program :
```
2 is a prime number.
3 is a prime number.
4 equals 2 * 2
5 is a prime number.
6 equals 2 * 3
7 is a prime number.
8 equals 2 * 4
9 equals 3 * 3
```

Note 1: The execution of the above program is as follows:

(*a*) The value of n starts with 2. So, the value of *x* in the range (2, 2) is empty. Thus the inner loop will not execute and the else part is executed. So we got the output "2 is a prime number.".

(*b*) Again, when n = 3, the value possible value of *x* from range(2,3) is 2 only. So the inner loop will execute only once. However the test condition of the if statement turns out to be false and there will be no more execution of the inner loop, so we got the output "3 is a prime number.".

(*c*) When *n* = 4, the possible values of *x* from range(2, 3) are 2 and 3 only. So the inner loop will execute two times. However the first test condition when *x* = 2 is true (*i.e.* 4 % 2 = 0), so the statements inside the if statement will execute. And we got the output "4 equals 2 * 2". The next loop when *x* = 3 will not execute because the break statement terminate the inner loop.

(*d*) Lastly, let us consider for *n* = 5. After this we are sure that you can analyze yourself for the remaining values of n. As before the possible values of *x* are 2, 3 and 4. So we know that the inner for loop will execute three times (*i.e.*, 5%2, 5%3 and 5%4). However, all the three conditions turn out to be false, so we got the output from the else part of the inner for loop.

Note 2: Precautions to be taken in using the `else` clause

Suppose if you write your program, in the following way shown in Fig. 6.6, the Python interpreter will not give error message because it is not a syntax error. Such type of error is known as Logical error.

In these cases, the `else` clause belongs to the `if` statement not for the loops. Let us write the above program 6.14 in this way to see the difference in the outputs:

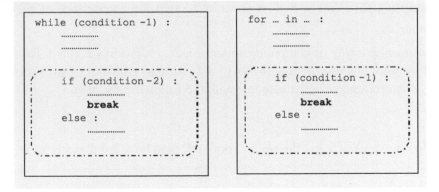

Fig. 6.6 wrong else clause with while and for loops

```
for n in range(2,10) :

    for x in range(2,n) :

        if n % x == 0 :

            print n, 'equals', x, '*', n/x

            break

    else : # see the difference here

        print n, ' is a prime number.'
```

The output will look like this
```
3 is a prime number.
4 equals 2 * 2
5 is a prime number.
5 is a prime number.
5 is a prime number.
6 equals 2 * 3
7 is a prime number.
7 is a prime number.
7 is a prime number.
7 is a prime number.
7 is a prime number.
8 equals 2 * 4
9 is a prime number.
9 equals 3 * 3
```

Example 6.15: Write a Python program to find the square root of a given number.

Solution: One way of computing square roots is Newton's method. Suppose that we want to know the square root of **a**. If we start with almost any estimate, **x**, we can compute a better estimate with the following formula:

$$y = \frac{x + a/x}{2}$$

Suppose, we want to get the square root of 4, then let a is 4 and x is 3.

```
a=4.0
x=3.0
epsilon = 0.00001
i=1
while True:
    print 'iteration = ', i,
    print 'x = ', x
    y = (x+a/x) /2
    if abs(y-x) < epsilon :
        break
    x=y
    i=i+1
```

Output of the program:
```
When a =4.0
iteration =  1 x =   3.0
iteration =  2 x =   2.16666666667
iteration =  3 x =   2.00641025641
iteration =  4 x =   2.00001024003
iteration =  5 x =   2.00000000003
when a = 50.0
iteration =  1 x =   3.0
iteration =  2 x =   9.83333333333
iteration =  3 x =   7.45903954802
iteration =  4 x =   7.08115772137
iteration =  5 x =   7.0710750004
when a = 80.0
```

```
iteration =  1 x =   3.0
iteration =  2 x =   14.8333333333
iteration =  3 x =   10.1132958801
iteration =  4 x =   9.0118372744
iteration =  5 x =   8.94452519234
iteration =  6 x =   8.94427191359
```

Important Point to Remember:

If you know how to use `for` loop, then see the program segment given below:

```
def getWordScore(word, n):
    score = 0
    for char in word:
        score = score + SCRABBLE_LETTER_VALUES[char]
    if len(word) == n:
        return ((score * len(word)) + 50)
    else:
        return score * len(word)
```

The above program can be written as :

```
def getWordScore(word, n):
    return (len(word) * sum(SCRABBLE_LETTER_VALUES[i] for i in
        word)) + (50 if len(word) == n else 0)
```

So, here are different ways of writing the programs. The best method is to understand easily to other new programmers.

EXERCISES

6.1. State whether the following statements are true or false.

(*i*) In a loop, if the body is executed **n** times, then the test condition is executed **n+1** times.

(*ii*) The number of times a control variable is updated always equal the number of loop iterations.

(*iii*) In a **for** loop expression, the starting value of the control variable must be less than its ending value.

(*iv*) **While** loops can be used to replace **for** loops without any change in the body of the loop.

(*v*) The use of **continue** statement is considered as unstructured programming.

(*vi*) The colon at the end of the while statement is not mandatory.

(*vii*) The **len()** function can't be used in while loops.

(*viii*) The **break** statement is used to skip a part of the statements in a loop.

(*ix*) The **else** statement can't be used with **for** or **while** loop.

(*x*) In a nested loop the **break** stamen will come out only from the inner loop.

(*xi*) Traversing in a list can be done without using a **for** loop.

6.2. Write the output of each of the following **range()** functions.

(*i*) `print range(5,10)`

(*ii*) `print range(0,10,3)`

(*iii*) `print range(0,10,2)`

(*iv*) `print range(2,2)`

6.3. What would be the output of each of the following code segment?

```
(i) words2 = ["room", "window","door"]
       for i in range(len(words2)) :
              print i, words[i]
```

```
(ii) words3 = "This is my name."
       for i in range(len(words3)) :
              print i, words3[i]
```

6.4. Convert the following **for** loop to a **while** loop statement.

```
sum = 0
for i in range(101):
       sum = sum + i
```

6.5. Convert the following **while** loop into a **for** loop statement.

```
sum = 0
i = 1
while sum < 101:
       sum = sum + i
       i += 1
```

6.6. Count the number of iterations in the following loops:

```
(i) i = 0
       while i < n:
              i += 1
```

```
(ii) for i in range(n):
              Print i
```

```
(iii) i = 3
       while i < n:
              i += 1
```

```
(iv) i = 3
       while i < n:
              i = i + 3
```

6.7. What will be the output of the following program segments?

```
(i)  for i in range(1, 6):
         j = 0
         while j < i:
             print j,
                     j += 1
(ii) i = 0
     while i < 7:
             for j in range(i, 1, -1):
                 print j,
             print("@@@")
             i += 1
(iii) i = 10
      while i >= 1:
          num = 1
          for j in range(1, i + 1):
              print num,
              print "***"
              num =num * 2
          print ' '
          i -= 1
(iv) i = 1
     while i <= 7:
         num = 1
         for j in range(1, i + 1):
             print num, "G"
             num += 2
         print
         i += 1
```

6.8. Write a **for** loop statement to print each of the following sequences of integers.

    (*a*) 1, 2, 4, 8, 16, 32, 64

    (*b*) 1, 3, 9, 27, 89, 243

    (*c*) –6, –4, –2, 0, 2, 4, 6

    (*d*) 1, 4, 6, 8, 9, 10, 12, 14, 15, 16, 18, 20

6.9. Change the following code from a **for** loop to a **while** loop:

```
for i in range(30, 0, -3):
    print i
```

6.10. What would be printed from the following code segment?

```
for i in range(1, 10):
    for j in range(1, i+1):
        print x, " ", y
```

6.11. Can you always convert any **while** loop into a **for** loop? Explain with an example.

6.12. The mathematician Srinivasa Ramanujan found an infinite series that can be used to generate a numerical approximation of π:

$$\frac{1}{\pi} = \frac{2\sqrt{2}}{9801} \sum_{k=0}^{\infty} \frac{(4k)!(1103+26390k)}{(k!)^4 * 396^{4k}}$$

Write a Python program to compute the value of p using this. It should use a while loop to compute terms of the summation until the last term is smaller than 1 e–15.

6.13. Write a Python program that computes and print a table of factorials for a given integer number, **n**.

[**Hints:** Factorial of $n = n! = 1 \times 2 \times 3 \times \ldots \times n$]

6.14. Write a Python program to print the following outputs using for loops.

(a)	(b)	(c)
*	11111	12345
**	2222	1234
***	333	123
****	44	12
*****	5	1

6.15. Write a Python program to compute the value of Euler's number e, which is used as the base of natural logarithm. The formula is given by:

$$e = 1 + \frac{1}{1!} + \frac{1}{2!} + \frac{1}{3!} + \frac{1}{4!} + \ldots + \frac{1}{n!}$$

The loop must terminate when the difference between two successive values of e is less than 0.00001.

6.16. Write Python programs to evaluate the following functions to 0.00001% accuracy.

$$(a)\ \sin x = x - \frac{x^3}{3!} + \frac{x^5}{5!} - \frac{x^7}{7!} + \frac{x^9}{9!} - \ldots$$

$$(b)\ \cos x = 1 - \frac{x^2}{2!} + \frac{x^4}{4!} - \frac{x^6}{6!} + \frac{x^8}{8!} - \ldots$$

Functions

INTRODUCTION

If we need to do the same work again, we could type the entire program again or place it in a loop. However, loops are most useful when we are repeating the same thing, but writing the same loop repeatedly in different parts of our program with slightly modified values in each one is not a proper way for a good programmer. For example, we need to find the sum of integers from 1 to 15, 21 to 40, and 38 to 60. If we write a program to add these three sets of numbers, our code might look like this:

```
sum = 0
for i in range(1, 16):
    sum = sum + i
print "Sum from 1 to 15 is", sum
sum = 0
for i in range(21, 41):
    sum = sum + i
print "Sum from 21 to 40 is", sum
sum = 0
for i in range(38, 61):
    sum = sum + i
print("Sum from 38 to 60 is", sum)
```

We have observed that the code is very similar, except that the starting and ending integers are different. Instead of writing these repetitive codes again and again, we can write a simplified code and then reuse it. This task can be done with the help of a function.

Python has **functions** that enable us to gather sections of code into more convenient groupings that can be called on when we have a need for them.

In this chapter, we will learn how to create and use our own functions. We can write our functions so that we can later interrogate them for information about how they behave and what we intend for them to do. So we will be learning in detail:

- How to design a function?
- How to integrate a function in a program?
- How functions communicate to each other?
- How nesting of functions can be achieved?

As the examples in this book get longer, typing the entire code block begins to be a burden. A single mistake causes us to retype in the entire block of code. When the program becomes very large and complex, the task of debugging, testing and maintaining becomes more difficult. So, if we divide a program into smaller segments or functional parts, then it is easier for us to code and debug them. Later, we can combine all the segments into a single unit.

We write programs that are saved as source code into files that can be opened, edited, and run without a great deal of work, whenever we want. To reach this far more convenient state of affairs, from here on we should type the programs into the main Editor window, and save the examples into a single folder from which we can reference them and run them anytime.

Note: We will be using the Editor provided by Enthought Canopy. We can use any one of the editors mentioned in Chapter 1. The Canopy editor is shown in Fig. 7.1

7.1 TYPES OF FUNCTIONS

Broadly functions are divided into 2 types.

(*a*) Built in functions and

(*b*) User defined functions.

7.1.1 Built in Functions

Some of the functions we have used, such as, `exp()`, `print()`, `input()` etc. are known as built-in functions. An example of built-in function is:

```
x = math.exp(1.0)
```

The Python has a number of built-in functions. They are listed in alphabetical order in Table 7.1.

Table 7.1: Built-in Functions

abs()	all()	any()	basestring()	bin()
bool()	bytearray()	callable()	chr()	classmethod()
cmp()	compile()	complex()	delattr()	dict()
dir()	divmod()	enumerate()	eval()	execfile()
file()	filter()	float()	format()	frozenset()
getattr()	globals()	hasattr()	hash()	help()
hex()	id()	input()	int()	isinstance()
issubclass()	iter()	len()	list()	locals()
long()	map()	max()	memoryview()	min()
next()	object()	oct()	open()	ord()
pow()	print()	property()	range()	raw_input()
reduce()	reload()	repr()	reversed()	round()
set()	setattr()	slice()	sorted()	staticmethod()
str()	sum()	super()	tuple()	type()
unichr()	Unicode()	vars()	xrange()	zip()
__import__()				

We will be explaining some of the commonly used built-in functions in the following chapters.

7.1.2 User Defined Functions

In order to make the use of a user defined function, we need to establish two elements that are related to functions:

1. Function definition and
2. Function call

Function definition:

The function definition is independent program module that is specially written to implement the requirements of the function. The program that calls the function is referred to as the *calling program*. A function definition shall include the following elements:

1. Python keyword def
2. Function name
3. List of parameters or arguments
4. A colon (mandatory for every function)
5. An indent (one indent = four blank spaces)
6. Function statements
7. A return statement.

The first four elements are grouped with the *function header* and remaining three is grouped with the *body of the function*.

The general syntax of a function definition to implement these two parts is given as follows:

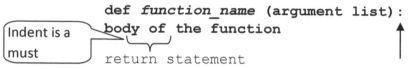

```
def function_name (argument list):
    body of the function
    return statement
```

Two precautions to be observed here in defining a function are:

(*a*) The colon at the end of the function header must be there and

(*b*) The function statements should be, with proper indent, if we want to keep inside the body of the function.

Suppose, if we write a function definition in the following way:

```
def function_name (argument list)  :
        statement 1
        statement 2
    statement 3
```

Here, **statement 1 and statement 2** belongs to the body of the function whereas **statement 3** does not belong to the function definition. So indentation will automatically take care the condition of being inside and outside of the body of the function.

The *function name* should be a valid Python identifier and therefore the same rules for the Python variables should follow. The name should be chosen appropriate to the task performed by the function. However, care must be exercised to avoid duplicating library routine names or operating system commands.

The return statement can take one of the following forms:

```
return
```

```
or
```

```
return expression
```

The first return will return None to the calling function. The second will return the value of the expression. It also may return the Boolean type, either True or False (or 0 or 1).

A function may have more than one or return statement depending on the certain conditions. For example:

```
if x >= y:
        return 1
    else :
        return 0
```

Let us start writing a small program of defining a function. The calculation of sum for different values of integers can be implemented in a simplified form as follows:

```python
def sum( no1, no2):
    result = 0
    for i in range(no1, no2 + 1):
        result = result + i
    return result
```

Now we can use this function for calculating different values of integers, as follows:

```python
print "Sum from 1 to 15 is", sum(1,16)
print "Sum from 21 to 40 is", sum(21, 41)
print "Sum from 38 to 60 is", sum(38, 61)
```

The output of the above program is:

```
Sum from 1 to 15 is 136

Sum from 21 to 40 is 651

Sum from 38 to 60 is 1188
```

The following example calculates the area of a circle.

Example 7.1: To find the area of a circle

```python
def area(radius):
    temp = math.pi * radius**2
    return temp
```

Here *area* is the *function name* and radius is the *argument*.

As we mentioned that we will be using Canopy editor for our examples. One of the reasons is that it provides the proper indentation in writing functions. An example to compare two values of x and y is shown in the following Canopy editor in Fig. 7.1. The bottom window(written as Python) of the editor shows the output of the program.

Fig. 7.1 Canopy Editor.

Function Call:

A function can be called using the function name followed by a list of actual arguments or parameters, if any, enclosed in parentheses. For example the function defined in Example 7.1 can be called as follows:

```
circle_area = area(5)
print circle_area
```

We can illustrate as:

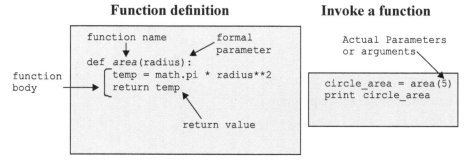

Important Points to remember:

1. The parameter names do not need to be same in the function definition. For example: we declare simply **r** in the calling program but the parameter name in the function definition is written as **radius**.

```
r = 5
circle_area = area(r)
print circle_area

def area(radius):
    temp = math.pi * radius**2
    return temp
```

2. If we are using more than one parameter, the list of the parameters must be separated by commas. For example :

```
def volume(length, breadth, thickness):
```

3. If the numbers of parameters are mismatch between the function definition and calling program, interpreter will generate an error.

Example 7.2: Write a "compare" function that returns

    (*a*) 1 if $x > y$,

    (*b*) 0 if $x = y$, and

    (*c*) –1 if $x < y$.

Answer: The function *compare* may be written as :

```
def compare(x,y) :
    if x > y :
        return 1
```

```
        elif x == y:
            return 0
        else :
            return -1
    x= compare (10,70)
    print x;
```

Note: To check this program using Python shell, we can do in two ways:

`>>> compare(10,70) # or`

`>>> print compare(10,70)`

Here we need two arguments for comparison the two values of x and y. On the other hand this function requires three return values according to the three conditions. It is a good idea to ensure that every possible path through the program has a return statement.

7.2 INCREMENTAL DEVELOPMENT

When we write larger functions, we spend more time in debugging. To deal with increasingly complex programs, we use a process called **incremental development**. The goal of incremental development is to avoid long debugging sessions by adding and testing only a small amount of code at a time.

Example 7.3: To find the distance between two points, given by the coordinates (x_1, y_1) and (x_2, y_2). By the Pythagorean theorem, the distance is given by:

$$\text{distance} = \sqrt{(x_2 - x_1)^2 + (y_2 - y_1)^2}$$

The first step is to think the number of inputs parameters and the return value in the function definition. In this case, the inputs are two points, which we can represent using four numbers x_1, y_1, x_2 and y_2. The return value is the distance, which is a floating-point value. Before we write the complete program let us write the following program segment.

```
    def distance (x1,y1,x2,y2):
        dx = x2 - x1
        dy = y2 - y1
        print "dx is=",dx          # double quote
        #print 'dy is=', dy        # single quote
        print 'dy is=%f' % (dy)    # format string
                                   # dy is=4.000000
    text = distance(1,2,4,6)
    print text
```

```
Output of this program segment:
dx is= 3
dy is= 4
None #  it returns nothing.
```

A few important points can be noted here: when we use print function, we can use both single and double quotes. Another way is to use format string, which is more convenient for displaying decimal values. Again, the last output line None means that the function does not return anything. If a function does not return anything python will return None.

If the function is working properly, it should display '*dx* is =3' and '*dy* is= 4'. If so, we know that the function is getting the right arguments and performing the first computation correctly. If not, there are only a few lines to check.

Next we compute the sum of squares of *dx* and *dy*:

```
def distance (x1,y1,x2,y2) :
    dx = x2 - x1
    dy = y2 - y1
    print "dx is=",dx # double quote
    print 'dy is=', dy # single quote
    ds = dx**2 + dy**2  # same as dx*dx + dy * dy
    print 'squared is: ', ds
    return 0.0 # return should be in the same indent,
               # can't outside function
x = distance(1,2,4,6)
print x # print distance(1,2,4,6)
```

```
Output of this Program segment:
dx is= 3
dy is= 4
squared is:   25
0.0 # see this 0.0 instead of None
```

When we check the output at this stage, if it shows 25, then we can compute the square root of ds. For computing square root, we can use the built in function provided by python, sqrt(), which is available in math module. Here are two ways for importing the math module, as explained below:

- from math import sqrt
- import math

The first one is used when we import only `sqrt ()` function. And the second one is used when we want to import more than one function. The syntax for using them is explained in the following program

```
from math import sqrt
def distance (x1,y1,x2,y2) :
    dx = x2 - x1
    dy = y2 - y1
    print "dx is=",dx # double quote
    print 'dy is=', dy # single quote
    ds = dx**2 + dy**2
    print 'squared is:', ds
    #result = math.sqrt(ds) #import math
    result = sqrt(ds) #from math import sqrt
x = distance(1,2,4,6)
print x
```

```
Ouput of this program segment:
dx is= 3
dy is= 4
squared is:   25
5.0
```

Note: When we use `from math import sqrt,` we can call simply `sqrt(ds).` And if we use `import math,` then we have to use the name of the module like `math.sqrt(ds).` If we omit this import statement we will get a message like,

```
# NameError: global name 'math' is not defined
```

The final version of the function normally doesn't display anything when it runs; it only returns a value, see the following program. The print statements we wrote are useful for debugging, but once we get the function working, we should remove them. Code like that is called **scaffolding** because it is helpful for building the program but is not part of the final product.

```
# Final Program
from math import sqrt
def distance (x1,y1,x2,y2) :
    dx = x2 - x1
    dy = y2 - y1
```

```
        ds = dx**2 + dy**2
        result = sqrt(ds)
        return result
    Final_Length = distance(1,2,4,6)
    print "\n Length =", Final_Length
```

```
Final Output
Length = 5.0
```

7.3 NESTING OF FUNCTIONS

Python permits nesting of functions freely. The ability of calling one function from within another function is called *nesting* or *composition*. Examples of nesting of functions are shown in Examples 7.4 and 7.5.

Example 7.4 : Let us write a function that takes two points, the center of the circle (*xc*, *yc*) and a point on the perimeter (*xp*, *yp*), and computes the area of the circle.

Our first step is to find the radius of the circle, which is the distance between the two points. We just wrote a function, distance, that does that:

```
from math import sqrt
def distance (xc,yc,xp,yp) :
    dx = xp - xc
    dy = yp - yc
    ds = dx**2 + dy**2
    result = sqrt(ds)
    return result
```

The next step is to find the area of a circle with that radius; we just wrote that, too:

```
from numpy import pi
def area(radius):
    temp = pi*radius**2
    return temp
```

The value of pi is also available with python using numpy. numpy is an extension to the Python programming language, adding support for large, multidimensional arrays and matrices, along with a large library of high level mathematical functions to operate on these arrays. We call the numpy module as from numpy import pi.

Combining these functions into a function say `circle_area()`, we can write

```
def circle_area(xc, yc, xp, yp):
    radius = distance(xc, yc, xp, yp)
    result = area(radius)
    return result
    # return area(distance(xc, yc, xp, yp))
Area= circle_area(1,2,4,6)
print "Area = ",Area
```

```
Output of this final program:
Area =   78.5398163397
```

The temporary variables `temp`,   `radius` and `result` are useful for debugging. The advantages for using these variables, that we can check and display the immediate values at any conditions. On the other hand, we can call the two functions without any variable as:

```
return area(distance(xc, yc, xp, yp))
```

7.4 BOOLEAN FUNCTION

Functions can return Booleans (means either True or False), which is often convenient for hiding complicated tests inside functions. For example:

```
def is_equal(x, y):
    if x != y:
        return False
    else:
        return True
```

Here `is_equal(x,y)` returns either True or False to indicate whether x is equal to y or not.

Here is an example, just check with python shell:

```
>>> is_equal(7, 8)
False
>>> is_equal(12, 12)
True
```

The advantages for using these functions make programs easier and more meaningful. Let us consider another example to show how and when to use these functions.

Example 7.5: Evaluate the expression $\dfrac{x}{y-z}$ for any given values of x, y and z.

Also explain how your program will care when the values of y and z are equal.

Our first step is to check the values of y and z is equal or not. If they are equal, then we have to print a message saying that the expression can't be evaluated. We wrote a function to compare the values:

```
def is_equal(x, y):
    if x == y:
        return True
    else:
        return False
def expression(x,y,z) :
    if is_equal (y,z) :
        print "Expression can't be evaluated."
        Print "because 1/0 is infinity (not defined)"
    else :
        result = float(x/(y-z))
        return result
x = expression(5,6,7)
print 'x = ', x
y= expression(5,7,7)
print 'y =', y
```

```
Output of this program segment will be :
x = -5.0
Expression can't be evaluated.
because 1/0 is infinity (not defined)
y = None
```

If we omit the `if statement` section and if we entered the same values of y and z, the following message will be generated by the python interpreter.

```
ZeroDivisionError: integer division or modulo by zero
```

Thus, the Boolean function is useful in such cases.

Example 7.6: Write a function is_between (x, y, z) that returns

True if $x <= y <= z$ or

False otherwise.

Here, the first step is to check the number of arguments. In this case we need 3 arguments of *x*, *y* and *z*. The incremental development of the program is explained below:

```
def is_between(x,y,z):
    if z >= y:
        if y >= x:
            return True
    else:
        return False
z1= is_between(2,3,6)
print z1 # True
x1= is_between(12,3,6)
print x1 # None   because no return statement is there
y1= is_between(2,12,6)
print y1 # False
```

In the above program, we are using two if statements and only one else part. In such case, all the conditions can't be fulfilled. For example, the value of x1, when x is larger than y and z, python returns None.

The final program may be written as :

```
def is_between(x,y,z):
    if z >= y:
        if y >= x:
            return True
        else : # to avoid None
            return False
    else:
        return False
big_x= is_between(12,3,6)
print big_x # output will be False
big_y= is_between(2,13,6)
print big_x # output will be False
big_z= is_between(2,3,16)
print big_x # output will be True
```

7.5 RECURSION FUNCTION

When a function calls the function itself, it is known as recursive function. In other words, the function invoke themselves. This function enables us to develop straightforward and simple solutions to an otherwise problem. For example Tower of Hanoi can be solved very easily if we use recursive function.

Let us see a few examples of recursive function.

Example 7.7: Calculation of factorial n using recursive function.

As we know that $n! = 1 \times 2 \times 3 \times 4 \times .... n$ or $n! = n \times (n-1)!$ and $0! = 1$

The definition says that the factorial of 0 is 1, and the factorial of any other value, n, is n multiplied by the factorial of $(n - 1)$.

So 3! is 3 times 2!, which is 2 times 1!, which is 1 times 0!. Putting it all together, 3! equals 3 times 2 times 1 times 1, which is 6. *i.e.*, $3! = 3 \times 2 \times 1$

The first step is to decide what the parameters should be. In this case it should be clear that factorial takes an integer:

```
def factorial(n):
```

If the argument happens to be 0, all we have to do is return 1:

```
def factorial(n):
    if n == 0:
        return 1
```

Otherwise, and this is the interesting part, we have to make a recursive call to find the factorial of $n - 1$ and then multiply it by n:

```
# Recursive Function
def factorial(n) :
    if n == 0 :
        return 1
    else :
        fact = n*factorial(n-1)
        return fact
x=factorial(5)
print "Factorial = ", x
```

Output of this program segment will be :
Factorial = 120

Explanation: Let us see how the recursive function executes the flow of sequence. We pass 5 as the value of *n*. In the first if statement *n* is not equal to 0 so it evaluates the else part, and it looks like

```
fact = 5 * factorial(4)
```

The function factorial (4) will be executed by calling the same function again. So, the new value of fact will be

```
fact = 5 * 4 * factorial(3)
```

Thus, by calling the function again and again, we will get

```
fact = 5 * 4 * 3 * factorial(2)

fact = 5 * 4 * 3 * 2 * factorial(1)

fact = 5 * 4 * 3 * 2 * 1 * factorial(0)
```

When *n* = 0 it will return 1 in the place of factorial (0). Thus the value of fact will be

```
fact = 5 * 4 * 3 * 2 * 1 * 1 =120
```

Note: If we can't get the correct output, adding a print statement just before each return statement displays the return value. Also, if possible, check the result by hand. If the function seems to be working, look at the function call to make sure the return value is being used correctly or not. Adding print statements at the beginning and end of a function can help make the flow of execution more visible.

Here is a version of factorial with many print statements:

```
def factorial(n):
    space = ' ' * (4 * n)
    print space, 'factorial', n
    if n == 0:
        print space, 'returning 1'
        return 1
    else:
        result = n * factorial(n-1)
        print space, 'returning', result
        return result
x=factorial(5)
print 'Factorial = ', x
```

```
Output of the above program segment is:
                        factorial 5
                   factorial 4
              factorial 3
          factorial 2
      factorial 1
  factorial 0
  returning 1
      returning 1
          returning 2
              returning 6
                  returning 24
                      returning 120
Factorial = 120
```

Example 7.8: Calculation of Fibonacci sequence using recursive function.

Another most common example of a recursively defined mathematical function is fibonacci sequence, which has the following definition :

Fibonacci $(0) = 0$

Fibonacci $(1) = 1$

Fibonacci $(n) =$ Fibonacci $(n - 1) +$ Fibonacci $(n - 2)$

The python code may be written as:

```
# Program for Fibonacci sequences
def fibonacci (n):
    if n == 0:
        return 0
    elif n == 1:
        return 1
    else:
        return fibonacci(n-1) + fibonacci(n-2)
fibo=fibonacci(5)
print 'Fibonacci = ', fibo
fibo=fibonacci(10)
print 'Fibonacci = ', fibo
```

```
Output of the above program segment is :
Fibonacci = 5
Fibonacci = 55
```

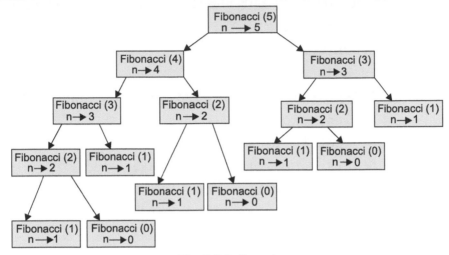

Fig. 7.2 Call graph.

Figure 7.2 shows the **call graph** for fibonacci with $n = 5$. A call graph shows a set of function frames, with lines connecting each frame to the frames of the functions it calls. At the top of the graph, fibonacci with $n = 5$ calls fibonacci with $n = 4$ and $n = 3$. In turn, fibonacci with $n = 4$ calls fibonacci with $n = 3$ and $n = 2$. Again, fibonacci with $n = 3$ calls fibonacci with $n = 2$ and $n = 1$. And so on.

Count how many times fibonacci(0) and fibonacci(1) are called. This is an inefficient solution to the problem, and it gets worse as the argument gets bigger. Such problems can be taken care by the concept of dictionary discussed in Chapter 9.

Example 7.9: To check a given string is palindrome or not.

A palindrome is a word that is spelled the same backward and forward, like "madam" and "malayalam". Recursively, a word is a palindrome if the first and last letters are the same and the middle is a palindrome.

The following are functions that take a string argument and return the first, last, and middle letters:

```
# Checking for palindrome:
def first(word):
    """Returns the first character of a string."""
    return word[0]
def last(word):
```

```
        """Returns all but the first character of a string."""
        return word[-1]
    def middle(word):
        """Returns all but the first and last characters
        of a string."""
        return word[1:-1]
    def is_palindrome(word):
        """Returns True if word is a palindrome."""
        if len(word) <= 1:
            return True
        if first(word) != last(word):
            return False
        return is_palindrome(middle(word))
    print is_palindrome('allen')
    print is_palindrome('madam')
    print is_palindrome('malayalam')
    print is_palindrome('redivider')
```

```
Output of the above program segment:
False
True
True
True
```

Example 7.10: Write an iterative function iterPower(base, exp) that calculates the exponential base^{exp} by simply using successive multiplication. For example, iterPower(base, exp) should compute base^{exp} by multiplying base times itself exp times. Write such a function below.

This function should take in two values - base can be a float or an integer; exp will be an integer $\geq$ 0. It should return one numerical value. Your code must be iterative - use of the **operator is not allowed (Courtesy : edX.)

Solution: In this example, using the concept of repeated multiplication, we can write as follows. Some of the conditions to be fulfilled are: (*i*) exp can't be negative value (*ii*) if exp becomes 0 then this function has to return 1 and (*iii*) if exp is 1, then the function will return the value of base.

```
        def iterPower(base, exp):
            '''
```

```
        base: int or float.
        exp: int >= 0
        returns: int or float, base^exp
        '''
        result = 1
        if exp < 0 :
            #print 'Negative values are not allowed'
            return None
        if exp == 0 :
            return result
        while exp != 0:
            result *= base
            exp -= 1
        return result
    test1 = iterPower(2,8)
    print 'Run1 =', test1
    test2 = iterPower(2,0)
    print Run2 = ', test2
    test3 = iterPower(2,-3)
    print 'Run3 = ', test3
```

```
Output of the above program:
Run1 = 256
Run2 = 1
Run3 =   None
```

In the above Example 7.10, we computed an exponential by iteratively executing successive multiplications. We can use the same idea, but in a recursive function.

Example 7.11: Write a function recurPower(base,   exp) which computes base^{exp} by recursively calling itself to solve a smaller version of the same problem. Your code must be recursive - use of the ** operator or looping constructs is not allowed.

Solution: As we know that recursive function will call the function itself inside the function. With this concept, the python program may be written as follows:

```
def recurPower(base, exp):
    '''
    base: int or float.
    exp: int >= 0
    returns: int or float, base^exp
    '''
    if exp <= 0 :
        return base
    else:
        return base * recurPower(base, exp -1)
t = recurPower(2,6)
print '2 to the power 6 =', t
t1 = recurPower(2,0)
print '2 to the power 0 =', t1
# Let us calculate for negative values afterwards,
t2 = recurPower(2,-3)
print '2 to the power -3 =', t2
```

Output of the above program:

```
2 to the power 6 = 64
2 to the power 0 = 1
2 to the power -3 = 1 # This is because of our program
```

The above function can be written without using the
else part also, as follows:

```
def recurPower(base, exp):
    if exp <= 0 :
        return 1
    return base * recurPower(base, exp-1)
```

The function recurPower(base, exp) from Example 5.11 computed
$base^{exp}$ by decomposing the problem into one recursive case and one base
case:

$$base^{exp} = base.base^{(exp-1)} \quad \text{if exp} > 0$$
$$base^{exp} = 1 \quad \text{if exp} = 0$$

Example 7.12: Another way to solve this problem just using multiplication (and remainder) is to note that

$$base^{exp} = \left(base^2\right)^{\frac{exp}{2}} \qquad \text{if exp} > 0 \text{ and exp is even}$$

$$base^{exp} = base.base^{exp-1}. \quad \text{if exp} > 0 \text{ and exp is odd}$$

$$base^{exp} = 1 \quad \text{if exp} = 0$$

(*i*) Write a procedure recurPowerNew which recursively computes exponentials using this idea.

(*ii*) Write a simple SimplePowerNew which computes exponentials without using recursion.

(*i*) Using recursive function

```
def recurPowerNew(base, exp):
    # Base case is when exp = 0
    if exp <= 0:
        return 1
    # Recursive case 1: exp > 0 and even
    elif exp % 2 == 0:
        return recurPowerNew(base*base, exp/2)
    # Otherwise, exp must be > 0 and odd, so use the
    # second recursive case.
    return base * recurPowerNew(base, exp - 1)
t = recurPowerNew(2,6)
print '2 to the power 6 =', t
t1 = recurPowerNew(2,5)
print '2 to the power 5 =', t1
```

```
Output of the above program:
2 to the power 6 = 64
2 to the power 5 = 32
```

(*ii*) Without using recursive function

In this case we can write very easily just following the given equation, as follows:

```
def SimplePowerNew(base, exp):
    result = 1
    if exp < 0 :
```

```
                return None
        elif exp == 1:
                return result
        elif (exp % 2 == 0):
                result = (base*base)**(exp/2)
                return result
        else :
                result = base*(base**(exp-1))
                return result
    t = SimplePowerNew(2,6)   # For even exponent
    print '2 to the power 6 =', t
    t1 = SimplePowerNew(2,5) # For even exponent
    print '2 to the power 5 =', t1
```

```
Output of the above program:
2 to the power 6 = 64
2 to the power 5 = 32
```

Example 7.13: Write a Python program to find the greatest common divisor of two positive integers. For example,

$$gcd(2, 12) = 2$$
$$gcd(12, 2) = 2$$
$$gcd(6, 12) = 6$$
$$gcd(9, 12) = 3$$
$$gcd(17, 12) = 1$$

(*i*) Without using recursive function

(*ii*) Using recursive function.

Solution:

We can write an iterative function, gcd2 (a, b), that implements this idea. One easy way to do this is to begin with a test value equal to the smaller of the two input arguments, and iteratively reduce this test value by 1 until you either reach a case where the test divides both *a* and *b* without remainder, or you reach 1. Another important condition is that the interchanging of the two values of the parameters will not change the GCD value. For example gcd (2, 12) is 2 and gcd (12, 2) will also be 2. We can implement it by interchanging the two values, as follows:

(*i*) Without using recursive function

```
def gcd2(m, n) :
    if (n > m) :
        m = m + n
        n = m - n
        m = m - n
    while (m % n != 0 ) :
        temp = n
        n = m % n
        m = temp
    return n
a = input( "Enter the first number :")
b = input( "Enter the second number :")
gcd1 = gcd2(a, b)
print 'The GCD(HCF) is ', gcd1
gcd2 = gcd2(2,12) # Here Second is greater than
first.
print 'The GCD of (2, 12) is ', gcd2
gcd3 = gcd2(12,2) # Here first is greater than second.
print 'The GCD of (12, 2) is ', gcd3
```

Output of the above program:
```
Enter the first number :12
Enter the second number :9
The GCD(HCF) is   3
The GCD of (2, 12) is 2
The GCD of (12, 2) is 2
```

(*ii*) Using recursive function

A clever mathematical trick (due to Euclid) makes it easy to find greatest common divisors. Suppose that a and b are two positive integers:

If b = 0, then the answer is a

Otherwise, gcd(a, b) is the same as gcd(b, a % b)

We write a function gcdRecur(a, b) that implements this idea recursively. This function takes in two positive integers and returns one integer. The Python program is as follows:

```
def gcdRecur(a,b):
    if b == 0:
        return a
    else :
        return gcdRecur(b, a%b)
t = gcdRecur(2, 12)
print 'The GCD of (2, 12) is ', t
t1= gcdRecur(12, 2) #= 2
print 'The GCD of (12, 2) is ', t1
t2 = gcdRecur(6, 12) #= 6
print 'The GCD of (6, 12) is ', t2
t3 = gcdRecur(9, 12) #= 3
print 'The GCD of (9, 12) is ', t3
t4 = gcdRecur(17, 12) # = 1
print 'The GCD of (17, 12) is ', t4
```

Output of the above Program:

```
The GCD of (2, 12) is  2
The GCD of (12, 2) is  2
The GCD of (6, 12) is  6
The GCD of (9, 12) is  3
The GCD of (17, 12) is  1
```

7.6 CHECKING TYPES : `isinstance ( )`

We know that we cannot calculate factorial for 3.5 etc. with the program we have written. The question is, how to take care of such situations in python? What will happen if we call `factorial` function with 3.5 as an argument?

```
>>> factorial(3.5)
```

```
RuntimeError: Maximum recursion depth exceeded
```

It gives an infinite recursion because this function will stop when the value of n becomes 0. Since n is not an integer, it will recurse forever. Because in the first recursive call, the value of n is 2.5, in the next, it is 1.5 and then 0.5 and −0.5 so on. Thus it becomes more negative and can never be 0.

In such cases, we can use the built-in function **isinstance** to verify the type of the argument. The complete program is given below:

```
def factorial(n):
```

```
    if not isinstance(n, int): # important line
        print 'Factorial is only defined for integers.'
        return None
    elif n < 0:
        print 'Factorial is not defined for negative
integers.'
        return None
    elif n == 0:
        return 1
    else:
        fact = n*factorial(n-1)
    return fact
x=factorial(-5)
print "Factorial = ", x
y=factorial(5.8)
print "Factorial = ", y
z=factorial(6)
print "Factorial = ", z
```

```
Output of the above program segment is :
Factorial is not defined for negative integers.
Factorial =  None
Factorial is only defined for integers.
Factorial =  None
Factorial =  720
```

The first case handles non-integers and the second catches negative integers. In both cases, the program prints an error message and returns None to indicate that something went wrong in the program. Using the built in function isinstance() can prove the correctness of the program code.

Note: We can calculate the factorial of floating-point numbers using gamma function also.

7.7 DESIGNING AND WRITING MODULES

Not only functions can be used to reduce redundant code but also to modularize code and improve a program's quality. In Python, the created module can be reused by importing into a program. The module file (extension with .py) should be placed in the same directory with other programs. A module can contain more than one function. Each function in a module must have a different name. If we define two functions with the same name in a module then the latter function definition will get the prevailage.

For example, the **random** and **math** are the modules defined in the Python library, and thus they can be imported into any Python program. Now let us try to define a module. Example 7.14 shows a program that prompts the user to enter two integers and displays their sum of the first number up to the second number.

Let us save the following code in the file sum1.py

Example 7.14: Sum of Integers: *sum1.py*

```
def sum( no1, no2):
    sum = 0
    for i in range(no1, no2 + 1):
        sum = sum + i
    return sum
```

The newly created module "sum1" is ready for use now. We can import this module like any other module in a program or script. Let us demonstrate the use of this sum function to a new program sum_module.py.

```
# sum_module.py
from sum1 import sum      # Calling the module
print "Sum from 1 to 15 is", sum(1,16)
print "Sum from 21 to 40 is", sum(21, 41)
print "Sum from 38 to 60 is", sum(38, 61)
```

We can also import the sum1 module using the following statement:

```
import sum1 #   NOT like "from sum1 import sum"
```

If we import in this way, then we would have to invoke sum function using dot operator as, sum1.sum(). The complete program is shown below:

```
import sum1
print "Sum from 1 to 15 is", sum1.sum(1,16)
print "Sum from 21 to 40 is", sum1.sum(21, 41)
print "Sum from 38 to 60 is", sum1.sum(38, 61)
```

```
The output of the above program:
Sum from 1 to 15 is 136
Sum from 21 to 40 is 651
Sum from 38 to 60 is 1188
```

7.8 GLOBAL AND LOCAL VARIABLES

The scope of a variable determines over what region of the program a variable is actually available for use. A variable created inside a function is referred to as a *local variable*. Local variables can only be accessed within a particular function. The scope of a local variable starts from its creation and continues to the end of the function that contains the variable. They are destroyed automatically when the function is exited.

Global variables are created outside all functions and are accessible to all functions in their scope. Consider the following examples.

Example 7.15: Scope of the variables

```
Global_Variable = 123
def function1():
    local_Variable = 45
    print " Global Variable = " ,Global_Variable
    print " Local Variable = ",local_Variable
function1()
# Print global variable outside the function
print " Global Variable (outside function)= ",Global_
Variable

# Try to print local variable outside the function
print " Local Variable = ",local_Variable  # Out of scope, so
                                        this gives an error
```

The global variable can be access from inside or outside the function. If we attempt to access the local variable from outside of the function, it gives an error:

```
NameError: name 'local_Variable' is not defined
```

If we create local variable with the same name of global variable, then the value of the global variable is overwritten by the local variable. The local variable will have precedence over the global variable in the function. However, if we call the global variable again from outside the function, we can get the original value.

Example 7.16: Overwriting of Global variable

```
Global_Variable = 123
def function2():
    Global_Variable = 456 # Same name
    print " Global Variable = " ,Global_Variable #
    displays 456
```

```
function2()
```

```
# Print global variable outside the function
```

```
print " Global Variable (outside function)= ",Global_
Variable
```

```
# displays 123
```

```
Output of the above program:
Global Variable =  456
Global Variable (outside function)=  123
```

We can bind a local variable in the global scope. We can also create a variable inside a function and use it outside the function. To do either, we can use a *global* statement, as shown in the following example.

Example 7.17: Local to Global variable

```
x = 100
def function3():
    global x
    x = x + 50
    print "x (Inside function)= ", x # displays 150
function3()
print "x (Outside function)= ", x # # also displays 150
```

Here the value of the global variable **x** is the same inside and outside of the function. It is possible because of the keyword global.

Note: It is not a good practice to allow global variables to be modified in a function, because by doing so it can make programs more prone to errors. However, the advantage of defining global constants is that all functions in the module can share them.

Example 7.18: Role of local variables

```
x = input("Enter a number: ")
if x > 5:
    y = 10
print "y =", y # This gives an error if y is not
created
```

The variable y will be created if the value of $x > 5$ otherwise the program will give an error "**NameError: name 'y' is not defined**" because *y* is not created.

If we enter any number greater than 5, then we can assign the value of *y* as 10, as follows:

```
Enter a number: 78
y = 10
```

On the other hand, let us try to find the value of a local variable created using a loop, as follows:

```
sum = 0
for i in range(10):
  sum += i
print "Value of i =", i
```

Here the variable i is created in the loop. After the loop is finished, the latest value of *i* was 9, so when we print the value of *i* outside the loop, it will give the value of 9 as:

```
Value of i = 9
```

7.9 DEFAULT ARGUMENTS

Python allows function arguments to have default argument values; if the function is called without the argument, the argument gets its default value. Furthermore, arguments can be specified in any order by using named arguments.

Example 7.19 demonstrates how to define functions with *default argument* values and how to invoke such functions.

Example 7.19: Default Arguments

```
def CalculateArea(height = 2, width=5):
    area = width * height
    print "Width = ", width, "\tHeight = ", height, \
        "\tArea = ", area
CalculateArea()
CalculateArea(width = 5.6)
CalculateArea(height = 9)
CalculateArea(width = 7, height = 5)
CalculateArea(4.5, 3.5)
CalculateArea(5)
```

The output of the above program will look like:

```
Width =  5           Height =  2       Area =  10
Width =  5.6         Height =  2       Area =  11.2
Width =  5           Height =  9       Area =  45
Width =  7           Height =  5       Area =  35
Width =  3.5         Height =  4.5     Area =  15.75
Width =  5           Height =  5       Area =  25
```

Explanation:

If we invoke the function without passing any arguments, so, by default, the program uses the value of height = 2 and width = 5, as follows:

```
CalculateArea()  # height = 2, width = 5
```

If we invoke the function by passing only one named argument, say width = 5.6, then the value of height will be 2 and width will be the new value.

```
CalculateArea(width = 5.6) # height = 2, width =5.6
```
```
CalculateArea(height = 9)# height = 9, width = 5
```

If we invoke the function by passing both named arguments, then the new values will overwrite the default values. Here the arguments can be specified in any order.

```
CalculateArea(width = 7, height = 5)# height = 5,
width = 7
```

Again, if we invoke the function without the named arguments, only passing by value, then the first value will assign to the first argument and second value to second argument and so on.

```
CalculateArea(4.5, 3.5) # height = 4.5, width = 3.5
```

If we invoke the function by passing only one value, then the first argument in the function definition will use it. The second will be using the default value.

```
CalculateArea(5) # height = 5, width = 5
```

Note: The function may have mix parameters with default arguments and non-default arguments. In such case, the non-default parameters must be defined before default parameters. For example:

```
CalculateArea(5, width = 4)
```

is valid, whereas

```
CalculateArea(width = 4, 5)
```

is not valid because non-keyword argument can't come after keyword argument.

EXERCISES

7.1. State the following are **true** or **false**:

(*a*) A function header begins with the def keyword followed by function's name and parameters, and ends with a semicolon.

(*b*) Parameters are optional; that is, a function does not have to contain any parameters.

(*c*) A function is called a void or None function if it does not return a value.

(*d*) A return statement can also be used in a void function for terminating the function and returning to the function's caller.

(*e*) The *arguments* that are passed to a function may or may not have the same number, type, and order as the parameters in the function header.

(*f*) A value-returning function can also be invoked as a statement in Python.

(*g*) The scope of a local variable starts from its creation and exists until the function returns.

(*h*) *Global variables* are created outside all functions and are accessible to all functions in their scope.

(*i*) The return statement can return multiple values.

(*j*) It is most likely result in logical error if there is a mismatch in data types between the actual and formal arguments.

7.2. Which of the following function headers are invalid and why?

```
(a) def CalculateArea(height , width = 5):
(b) def CalculateArea(height = 5 , width):
(c) def CalculateArea(5 , width = 5):
(d) def CalculateArea(height = 5 , 5):
(e) def CalculateArea(5 , 5):
```

7.3. Find out the logical and syntax errors, if any, in the following program segments:

```
(a) def sum( no1, no2):
        sum = 0
        for i in range(no1, no2 + 1):
            sum += i
        return result
(b) def sum( no1, no2):
        result = 0
        for i in range(no1, no2 + 1):
            result = result + i
            return result
```

```
(c) def sum( no1, no2):
            result = 0
            for i in range(no1, no2 + 1):
                result = result + i
      return result
```

7.4. Two functions are defined below. Which function is more meaningful and why? Can you see any difference when you run the program?

```
(a) def showGrade(marks):
      if marks >= 75.0:
          print('Distinction')
      elif marks >= 60.0:
          print('First Division')
      elif marks >= 50.0:
          print('Second Division')
      elif marks >= 40.0:
          print('Third Division')
      else :
          print('Fail')
(b) def showGrade(marks):
      if marks >= 75.0 and marks <= 100:
          print('Distinction')
      elif marks >= 60.0 and marks < 75:
          print('First Division')
      elif marks >= 50.0 and marks < 60:
          print('Second Division')
      elif marks >= 40.0 and marks < 50:
          print('Third Division')
      elif marks >= 0.0 and marks < 40:
          print('Fail')
      else :
          print('Fail')
```

7.5. Identify and correct the errors in the following program:

```
def function1(no1, no2):
    function2(3.4)
def function2(no):
    if no > 0:
```

```
            return 1
        elif no == 0:
            return 0
        elif no < 0:
            return -1
    function1(2, 3)
```

7.6. Show the output of the following code:

```
def main():
    print(min(5, 6))
def min(n1, n2):
    smallest = n1
    if n2 < smallest:
        smallest = n2
main()
```

7.7. Find out error, if any, in the following function definition:

```
def CalculateArea(height , width=5):
    area = width * height
    print "Width = ", width, "\tHeight = ",\
                    height, "\tArea = ", area
```

7.8. Assuming that exercise **7.7** has no error, which of the function calls are valid and why?

```
CalculateArea()
CalculateArea(width = 5.6)
CalculateArea(height = 9)
CalculateArea(width = 7, height = 5)
CalculateArea(4.5, 3.5)
CalculateArea(4, width = 4)
CalculateArea(width = 4, 4)
```

7.9. Show the output of the following code:

```
def fun(w = 10, h = 20):
    print w, h
fun()
fun(w = 5)
fun(h = 24)
fun(4, 5)
```

7.10. What are the benefits of using a function?

7.11. How do you define a function? How do you invoke a function? Explain with an example.

7.12. Can you have a **return** statement in a **None** function? Does the **return** statement in the following function cause syntax errors?

```
def Function(x, y):
    print x + y
    return
```

7.13. Write a function exchange to interchange the values of two variables, say *a* and *b*. Illustrate the use of this function, in a calling function. Assume that *a* and *b* are defined as global variables.

7.14. Write a recursive function to evaluate

$$f(x) = x - \frac{x^3}{3!} + \frac{x^3}{5!} - \frac{x^3}{7!} + \dots$$

8

List

INTRODUCTION

The preceding chapters so far have described structured commands and problem solving involving generally simple variables. Python like other programming languages has user friendly features for large numbers of variables or arrays and subscripted variables. In Python they can be proceed using List statements. This chapter describes the usefulness of **List** in Python programming. The basics of how to create a list and common operations of list that frequently used are explained in detail. How to access list elements by using indexed variables and creating a sublist from a larger list with the help of the slicing operator are also described with examples. Commonly used operations like traversing the elements in a list using a `for loop`, comparing the contents of two lists, invoking the list's important built-in methods, copying the contents from one list to another and applications of list in program development are explained with examples. It also include various applications of the important techniques of Sorting, Selection and Insertion sort, in lists with diagrams. The concept of representing data in a two dimensional list, accessing elements by using row and column indexes and concepts of multidimensional lists are also included with illustrative examples.

8.1 DEFINITION

Python has six built-in types of sequences. They are lists, tuples, strings, unicode strings, buffer objects, and xrange objects. This chapter concentrates on lists. A **list** is a sequence of values. The values in a list are called **elements** or sometimes **items**. The items of a list are separated by commas. The values of a list may be of any type. There are several ways to create a new list; the simplest is to enclose the elements in square brackets ([and]), for example:

```
[1, 2, 3, 4, 5 ] # a list of integer values
['respect', 'and', 'regard']# list with characters
```

The first example is a list having five integers. The second is a list of three strings. The elements in a list may have different data types. For example,

```
[12, 9.6, 'copy', [6, 7]] # list of mixed data types
```

The above list contains an integer, a float, a string, and another list. A list within another list is said to be **nested list**.

A list that contains no elements is called an empty list; we can create one with empty brackets, [ ].

We can assign list values to variables, as follows:

```
S= ['python', 'programming', 'very', 'easy']
N= [12, 34, 56]
empty = [ ]# an empty list
print S, N, empty
```

Output of this program segment will be

```
['python', 'programming', 'very', 'easy'] [12, 34, 56] []
```

Note: We used Enthought canopy for scripting our programs. We can also use python shell as follows:

```
>>> s= ['python', 'programming', 'very', 'easy']
>>> N= [12, 34, 56]
>>> empty = []
>>> print s, N, empty
['python', 'programming', 'very', 'easy'] [12, 34, 56] []
```

Using bracket operator, we can access the elements of a list. The expression inside the brackets specifies the index. By default, the indices start at 0. For example: `print  S[0]` will print `python` where S is the list we have defined.

Note: Creating Lists with list class

To create a list, we also can use **list**'s constructor, as follows:

```
list1 = list() # Create an empty list
print list1
list2 = list([2, 3, 4]) # Create a list with elements
2, 3, 4
print list2
```

```
list3 = list(["red", "green", "blue"]) # Create a
list with strings
print list3
list4 = list(range(3, 6)) # Create a list with
elements 3, 4, 5
print list4
list5 = list("abcd") # Create a list with characters
a, b, c, d
print list5
Output:
[]
[2, 3, 4]
['red', 'green', 'blue']
[3, 4, 5]
['a', 'b', 'c', 'd']
```

However, we can create a list by using the simpler form:

```
list1 = [ ] # Same as list()
list2 = [2, 3, 4] # Same as list([2, 3, 4])
list3 = ["red", "green", "blue"] # Same as list(["red",
                                  # "green", "blue"])
```

The elements in a list are separated by commas and are enclosed by a pair of brackets ([ ]).

Let us illustrate one more example:

```
strings1 = ['Computer', 'Maths', 'Physics']
numbers = [12,34,56]
mixed = ['shubha', 1, 45, 78, 'Kanta']
# Mixed data type is allowed in Python
empty =[] # Empty list has no elements
print 'Strings = ', strings1
print 'Numbers = ', numbers
print 'Mixed list =',mixed
print 'Empty list =', empty
numbers[1]= 78 # elements in a list is changeable.
```

```
print 'New List =', numbers
print 'String[0] = ', strings[0]
```

The output of the above program segment is:
```
Strings = ['Computer', 'Maths', 'Physics']
Numbers = [12, 34, 56]
Mixed list = ['shubha', 1, 45, 78, 'Kanta']
Empty list = [ ]
New List = [12, 78, 56]
String[0] = Computer
```

From the above example we have seen that the elements of a list are changeable. In other words, we say that lists are mutable. When the bracket operator appears on the left side of an assignment, it identifies the element of the list that will be assigned. Using python shell, we can check:

```
>>> numbers = [12, 34, 56]
>>> print numbers[0]
12
>>> numbers[1] = 78
>>> print numbers
[12, 78, 56]
```

The one-eth element of numbers, which used to be 34, is now 78. In the same manner we can assign different values to different data types. Another example, we can check

```
>>> strings1 = ['Computer', 'Maths', 'Physics']
>>> strings1[2] = ' Chem'
>>> print strings1
['Computer', 'Maths', 'Chem']
```

The relationship between indices and elements of a list is called a **mapping**; each index "maps to" one of the elements. Figure 8.1 shows the state diagram for strings1 and numbers lists:

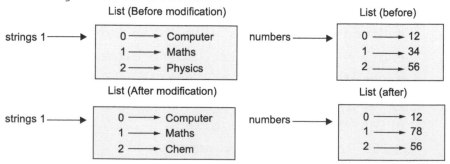

Fig. 8.1 State diagram.

Lists are represented by boxes with the word "list" outside and the elements of the list inside. strings1 refers to a list with three elements indexed 0, 1 and 2. List for numbers contains three elements; the diagram shows that the value of the second element has been reassigned from 34 to 78.

Some of the properties of List indices are:

- Any integer expression can be used as an index.
- If you try to read or write an element that does not exist, you get an IndexError.
- If an index has a negative value, it counts backward from the end of the list.

8.2 THE in OPERATOR

The in operator also works within lists. For example:

```
>>> strings1 = ['Computer', 'Maths', 'Physics']
>>> print 'Maths' in strings1
True
>>> print 'maths' in strings1
False
```

The above code is to execute with python shell. If you want to use editor, you can write as follows:

```
strings1 = ['Computer', 'Maths', 'Physics']
print 'Maths' in strings1
print 'maths' in strings1
```

8.3 TRAVERSING IN A LIST

The most common way to traverse the elements of a list is with a for loop. The syntax is :

```
for variable_name in list_name :
    print variable_name
```

The bold words can be named by the user however others are python keywords. This works well if we need to read only the elements of the list. But if we want to write or update the elements, we need indices. A common way to do that is to combine the functions range and len, as follows:

```
for i in range(len(numbers)):
    numbers[i] = numbers[i] * 2
```

This loop traverses the list and updates each element. The `range()` and `len()` are python built in functions. `len()` returns the number of elements in the list. The `range()` function returns a list of indices from 0 to $n-1$, where n is the length of the list. Each time through the loop i gets the index of the next element. The initial value of i is 0 as we mentioned. The assignment statement in the body uses the variable **i** to read the old value of the element and to assign the new value in the list. Here in this example, the old value is multiplied by 2. Let us write a program segment to explain this:

```
strings1 = ['Computer', 'Maths', 'Physics']
numbers = [12,78,56]
mixed = ['shubha', 1, 45, 78, 'Kanta']
for string in strings1 :
    print string
for number in numbers :
    print number
for i in mixed :
    print i
number2=[2,3,4,5,6] # defining a new list
    print number2
for i in range(len(number2)) :
    number2[i] = number2[i] * 2
    print number2
```

```
Output of the above program segment is:
Computer
Maths
Physics
12
78
56
shubha
1
45
78
Kanta
[2, 3, 4, 5, 6]
[4, 6, 8, 10, 12]
```

Note: A for loop over an empty list never executes the body:

```
for j in [ ]:
print 'This line won't executes at all.'
```

8.4 NESTED LIST

If a list contains another list within itself, it is known as nested list. For example,

```
nested_list=  ['test',  12,  [1,3,45],  ['com',
'abc', 'ph']]
```

The length of this list is four, not eight as it would appear. We can use **for loop** for traversing a nested list. Now let us take an example. The elements can be multiplied by 2 as we have seen in the above example. Now let us observe the difference of * operator in numbers and strings in a nested list.

```
nested_list = ['test',12,[1,3,45],['com','abc',
'physics']]
print nested_list
for j in nested_list :
     print j
for j in range(len(nested_list)) :
# Length of the List =4 not 8
     nested_list[j] = nested_list[j] *2
print nested_list
```

```
Output of the above program segment:
['test', 12, [1, 3, 45], ['com', 'abc', 'physics']]
test
12
[1, 3, 45]
['com', 'abc', 'physics']
['testtest', 24, [1, 3, 45, 1, 3, 45], ['com',
'abc', 'physics', 'com', 'abc', 'physics']]
```

The len() returns four for the above nested list. It gives length of *one* for the inner list though it has more than one element. Note the difference of print statements *with loop* and *without loop*. And another interesting part is that when we multiply by 2, strings elements and inner lists get doubled of its length. Let us see more on list operations.

Note: Python has a basic notion of a kind of data structure called a *container*, which is basically any object that can contain other objects. The two main kinds of containers are sequences (such as lists and tuples) and mappings (such as dictionaries). While the elements of a sequence are numbered, each element in a mapping has a name (also called a key). A container type is neither a sequence nor a mapping.

8.5 LIST OPERATIONS

The + operator concatenates lists:

```
>>> a = [10, 20, 30]
>>> b = [40, 50, 60]
>>> c = a + b
>>> print c
[10, 20, 30, 40, 50, 60]
```

Similarly, the * operator repeats a list a given number of times:

```
>>> [2] * 4
[2, 2, 2, 2]
>>> [1, 2, 3] * 3
[1, 2, 3, 1, 2, 3, 1, 2, 3]
```

The first operation repeats [2] four times. The second operation repeats the list [1, 2, 3] three times. If the elements are characters instead of numbers, it will repeat the multiplier number of times. For example:

```
# The + operator concatenates lists:
a = [10, 20, 30]
b = [40, 50, 60]
c = a + b
print c
d = [2] * 4
print d
print [1, 2, 3] * 3
#This repeats the list [1, 2, 3] THREE times
e = ['a', 'b'] * 2
print e
```

```
Output of this program segment:
[10, 20, 30, 40, 50, 60]
[2, 2, 2, 2]
[1, 2, 3, 1, 2, 3, 1, 2, 3]
['aa', 'bb']
```

8.6 LIST SLICES

The slice operator can also works with lists. For example,

```
>>> a = [1, 2, 3, 4, 5, 6, 7]
>>> a[1:4]
[2, 3, 4]
>>> a[:5]
[1, 2, 3, 4, 5]
>>> a[3:]
[4, 5, 6, 7]
```

If we omit the first index, the slice starts at the beginning. If we omit the second, the slice goes to the end. So if we omit both indices, the slice is a copy of the whole list.

```
>>> a[ : ]
[1, 2, 3, 4, 5, 6, 7]
```

Since lists are mutable, it is often useful to make a copy before performing operations that fold, spindle or mutilate lists.

A slice operator on the left side of an assignment can update multiple elements:

```
>>> b = ['a', 'b', 'c', 'd', 'e', 'f']
>>> b[1:3] = ['x', 'y']
>>> print b
['a', 'x', 'y', 'd', 'e', 'f']
```

Let us write a program using Canopy editor.

```
# List slices : using slice operator
t = ['a', 'b', 'c', 'd', 'e', 'f']
print t[1:3]
print t[:4]
print t[3:]
print t[:]
```

```
t1 = ['a', 'b', 'c', 'd', 'e', 'f']
t1[1:3] = ['x', 'y']
print t1
```

```
Output of the above program segment:
['b', 'c']
['a', 'b', 'c', 'd']
['d', 'e', 'f']
['a', 'b', 'c', 'd', 'e', 'f']
['a', 'x', 'y', 'd', 'e', 'f']
```

Again, A list can contain other list, too. For example if we want to create a database, then:

```
>>> name1=['Chatterjee', 65]
>>> name2=['Manju', 58]
>>> database =[name1, name2]
>>> print database
[['Chatterjee', 65], ['Manju', 58]]
```

Example 8.1: Write a Python program that asks you for a year, a month (as a number from 1 to 12), and a day (1 to 31), and then prints out the date with the proper month name and so on.

Solution:

```
#Print out a date, given year, month, and day as numbers
months = [
'January',
'February',
'March',
'April',
'May',
'June',
'July',
'August',
'September',
'October',
'November',
```

```
'December'
]
# A list with one ending for each number from 1 to 31
endings = ['st', 'nd', 'rd'] + 17 * ['th'] \
+ ['st', 'nd', 'rd'] + 7 * ['th'] \
+ ['st']
year = raw_input('Year: ')
month = raw_input('Month (1-12): ')
day = raw_input('Day (1-31): ')
month_number = int(month)
day_number = int(day)
# Remember to subtract 1 from month and day to get a
# correct index
month_name = months[month_number-1]
ordinal = day + endings[day_number-1]
print month_name + ' ' + ordinal + ', ' + year
```

Output of this program:

Year: 1990

Month (1-12): 7

Day (1-31): 9

July 9th, 1990

Note: A Python list's size is flexible. It can grow and shrink on demand.

8.7 LIST FUNCTIONS

Python has several built-in functions that can be used with lists. Some of the commonly used functions are summarized in Table 8.1. These operations are explained in the following sections with examples.

Table 8.1: Commonly used Functions

Function name	Description
len(s)	Length of the list, s, *i.e.*, the number of elements in the list, s.
min(s)	The smallest element in the list, s.
max(s)	Largest element in the list, s.
sum(s)	Sum of all numbers in the list, s.
random.suffle(s)	Shuffle the elements in the list, s.

The `len()` function returns the number of elements in the list.

```
>>> list1= [12, 34, 56, 78, 90, 4, 2, 11]
>>> len(list1)
8
```

The `max()` and `min()` functions return the elements with the greatest and lowest values in the list respectively.

```
>>>max(list1)
90
>>>min(list1)
2
>>>sum(list1)
287
```

To shuffle the elements we may use the the `shuffle()` function from the random module as follows:

```
>>> import random
>>> random.shuffle(list1)
>>> list1
[78, 2, 12, 4, 56, 34, 11, 90]
```

Note: If you are using older version of Python, you may get a warning message when you call the sum() function, as follows:

```
Traceback (most recent call last):
  File "<pyshell#20>", line 1, in ?
    sum(list1)
NameError: name 'sum' is not defined
```

8.8 LIST METHODS

We can use the list class's methods to manipulate the list. Most of the commonly used methods are summarized in Table 8.2.

Table 8.2: Commonly used List Methods

Methods	Descriptions
`append(s)`	Add an element, s to the end of the list.
`extend(s)`	Appends all the elements of list, s to the calling list.
`sort()`	Sort the elements in the list in ascending order.
`count(s)`	Returns the number of times element, s appears in the list.

Contd...

index(s)	Returns the index of the **first** occurrence of element, x in the list.
insert(s1,s2)	Insert the element s2 at a given index, s1. Note that the first element in the list has index 0 (not 1).
pop(s)	Removes the element at the given position, s and returns it. If the position is not specified, pop() removes the last element of the list and return it.
remove(s)	Removes the first occurrence of the element, s from the list. Here s represents the element not the index of the element.
reverse()	Reverse the elements in the list.

Python provides methods that operate on lists. The append(x) adds a new element x to the end of a list:

```
>>> a = [1, 2, 3, 4]
>>> a.append(5)
>>> print a# In Python shell, we can omit print
            # statement
[1, 2, 3, 4, 5]
```

If we give the argument as a list in append(s) method rather than an integer or character, it will give us a nested list, as follows:

```
>>> a = [1, 2, 3, 4]
>>> b = [6, 7, 8]
>>> a.append(b)
>>> a
[1, 2, 3, 4, [6, 7, 8]]
```

The extend() takes a list as an argument and appends all of the elements:

```
>>> b = [1, 2, 3]
>>> c = [4, 5]
>>> b.extend(c) # here argument is a list.
>>> print b
[1, 2, 3, 4, 5]
```

This example leaves c unmodified and appends only at b list.

Note: If we use the argument of the extend() method as an integer value rather than a list, we will get an error message as follows:

```
>>> list1 =[1, 2, 3, 4]
>>> list1.extend(12)
Traceback (most recent call last):
  File "<pyshell#26>", line 1, in ?
    list1.extend(12)
TypeError: list.extend() argument must be a sequence
```

`sort()` arranges the elements of the list from smallest to largest:

```
>>> t = ['d', 'c', 'e', 'b', 'a']
>>> t.sort()
>>> print t
['a', 'b', 'c', 'd', 'e']
```

The `sort()` method can accepts integers or characters as its input values.

```
>>> s =[12, 3, 45, 77, 6, 98, 3]
>>> s.sort()
>>> s
[3, 3, 6, 12, 45, 77, 98]
```

All list methods are void; they modify the list and return `None`. For example

```
>>> t1 = t.sort()
>>>print t1
None
```

The `count(s)` returns the count of element, s in the list. If the element is not in the list, it will return 0.

```
>>> list1 = [1, 3, 5, 78, 87, 4, 3, 13]
>>> list1.count(3)
2
>>> list1.count(23)
0
```

The `index(x)`   return the index of the first occurrence of the element, x

```
>>> list1 = [1, 3, 5, 78, 87, 4, 3, 13]
>>> list1.index(3)
1
```

In the above example, the element, 3 occurs two times in the list. The first one is in index 1 and the second occurrence is in index 6.

The `insert ()` method can be used in the following way:

```
>>> list1 = [1, 3, 5, 78, 87, 4, 3, 13]
>>> list1.insert(4,66)
>>> list1
[1, 3, 5, 78, 66, 87, 4, 3, 13]
```

Again, the `pop()` method can be used in two different ways : with and without arguments. If we give the position as argument, then it returns the element by

removing it from the position of the list. If no argument is given, then the last
element will be removed.

```
>>> list1 = [1, 3, 5, 8, 7, 10, 20]
>>> list1.pop(5)    # with argument: 5 is the
position of 10
                     # the element in the list.
>>> list1#  the  new  list  after  removing  the
element
[1, 3, 5, 8, 7, 20]
>>> list1.pop()# without argument
20
>>> list1 # the last element is removed.
[1, 3, 5, 8, 7]
```

The remove() method removes the element permanently from the list.

```
>>> list1 = [12, 3, 34, 6, 56, 99, 85, 78, 90]
>>> list1.remove(85)
>>> list1
[12, 3, 34, 6, 56, 99, 78, 90]
```

Note 1: If the element is not in the list, it will give an error message as follows:
```
>>> list1.remove(86)
Traceback (most recent call last):
  File "<pyshell#45>", line 1, in ?
    list1.remove(86)
ValueError: list.remove(x): x not in list
```
Note 2: The basic difference between pop() and remove() methods is
that the element removed by pop() can be reused by assigning it to a variable
whereas the element removed by remove() method is permanently deleted.

The reverse() method can be called as follows:

```
>>> list1 = [12, 3, 34, 6, 56, 99, 78, 90]
>>> list1.reverse()
>>> list1
[90, 78, 99, 56, 6, 34, 3, 12]
```

Here are some examples that use append(), extend() and sort()
methods

```
# List methods (or functions): append(), extend(), sort()
x =['a', 'b', 'c']
x.append('d') # here append takes One character as an
              # arguments
print 'x = ',x
y =['x', 'y', 'z']
x.append(y) # here append takes a list as an argument
print 'New x = ',x
# check the output , a nested list is formed
a1 =['a','b','c']
b1 =['x', 'y', 'z']
a1.extend(b1)
print 'a1 = ',a1
# a normal list is formed
s = ['d', 'c', 'e', 'b', 'a', 'p']
s.sort()
print 'Sorted s = ',s
z=s.sort()
print 'Return value of s = ', z
# None because list methods does not return anything
t1 = [ 23, 45, 2, 5, 67, 78, 45]
t1.sort()
print 'Sorted t1 = ',t1
# sort() works for both numbers and characters
```

Output of the above program:
```
x = ['a', 'b', 'c', 'd']
New x = ['a', 'b', 'c', 'd', ['x', 'y', 'z']]
a1 = ['a', 'b', 'c', 'x', 'y', 'z']
Sorted s = ['a', 'b', 'c', 'd', 'e', 'p']
Return value of s = None
'Sorted t1 = [2, 5, 23, 45, 45, 67, 78]
```

From the above example we have seen that append() can accept different arguments. When we pass a character as an argument, it appends at the end. But when we pass a list as an argument it creates a nested list. However, extend() accepts a list as argument but it does not create a nested list which is more useful in list applications. Lastly sort() can be used for sorting numbers and character elements in a list.

8.9 SPLITTING A STRING INTO A LIST

The string class contains the `split()` method, which is very useful for splitting items in a string into a list.

```
>>> item = "This is a list".split() # no argument
>>> item
['This', 'is', 'a', 'list']
```

With this method `split()`, it splits the given string "This is a list" into a list `['This', 'is', 'a', 'list']`. In this case the strings are delimited by spaces, by default. However, we can use a non-space delimiter as follows:

```
>>> item2 = "09/08/2015".split("/") # with argument
>>> item2
['09', '08', '2015']
```

8.10 INPUTTING LIST FROM THE CONSOLE/KEYBOARD

We may often need code that reads data from the console into a list. We can enter one data per line and append it to a list using a loop. The following code reads eight numbers *one per line* into a list. (Use an Editor)

```
list1 = []
print("Enter Eight Numbers (Press Enter): ")
for i in range(8):
    list1.append(input())
print list1
```

```
Output of the above Program:
Enter Eight Numbers (Press Enter):
12
34
56
78
90
21
43
65
[12, 34, 56, 78, 90, 21, 43, 65]
```

Sometimes it is more convenient to enter the data in one line separated by spaces. In such case, we can use the string's split() method to extract data from a line of input. For example, the following code reads eight numbers separated by space from one line into a list.

```
str1 = raw_input("Enter Eight numbers :")
list1 = str1. split()
list2 = [eval(x) for x in list1]
print list2
```

Output of the above program:

Enter Eight numbers: 2 3 4 5 6 7 7 8

[2, 3, 4, 5, 6, 7, 7, 8]

Enter Eight numbers: 12 34 45 56 67 78 80 90 123 189

[12, 34, 45, 56, 67, 78, 80, 90, 123, 189]

Invoking `raw_input()` reads a string. Using `str1.split()` extracts the items delimited by spaces from a string str1 and returns the items in a list. The `for` loop creates a lists of numbers by converting the items into numbers. However, this program can accept more than eight numbers as shown above.

Note: Change the above program as below, by changing raw_input() by input(), and see the difference:

```
str1 = input("Enter Eight numbers :")
list1 = str1. split()
list2 = [eval(x) for x in list1]
print list2
```

8.11 SHIFTING LISTS

Sometimes we need to shift the elements left or right. Python does not provide such a method in the list class, but we can write the following function to perform a left shift.

A. Left Shift

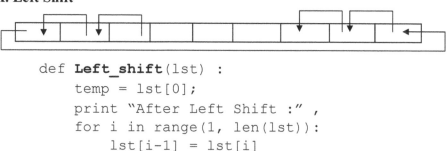

```
def Left_shift(lst) :
    temp = lst[0];
    print "After Left Shift :" ,
    for i in range(1, len(lst)):
        lst[i-1] = lst[i]
```

```
        lst[len(lst) - 1] = temp
        print lst
    list1 = [2, 3, 45, 6, 78]
    print "Before left Shift : ", list1
    Left_shift(list1)
```

Output of the above program:

```
Before left Shift : [2, 3, 45, 6, 78]
After left Shift : [3, 45, 6, 78, 2]
```

B. Right Shift

There are many ways for implementing the *right shift* of the elements in a list. One of the easiest ways to perform a right shift is shown below.

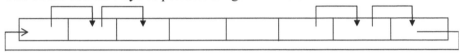

```
    def Right_shift(lst):
        no_of_elements = len(lst)-1
        Last_value = lst[no_of_elements]
        print "After Right Shift :" ,
        for i in range(no_of_elements, 0,-1):
            lst[no_of_elements] = lst[no_of_
            elements-1]
            no_of_elements -= 1
        lst[0] = Last_value
        print lst
    list2 = [2, 3, 45, 6, 78]
    print "Before Right Shift : ", list2
    Right_shift(list2)
```

Output of the above Program:

```
Before Right Shift :  [2, 3, 45, 6, 78]
After Right Shift : [78, 2, 3, 45, 6]
```

8.12 SIMPLIFYING CODING WITH LIST

With lists, we can simplify coding for certain tasks. For example, suppose we want to obtain the English month name for a given month in number. If the month names are stored in a list, the month name can be accessed simply via index. The following sample code prompts the user to enter a month number and displays its month name:

```
months = ["January", "February", "March",...,"December"]
month_number = input("Enter a month number ( 1 to 12 ) :")
print("The month is :", months[month_number - 1])
```

If the `months` list is not used, we would have to determine the month name using a lengthy multi-way `if-else` statements as follows:

```
if month_number == 1 :
     print " The month is January"
elif month_number == 2:
     print " The month is February"
elif month_number == 3:
     print " The month is March"
...
else :
     print " The month is December"
```

Example 8.2: Write a function called SUM that takes a list of integers and add up the elements.

Answer:

```
def SUM(t):     # t should be a list
     total = 0
     for x in t : # we can use "range(len(t))" also.
          total += x # equivalent to "total = total + x"
          #print total # debugging line, remove after
                    # program works properly
     return total
t=[1, 2, 3, 4]
s=SUM(t)
print 'Sum of the elements of the list = ',s
print "\nThe sum of the elements using built in
function:"
print sum(t) # Built in Functions
s=sum(t) # An operation like this that combines
#a sequence of elements into a single value is
#sometimes called reduce.
(Please keep the # symbol at the beginning of
the line.)
print s
```

```
Output of this program segment:
1 3 6
Sum of the elements of the list = 10
The sum of the elements using built in function:
10
```

The built in function sum() works in the same way. One important difference in using indent is explained below:

A.
```
def SUM(t):
        total = 0
        for x in t :
               total += x
        return total
```
If we write **return total** just after total += *x*, without removing an indent, we will get the first element as a return value. In this case 1 will get as return value

B.
```
def SUM(t):
        total = 0
        for x in t :
               total += x
        return total
```
If we write **return total** just after total += *x*, by removing an indent, we will get the correct return value. In this case 10 will get as return value

Example 8.3: Write a function called nested_sum that takes a nested list of integers and add up the elements from all of the nested lists.

Answer: Here the sum() function will not work as before. So we have to write a program. The advantage of writing user defined function makes it simpler. In this program we have to put a condition to check a nested list. After that we know how to sum up the elements of a list.

```
a=[1, 2, 3, 4, [5, 6]]
# s=sum(a) will not work here
def nested_sum (L) :
    total = 0
    for i in L :
    if isinstance(i,list) :
        print 'A nested list is found.'
        total += nested_sum (i)
        print 'Total(inside function) = ', total
    else :
        total +=i
        print 'Normal List = ', total
        return total
```

```
result = nested_sum (a)
print '\nSum of nested list = ', result
```

Output of the above program :
```
Normal List = 1
Normal List = 3
Normal List = 6
Normal List = 10
A nested list is found.
Normal List = 5
Normal List = 11
Total(inside function) = 21
Sum of nested list = 21
```

The print statements inside the function is not required if we get the correct output. But it is recommended to see how the code checks the flow of program. From the output we know that when an inner list is found, it prints a message "A nested list is found.". After this the sum of inner list takes place and overall sum is returned to the calling function.

Example 8.4: Write a Python program to find the average value of a given **n** numbers. And also print the numbers which are greater than the average value.

Solution:
```
NUMBER_OF_ELEMENTS = input("For how many numbers\
do you want to find Average? ")
numbers = []
larger = []
Sum = 0.0
for i in range(NUMBER_OF_ELEMENTS):
    value = input("Enter a new number:")
    numbers.append(value)
    Sum += value
average = float(Sum / NUMBER_OF_ELEMENTS)
count = 0 # The number of elements above average
for i in range(NUMBER_OF_ELEMENTS):
    if numbers[i] > average:
        larger.append(numbers[i])
        count += 1
print "Average :", average
print "Number of elements above the average \
is/are :", count
print "The numbers are :", larger
```

```
Output of the above program:
For how many numbers do you want to find Average? 8
Enter a new number: 6
Enter a new number: 8
Enter a new number: 12
Enter a new number: 5
Enter a new number: 16
Enter a new number: 22
Enter a new number: 19
Enter a new number: 7
Average : 11.875
Number of elements above the average is/are : 4
The numbers are : [12, 16, 22, 19]
```

Note 1:

The Python interpreter cannot determine the end of the statement written in multiple lines. We can place the *line continuation symbol* (\) at the end of a line to tell the interpreter that the statement is continued on the next line. For example, the following statement

```
sum = 1 + 2 + 3 + 4 + \
5 + 6
```

is equivalent to

```
sum = 1 + 2 + 3 + 4 + 5 + 6
```

In the above program, we used the continuation symbol to tell the interpreter that the statement is continued on the next line.

```
    NUMBER_OF_ELEMENTS = input("For how many
    numbers do you \ want to find Average?")
```

Note 2: The built-in function eval () :

We can use the function **eval** to evaluate and convert it to a numeric value.

For example, eval("34.567") returns 34.567, eval("1234") returns 1234, and eval("5 + 8") returns 13.

Again,

```
variable = input("Enter a value:")
```

The value entered is a string. So we can convert into numeric value as:

```
variable = eval(input("Enter a value: "))
```

8.13 COPYING LISTS

To copy the data from one list to another, we have to copy individual elements from the source list to the target list. Copying of the list cannot be obtained by using the simple assignment statement (=):

list2 = list1

In this case, it will not copy the contents of the list referenced by list1 to list2. Instead, it merely copies the reference value from list1 to list2. After this statement, list1 and list2 will have the same list, as shown in Fig. 8.2. The list previously referenced by list2 is no longer referenced; it becomes garbage. The memory occupied by list2 will be automatically collected and reused by the Python interpreter.

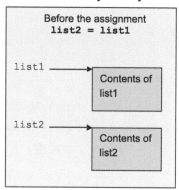 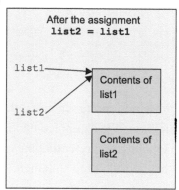

Fig. 8.2 Before the assignment statement, list1 and list2 had separate memory locations. After the assignment statement, the list1 reference value is passed to list2 (*i.e.*, they have the same memory locations).

Here is an example to illustrate this concept:

```
>>> list1 = [2,3,4,5]
>>> list2 = [5,4,6,7,8]
>>> id(list1) # The reference of list1
12512716
>>> id(list2) # The reference of list2
12850348
>>> list2 = list1
>>> id(list2)
12512716
```

The two lists list1 and list2 are created with different references. After assigning list1 to list2, list2's id is same as list1's id. Now list1 and list2 refer to the same object.

To get a duplicate copy of list1 into list2, we can use:

```
list3 = [x for x in list1] or list4 = [] + list1
```

The following illustrate this

```
>>> list1 = [2,3,4,5]
>>> list3 = [x for x in list1]
>>> list3
[2, 3, 4, 5]
>>> id(list3)
12908900
>>> list4 = [] + list1
>>> list4
[2, 3, 4, 5]
>>> id(list4)
12605396
```

8.14 PASSING LISTS TO FUNCTIONS

We know that list is mutable *i.e.*, changeable. When we pass a list to a function, the contents of the list may change after the function call.

We can pass a list to a function just like passing an object to a function. For example, the following function displays the elements in a list:

```
def List_print(list1):
    for element in list1:
        print element
list2= [2,4,5,6,7]
List_print(list2)
print "\nAnonymous List:"
List_print([1,4,5,7,9,10])
```

```
Output of the above program:
2 4 5 6 7
Anonymous List:
1 4 5 7 9 10
```

We can invoke it by passing a list. For instance, the list list2 is passed to the function List_print to display the contents of the list. Again, we can pass a list directly to the function. There is no explicit reference variable for the list. Such a list is called an *anonymous list*.

Since a list is mutable object, the contents of a list may change in the functions. For example:

8.15 SEARCHING LISTS

Searching is the process of looking for a specific element in a list. The `list` class provides the `index()` method for searching and returning the index of a matching element from a list.

Searching is an important operation in any computer programming. Many algorithms are devoted to searching. This section discusses two commonly used approaches : *linear searches* and *binary searches*.

8.15.1 The Linear Search Method

The linear search approach compares the key element sequentially with each element in the list. It continues to do so until the key matches an element in the list or the list is exhausted without a match is being found. If a match is found, the linear search returns the matching element's index in the list. if no match is found, the search returns -1. The `linearSearch` method is given below:

```
def LinearSearch(key, list1):
    for i in range(len(list1)):
        if key == list1[i] :
            print "Found at index :",
            return i
    else:
        print "Not Found : ",
        return -1 # if no match is found
list1 = [1,3,5,6,7,8,12,15,18]
search1 = LinearSearch(6, list1)
print search1
search3 = LinearSearch(4, list1)
print search3
```

```
Output of the above Program:
Found at index : 3
Not Found :   -1
Found at index : 8
```

The linear search function compares the key with each element in the list. The elements can be in any order. Since the execution time of a linear search increases linearly as the number of list elements increases. A linear search is therefore inefficient method especially when the list is a large one.

8.15.2 The Binary Search Method

A binary search is another common approach for a list of values. For a binary search to work, the elements in the list must be in sorted order. Assume that the list is in ascending order, a binary search first compares the key with the element in the middle of the list. Consider the following three cases:

   (*i*) If the key is less than the list's middle element, we need to continue to search for the key only in the first half of the list.

   (*ii*) If the key is equal to the list's middle element, the search ends with a match.

   (*iii*) If the key is greater than the list's middle element, we need to continue to search for the key only in the second half of the list.

The binary search function eliminates half of the list after each comparison. Suppose that the list has n elements. For convenience, let n be a power of 2. After the first comparison, $n/2$ elements are left for further search; after the second comparison, $(n/2)/2$ elements are left. After the kth comparison, $n/2^k$ elements are left for further search. When only one element is left in the list, and we need only one more comparison. Therefore,

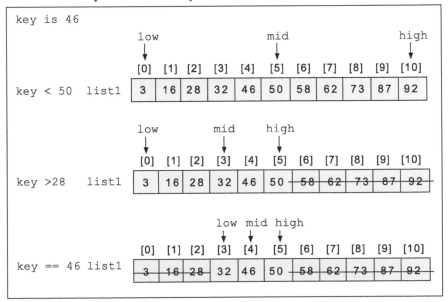

Fig. 8.3 A binary search eliminates half of the list after each comparison.

in the worst-case scenario when using the binary search approach, we need comparisons to find an element in the sorted list. In the worst case for a list of 1024 elements, the binary search requires only 11 comparisons, whereas a linear search requires 1,023 comparisons in the worst case.

Let us start with an example. Consider a list, list1=[3, 16, 28, 32, 46, 50, 58, 62, 73, 87, 92], with key = 46. The Fig. 8.3 shows the constructive steps of the search method. The portion of the list being searched shrinks by half after each comparison. Let **low** and **high** denote the first index and last index of the list , respectively. Initially, **low** is **0** and **high** is **len(list1)–1**. Let **mid** denote the index of the middle element, so **mid** is **(low + high) // 2**.

The next task is to implement it in Python.

```python
def BinarySearch(key, list1) :
    low = 0
    high = len(list1) - 1
    while high >= low :
        mid = (high + low) // 2
        if key < list1[mid] :
            high = mid -1
        elif key == list1[mid]:
            print "Key is found",
            return mid# we can return key  also.
        else :
            low = mid + 1
    print "Not Found :",
    return -1 # if not found in the list
list1=[3, 16, 28, 32, 46, 50, 58, 62, 73, 87, 92]
result = BinarySearch(46, list1)
print result
result1 = BinarySearch(47, list1)
print result1
```

```
Output of the above program:
Key is found 4
Not Found :   -1
```

Let us see how the program works. The value of the key is given as 46 in the first run of the program. So the value of `low = 0, high = len(list1)-1 = 11-1 =10` and `mid = (10+0) /2 = 5`. The while loop will be executed because the condition `high >= low` is true *i.e.*, 10>=0. Inside the loop, in the first run, the `if` condition `key < list1[mid]` *i.e.*, 46 < 50 is *true*, so the new value of `high` will be `mid -1 = 5 -1 =4`. In the second execution of the while loop, the new value of `mid` will be `0 + 4 = 4`. In this case the second condition of else if part is true, so the function will return the index. We can return both index and corresponding value of the key also by the same function.

In the second run of the program when the key is 47, the while loop can't get the index, thus it will return −1.

Note: Why not − 1?

When the key is not found, **low** is the insertion point where a key would be inserted to maintain the order of the list. It is more useful to return the insertion point than −1. The function must return a negative value to indicate that the key is not in the list. Can it simply return–**low**? No. If the key is less than **list1[0]**, **low** would be **0**. −0 is **0**. This would indicate that the key matches **list1[0]**. A good choice is to let the function return −**low** − **1** if the key is not in the list. Returning −**low** − **1** indicates not only that the key is not in the list, but also where the key would be inserted.

This can be done simply by changing `return -1` by `return -low -1` in the last line of the function above.

8.16 SORTING LISTS

There are many strategies for sorting elements in a list. Selection sorts and insertion sorts are two common approaches.

Sorting, like searching, is a common task in computer programming. The **list** class provides the **sort** method for sorting a list. Many different algorithms have been developed for sorting. This section introduces two simple, intuitive sorting algorithms: *selection sort* and *insertion sort*. By using these algorithms, we will learn valuable techniques for developing and implementing other algorithms.

8.16.1 Selection Sort

Suppose that we want to sort a list in ascending order. A *selection sort* finds the smallest element in the list and swaps it with the first element. It then finds the smallest from the remaining and swaps it with the first element in the remaining list, and so on, until only a single element remains. Figure 8.4 shows the sort of the list [12, 45, 3, 89, 7, 11, 9] using a selection sort.

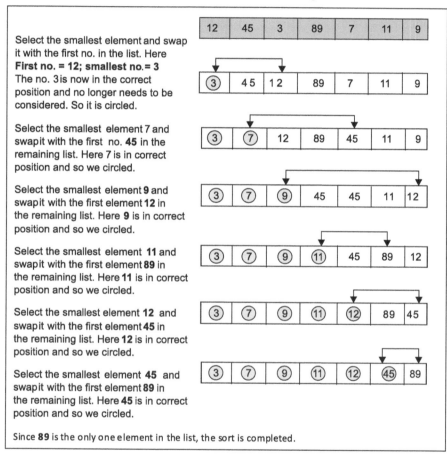

Fig. 8.4 The Selection sort repeatedly selects the smallest element and swaps it with the first element in the remaining list.

The next step is to implement with Python. We know that the important part is to find the smallest element in the list and swap it with the first element and continue it till the last element. The Python program is given below:

```
def SelectionSort( list1) :
    print "Steps of Selection Sort:"
    for i in range(len(list1) - 1) :
```

```
            smallest_element = list1[i]
            index_to_smallest = i
            #To find the smallest element in the List
            for j in range(i+1, len(list1)) :
                if smallest_element > list1[j] :
                    smallest_element = list1[j]
                    index_to_smallest = j
            #Swap list1[i]  with list1[index_to_smallest]
            # if necessary
            if index_to_smallest != i :
                list1[index_to_smallest] = list1[i]
                list1[i] = smallest_element
        list1 = [12, 45, 3, 89, 7, 11, 9]
        print "List elements before sorting:", list1
        SelectionSort(list1)
        print "List elements after sorting:", list1
```

Output of the above program :
```
List elements before sorting: [12, 45, 3, 89, 7,
11, 9]
Steps of Selection Sort:
[12, 45, 3, 89, 7, 11, 9]
[3, 45, 12, 89, 7, 11, 9]
[3, 7, 12, 89, 45, 11, 9]
[3, 7, 9, 89, 45, 11, 12]
[3, 7, 9, 11, 45, 89, 12]
[3, 7, 9, 11, 12, 89, 45]
List elements after sorting: [3, 7, 9, 11, 12, 45,
89]
```

8.16.2 Insertion Sort

The insertion-sort algorithm sorts a list of values by repeatedly inserting a new element into a sorted sublist until the whole list is sorted. Figure 8.5 shows how to sort the list [12, 45, 3, 89, 7, 11, 9] using an insertion sort.

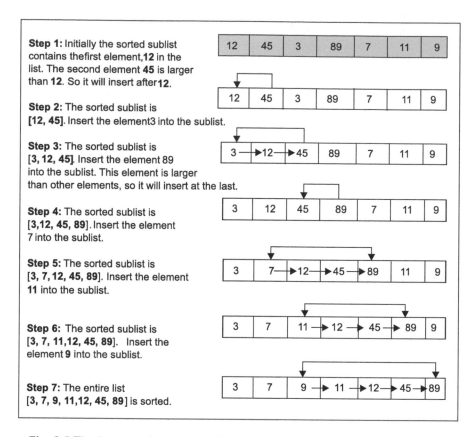

Step 1: Initially the sorted sublist contains thefirst element,**12** in the list. The second element **45** is larger than **12**. So it will insert after**12**.

Step 2: The sorted sublist is [**12, 45**]. Insert the element**3** into the sublist.

Step 3: The sorted sublist is [**3, 12, 45**]. Insert the element **89** into the sublist. This element is larger than other elements, so it will insert at the last.

Step 4: The sorted sublist is [**3,12, 45, 89**].Insert the element **7** into the sublist.

Step 5: The sorted sublist is [**3, 7,12, 45, 89**]. Insert the element **11** into the sublist.

Step 6: The sorted sublist is [**3, 7, 11,12, 45, 89**]. Insert the element **9** into the sublist.

Step 7: The entire list [**3, 7, 9, 11,12, 45, 89**] is sorted.

Fig. 8.5 The Insertion Sort repeatedly inserts a new element into a sorted list.

The algorithm may be described as follows:

```
for i in range(1, len(list1)):
    insert list1[i] into a sorted sublist list1[0:i]so that
    list1[0:i+1] is sorted.
```

The Python program may be implemented as follows:

```
def InsertionSort(list1):
    print "Steps of Insertion Sort:"
    for i in range(1, len(list1)):
    #insert the element list1[i] into a sorted sublist
        currentElement = list1[i]
        k = i - 1
        while k >= 0 and list1[k] > currentElement :
            list1[k+1] = list1[k]
            k = k - 1
```

```
                    #insert the current element into list1[k+1]
                    list1[k+1] = currentElement
                    print list1
        list1 = [12, 45, 3, 89, 7, 11, 9]
        print "List elements before sorting:", list1
        InsertionSort(list1)
        print "List elements after sorting:", list1
```

Output of the above program:

List elements before sorting: [12, 45, 3, 89, 7, 11, 9]
Steps of Insertion Sort:
[12, 45, 3, 89, 7, 11, 9]
[3, 12, 45, 89, 7, 11, 9]
[3, 12, 45, 89, 7, 11, 9]
[3, 7, 12, 45, 89, 11, 9]
[3, 7, 11, 12, 45, 89, 9]
[3, 7, 9, 11, 12, 45, 89]
List elements after sorting: [3, 7, 9, 11, 12, 45, 89]

The `InsertionSort(list1)` function sorts the lists of elements. The function is implemented with a nested `for` and `while` loops. The outer `for` loop is iterated in order to obtain a sorted sublist, which ranges from `list1[0]` to `list1[i]`. The inner `while` loop inserts `list1[i]` into the sublist from `list1[0]` to `list1[i-1]`. The steps of this sorting technique is shown above.

8.17 TWO-DIMENSIONAL LISTS

So far we have discussed how to use a list to store linear collections of elements. There could be situations where a table of values will have to be stored in multi dimensional list. A *two-dimensional list* is a list that contains other lists as its elements. We can use a list to store two-dimensional data, such as a matrix or a table. For example, the following table, which gives the marks obtained by four students in four subjects, can be stored in a list named **marks**.

	Physics	Chemistry	Computer Sc.	Mathematics
Student1	67	89	82	90
Student2	87	66	78	75
Student3	78	76	80	82
Student4	80	88	76	72

```
marks = [
            [67,  89,  82,  90],
            [87,  66,  78,  75],
            [78,  76,  80,  82],
            [80,  88,  76,  72]
        ]
```

In this way, a two-dimensional list can be used to store two-dimensional data. In other words, it is considered as nested list.

8.17.1 Processing Two-Dimensional Lists

A value in a two-dimensional list can be accessed through a row and column index. We can think of a *two-dimensional list* as a list that consists of rows. Each row is a list that contains the values. The rows can be accessed using the index, conveniently called a *row index*. The values in each row can be accessed through another index, called a *column index*. So, the above two-dimensional list **marks** can be illustrated explicitly as follows in Fig. 8.6.

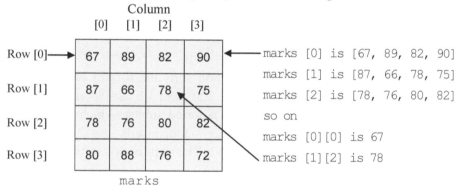

Fig. 8.6 Representation of the values in a two-dimensional list.

8.17.2 Initializing Lists with Input Values

Each value in a two dimensional list can be accessed using the row and column indexes. The following loop will initialize a two dimensional list with user input values:

```
matrix = [] # Create an empty list
Rows = input("Enter the number of rows:")
Columns = input("Enter the number of columns:")
for row in range(Rows):
```

```
matrix.append([]) # Add an empty new row
    for column in range(Columns):
        value = input("Enter an element & press Enter:")
        matrix[row].append(value)
print "The matrix is :"
print matrix,
```

The output of the above program:
First Run:
Enter the number of rows: 2
Enter the number of columns: 2
Enter an element & press Enter: 12
Enter an element & press Enter: 34
Enter an element & press Enter: 56
Enter an element & press Enter: 78
The matrix is :
[[12, 34], [56, 78]]
Second Run:
Enter the number of rows: 3
Enter the number of columns: 3
Enter an element & press Enter: 12
Enter an element & press Enter: 34
Enter an element & press Enter: 56
Enter an element & press Enter: 78
Enter an element & press Enter: 90
Enter an element & press Enter: 98
Enter an element & press Enter: 87
Enter an element & press Enter: 76
Enter an element & press Enter: 65
The matrix is :
[[12, 34, 56], [78, 90, 98], [87, 76, 65]]

8.17.3 Initializing Lists with Random Values

We can use the random module to initialize the list with random values. The following program initializes a list that stores random values between **1** and **50**. Here the list is filled with integer values using the randint(1,   50 function from random module.

```
import random
matrix = [] # Create an empty list
Rows = input("Enter the number of rows: ")
Columns = input("Enter the number of columns: ")
for row in range(Rows):
    matrix.append([]) # Add an empty new row
    for column in range(Columns):
        matrix[row].append(random.randint(1, 50))
print "\n The new matrix is :"
print matrix
```

Output of the above program:
```
Enter the number of rows: 3
Enter the number of columns: 3
The new matrix is :
[[17, 46, 11], [36, 17, 33], [49, 7, 37]]
Enter the number of rows: 2
Enter the number of columns: 2

The new matrix is :
[[41, 10], [41, 25]]
```

8.17.4 Printing Two Dimensional List

Sometimes we want to print a two dimensional list in proper matrix form. For example, a 2 × 2 matrix takes the following form:

$$41 \quad 10$$
$$45 \quad 25$$

However, the two dimensional list, printed above is as follows:

```
[[41, 10], [45, 25]]
```

Though the concepts are same, the first representation gives a better look. Printing a two-dimensional list in proper matrix form, with each element in the list, can be done by using two nested loops like the following:

```
matrix = [[11, 12, 13], [14, 15, 16], [17, 18, 19]]
for row in range(len(matrix)):
    for column in range(len(matrix[row])):
        print matrix[row][column],
    print # print a new line
```

Output of the above program segment:
```
11 12 13
14 15 16
17 18 19
```
Note: Change the last line in the above program by
"print '\n'"
and see the difference.

Another way to print the elements of a two dimensional list in matrix form may be written as follows:

```
matrix = [[11, 12, 13], [14, 15, 16], [17, 18, 19]]
for row in matrix:
    for value in row:
        print value,# end = " ")
    print # print a new line.
```

The output will be same as above, but the advantage is that summing of the elements of a list can be done easily with this concept.

Note: Check the following program, if you have difficulty in understanding the above program segment
```
matrix = [[11, 12, 13], [14, 15, 16], [17, 18, 19]]
for row in matrix:
    print row# value,# end = " ")
print
```
The output will look like this:
[11, 12, 13]
[14, 15, 16]
[17, 18, 19]

8.17.5 Summing All Elements

We can sum all the elements of a list. It may be a simple one dimensional list or a two dimensional list. As we know a two dimensional list is represented by a nested list. We can use the built-in function sum() provided by Python, or we can write our own way. For better understanding, let us start it without using the built-in function.

Use a variable named **total** to store the sum. Initially, **total** is **0**. Add each element in the list to **total** by using a loop like this:

```
matrix = [[1, 2, 3], [4, 5, 6], [7, 8, 9]]
total = 0 #initialized to zero
for row in matrix:
        for value in row:
                total = total + value
print "Total = ", total # Print the total
```

Output of the above program:
```
Total =   45
```
Note 1: For One dimensional list, we can do it very easily as follows:
```
    matrix = [1, 2, 3, 4, 5, 6, 7, 8, 9, 10]
    total = 0
    for value in matrix:
            total = total + value # same as total +=
    value
    print "Total = ", total
will display
Total =   55
```
Note 2: If we used the built-in function, then,
```
        matrix = [1, 2, 3, 4, 5, 6, 7, 8, 9, 10]
        print sum(matrix)
```

8.17.6 Summing Elements by Column

Let us define a 2 dimensional matrix as shown below. From the figure we know that the sum of the first column is $1 + 4 + 7 = 12$.

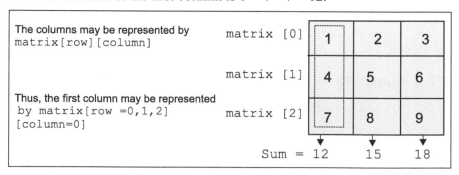

Fig. 8.7 A two dimensional matrix showing the column with dotted line.

The Python program may be implemented as follows:

```
matrix = [[1, 2, 3], [4, 5, 6], [7, 8, 9]]
for column in range(len(matrix[0])):
    total = 0
    for row in range(len(matrix)):
        total += matrix[row][column]
    print "Sum for column", column, "is", total
```

Output of the above program:

```
Sum for column 0 is 12
Sum for column 1 is 15
Sum for column 2 is 18
```

Note: In the statement:

```
    for column in range(len(matrix[0])):
```

we can change to:

```
    for column in range(len(matrix[1])):
```

or

```
    for column in range(len(matrix[2])):
```

Because the matrix we considered here, have the same rows and columns.

8.17.7 Finding the Row with the Largest Sum

In this case, first of all, we add the first row and assign it to a variable, Largest_row. Compare it with the sum of the other rows. If any of the other rows has a higher value, then, we simply assign it to the variable, Largest_row. The complete Python program is shown below:

```
matrix = [[41, 2, 3], [4, 5, 26], [7, 8, 9]]
Largest_row = sum(matrix[0]) # Get sum of the
first row
index_Row = 0
    for row in range(1, len(matrix)):
        if sum(matrix[row]) > Largest_row:
            Largest_row = sum(matrix[row])
            index_Row = row
    print"Row", index_Row, "has the maximum sum of", \
Largest_row
```

Output of the above program:

Row 2 has the maximum sum of 24

Note: Change the matrix in different ways, like

matrix = [[1, 2, 3], [4, 5, 26], [7, 8, 9]]

matrix = [[41, 2, 3], [4, 5, 6], [7, 8, 9]]

And check the outputs.

8.17.8 Random Shuffling

We can shuffle all the elements in a two-dimensional list. To accomplish this, for each element **matrix[row][column]**, randomly generate indexes **i** and **j** using **randint()** and swap **matrix[row][column]** with **matrix[i][j]**, as follows:

```
import random
matrix = [[11, 12, 13], [14, 15,16], [17, 18, 19]]
print "Matrix before Shuffle:"
print matrix
for row in range(len(matrix)):
    for column in range(len(matrix[row])):
        i = random.randint(0, len(matrix) - 1)
        j = random.randint(0, len(matrix[row]) - 1)
# Swap matrix[row][column] with matrix[i][j]
        matrix[row][column], matrix[i][j] = \
matrix[i][j], matrix[row][column]
print "Matrix after shuffle:"
print matrix
```

Output of the above program:

Matrix before Shuffle:

[[11, 12, 13], [14, 15, 16], [17, 18, 19]]

Matrix after shuffle:

[[19, 13, 14], [12, 17, 11], [18, 16, 15]]

Note: We can shuffle the elements in a one-dimensional list easily by using the **random.shuffle(list)** as follows:

>>> import random

```
>>> list1= [12, 3, 4, 56, 78, 9]
>>> random.shuffle(list1) # Shuffle the elements in
list1
>>> list1
[12, 56, 4, 3, 9, 78]
```

8.17.9 Passing Two-Dimensional Lists to Functions

When passing a two-dimensional list to a function, the list's reference is passed to the function. And a function also can return a two-dimensional list. The following example shows about this. The first function, **GetMatrix()**, returns a two-dimensional list, and the second function, **Sum(matrix1)**, returns the sum of all the elements in a matrix.

```
def GetMatrix():
    matrix = [] # Create an empty list
    Number Of Rows = input("Enter the number\
                    of rows:")
    Number Of Columns = input("Enter the number\
                    of columns:")
    for row in range(Number Of Rows):
        matrix.append([]) # Add an empty new row
        for column in range(Number Of Columns):
            value = input("Enter a value and press
            Enter:")matrix[row].append(value)
    return matrix
def Sum(matrix1):
    total = 0
    for row in matrix1:
        total += sum(row)
    return total
matrix = GetMatrix()
#printing the matrix in proper way:
print "The matrix is:"
```

```
    for row in matrix:
        for value in row:
            print value,
        print
    sum_of_matrix = Sum(matrix)
    # Display sum of elements
    print "\nSum of all elements is", sum_of_matrix
```

Output of the above program:

```
Enter the number of rows: 3
Enter the number of columns: 3
Enter a value and press Enter: 2
Enter a value and press Enter: 3
Enter a value and press Enter: 4
Enter a value and press Enter: 5
Enter a value and press Enter: 6
Enter a value and press Enter: 7
Enter a value and press Enter: 8
Enter a value and press Enter: 9
Enter a value and press Enter: 10
The matrix is:
2 3 4
5 6 7
8 9 10
Sum of all elements is 54
```

8.18 APPLICATION: FINDING THE CLOSEST PAIR

This section presents a geometric problem for finding the closest pair of points from a set of points. The closest-pair problem is to find the two points that are nearest to each other. In Fig. 8.8, for example, points **(1, 1)** and **(2, 0.5)** are closest to each other. An intuitive approach is to compute the distances between all pairs of points and find the one with the minimum distance, as implemented below.

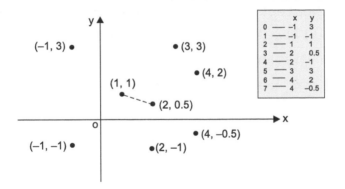

Fig. 8.8 Set of points can be represented in a nested list.

The distance between two points $(x1, y1)$ and $(x2, y2)$ can be computed using the formula

$$\text{distance between two points} = \sqrt{(x2 - x1)^2 + (y2 - y1)^2}$$

This can be done with the following program segment.

```
def distance(x1, y1, x2, y2):
    return ((x2 - x1) * (x2 - x1) + (y2 - y1) * (y2 - y1)) ** 0.5
```

or

```
from math import sqrt
def distance(x1, y1, x2, y2):
    return (sqrt((x2 - x1) * (x2 - x1) + (y2 - y1) * (y2 - y1)))
```

Next step is to find the nearest points from the given set of points. This can be done with the help of the function, `distances(x1, y1, x2, y2)` explain above. Another function **nearestPoints(points)** returns the indexes of the two nearest points in the two-dimensional list `points`. The program uses the variable **shortestDistance** to store the distance between the two nearest points, and the indexes of these two points in the **points** list are stored in **p1** and **p2**. The following Python program explains about this function.

```
def nearestPoints(points):
    # p1 and p2 are the indexes in the points list
    p1, p2 = 0, 1 # Initial two points
    #Initialize shortestDistance =[0,0],[0,1]&[1,0],
[1,1]
```

```
        shortestDistance  =  distance(points[p1][0],
points[p1][1], points[p2][0], points[p2][1])
# Compute distance between every two points
    for i in range(len(points)):
        for j in range(i + 1, len(points)):
            d = distance(points[i][0], points[i][1],
                    points[j][0], points[j][1])
            if shortestDistance > d:
                p1, p2 = i, j #Update p1, p2
                shortestDistance = d #New shortestDistance
    return p1, p2
```

In the above program, for each point at index **i**, the program computes the distance between **points[i]** and **points[j]** for all **j > i**. Whenever a shorter distance is found, the variable **shortestDistance** and **p1** and **p2** are updated.

The complete program is shown below. The program prompts the user to enter the points and then displays the nearest two points. The points are read from the console and stored in a two-dimensional list named **points**. The program invokes the **nearestPoints(points)** function to return the indexes of the two nearest points in the list.

```
def distance(x1, y1, x2, y2):
    return ((x2 - x1) * (x2 - x1) + (y2 - y1) * y2 -
y1)) ** 0.5
def nearestPoints(points):
    # p1 and p2 are the indexes in the points list
    p1, p2 = 0, 1 # Initial two points

    #Initialize shortestDistance=[0,0],[0,1]&[1,0],
    [1,1]
        shortestDistance  =  distance(points[p1][0],
points[p1][1], points[p2][0], points[p2][1])
```

```
# Compute distance between every two points
    for i in range(len(points)):
        for j in range(i + 1, len(points)):
            d = distance(points[i][0], points[i][1],
                        points[j][0], points[j][1])
            if shortestDistance > d:
                p1, p2 = i, j #Update p1, p2
            shortestDistance = d #New shortestDistance
    return p1, p2
numberOfPoints = input("Enter the number of points:
")
# Create a list to store points
points = []
print "Enter", numberOfPoints, "points:",
for i in range(numberOfPoints):
    point = 2 * [0]
    point[0], point[1] = \
    input("Enter coordinates separated by a comma: ")
    points.append(point)

p1, p2 = nearestPoints(points)
print "The closest two points are (" +\
str(points[p1][0]) + ", " + str(points[p1][1]) + ")\
and (" + str(points[p2][0]) + ", " + str(points[p2]
[1]) + ")"
```

Output of the above Program:
```
Enter the number of points: 8
Enter 8 points:
Enter coordinates separated by a comma: -1, 3
Enter coordinates separated by a comma: -1, -1
Enter coordinates separated by a comma: 1, 1
Enter coordinates separated by a comma: 2, .5
Enter coordinates separated by a comma: 2, -1
Enter coordinates separated by a comma: 3, 3
Enter coordinates separated by a comma: 4, 2
Enter coordinates separated by a comma: 4, -.5
  The closest two points are (1, 1) and (2, 0.5)
```

Note: In the above program, there might be more than one closest pair of points with the same minimum distance. The above program finds one such pair. We can modify the program to find all the closest Pairs. We left it for you as an exercise.

It is cumbersome to enter all points from the keyboard. We may store the input in a file, with a name such as *Nearest_Points.txt*, and run the program using the following command from a command window:

>>>python function name < Text file name. For example,

>>>**python FindNearestPoints < FindNearestPoints.txt**

8.19 MULTIDIMENSIONAL LISTS

A two-dimensional list consists of a list of one-dimensional lists and a three-dimensional list consists of a list of two-dimensional lists. We can represent n-dimensional lists for any integer *n*. For example, we can use a three-dimensional list to store the values for 3-dimensional axes *x*, *y* and *z*.

The following syntax creates a three-dimensional list co_ordinates.

```
                    co_ordinates = [
x[0] ────► [[10, 20], [15, 30]],          co_ordinates[0][1 [0]=15
x[1] ────► [[12, 18], [14, 25]],
x[2] ────► [[15, 30], [18, 35]],          co_ordinates[3][0][1]=25
x[3] ────► [[20, 25], [10, 18]],
                    ]
```

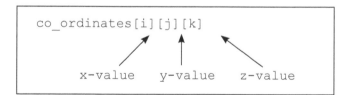

The above figure depicts the meaning of the values in the list.

A multidimensional list is a list in which each element is another list. More specifically, a three-dimensional list consists of a list of two-dimensional lists, and a two-dimensional list consists of a list of one-dimensional lists. For example, co_ordinates[0] and co_ordinates[1] are two-dimensional lists, while co_ordinates [0][1] co_ordinates [1][0], and co_ordinates [1][1] are one-dimensional lists and each contains two elements. len(co_ordinates) is 4, len(co_ordinates [0]) is 2, and len(co_ordinates [0][0]) is 2.

Let us start with some examples:

```
m1 = [
[[11, 12], [10, 21]],
[[15, 13], [14, 15]]
]
print "m1[0][1][0] =",m1[0][1][0]
```

will display **10**.

We can add a value to each of the elements in a three dimensional list, as follows:

```
def f(matrix):
    for i in range(len(matrix)):
        for j in range(len(matrix [i])):
            for k in range(len(matrix [j])):
                matrix [i][j][k] += 1

def printMatrix(m):
    for i in range(len(m)):
        for j in range(len(m[i])):
            for k in range(len(m[j])):
                print m[i][j][k],
            print
matrix1 = [
[[0, 0], [0, 1]],
[[0, 0], [0, 1]]
]
printMatrix(matrix1)
f(matrix1)
print "Matrix after adding a value:"
printM(matrix1)
```

Output of the above program:
```
0 0
0 1
0 0
0 1
```

```
Matrix after adding a value:
1 1
1 2
1 1
1 2
```

Till now we discussed the use of Python built-in functions **len**, **min**, **max**, and **sum** to return the length of a list, the minimum and maximum elements in a list, and the sum of all the elements in a list. The important usages of the index operator [] to reference an individual element in a list is also highlighted. The use concatenation operator + to concatenate two lists and the repetition operator * to duplicate elements are illustrated with examples..The slicing operator [:] to get a sublist, and the **in** and **not in** operators to check whether an element is in a list or not have described with examples.

We have also learned that the methods **append**, **extend**, **insert**, **pop**, and **remove** can be used for the manipulation of the list elements. A few important search and sorting techniques have been highlighted with example.

EXERCISES

8.1. State whether the following statements are true or false:

(*a*) Every element in a list must have the same type.

(*b*) A list's size is fixed after it is created.

(*c*) A list can have duplicate elements.

(*d*) The elements in a list can be accessed via an index operator.

(*e*) The shuffle function in the random module to is to shuffle the elements in a list.

(*f*) The index of the first element in a list starts with 1.

(*g*) The concatenation operator + is used to concatenate two lists of same size.

(*h*) The repetition operator * is used to duplicate elements of different sizes.

(*i*) The slicing operator [:] is used to get a sublist from a given list.

(*j*) We can use a `for` loop to traverse all elements in a list.

(*k*) We cannot use a `while` loop to traverse all elements in a list.

(*l*) We can use the comparison operators to compare the elements of two lists.

(*m*) We can use the `reverse` methods to sort the elements in a list.

(*n*) Anonymous list is a list of one element only.

(*o*) A two-dimensional list can be used to store two-dimensional data such as a table and a matrix.

(*p*) A two-dimensional list is a list. Each of its elements is also a list.

8.2. Given a list, `list1 = [10, 11, 12, 13, 14]`, what is the list after applying each of the following statements? Assume that each line of code is independent.

```
list1.append(20)
list1.insert(1, 25)
list1.extend([21, 22])
list1.remove(3)
list1.pop(2)
list1.pop()
list1.sort()
list1.reverse()
random.shuffle(list1)
```

8.3. Given a list, `list1 = [10, 11, 12, 13, 14]`, what is the list after applying each of the following statements?

```
list1.index(1)
list1.count(1)
list1.count(list1)
sum(list1)
len(list1)
max(list1)
min(list1)
```

8.4. Given `list1 = [10, 11, 12, 13, 14]` and `list2 = [18, 19, 20]`, what is the return value of each of the following statements?

```
list1 + list2
2 * list2
list2 * 2
list1[1 : 3]
list1[3]
```

8.5. How do you create an empty list and a list with the two integers 1 and 2?

8.6. Given `list1 = [10, 11, 12, 13, 14, 0]`, how many elements are in `list1`? What is the index of the last element in `list1`? What is `list1[2]`? What is `list1[-2]`?

8.7. Write a function named `shuffle1()` to shuffle a list without using `random.shuffle(list1)` method. Write a Python program that prompts the user to enter a list of numbers, invokes the function to shuffle the numbers, and displays the numbers.

8.8. Write a function `find_gcd()` that returns the greatest common divisor (GCD) of integers in a list. Write a Python program that prompts the user to enter five numbers, invokes the function to find the GCD of these numbers, and displays the GCD.

8.9. Write a function, RemoveDuplicates() that returns a new list by eliminating the duplicate values in the list. Write a Python program that reads in a list of integers, invokes the function, and displays the result.

8.10. Write a Python program that reads some integers between 1 and 100 and counts the occurrences of each numbers. Here is a sample run of the program:

```
Enter integers between 1 and 100:1 2 2 3 3 4 5 5 6…

1 occurs 2 times

2 occurs 1 times

3 occurs 2 time

4 occurs 1 time

5 occurs 2 times …
```

8.11. Write a Python program that returns the sum of all the elements in a specified column in an $m \times n$ matrix.

8.12. Write a Python program that sums all the numbers of the major diagonal in an $m \times n$ matrix.

8.13. Write a Python program to find the product of two matrices. It will show a proper message if the product cannot be find out due to the mismatch in the row and column of the two matrices.

8.14. Write a Python program that invokes a function find() to perform the following tasks.

(*a*) Receive a character list or a string and a single character

(*b*) Returns *True* if the specified character is found in the list, o otherwise.

8.15. Write a function that takes an integer parameter m representing the month number of the year and returns the corresponding name of the month. For example, if $m = 6$, the month is June.

9

Dictionaries

INTRODUCTION

A dictionary is a new concept in Python that stores a collection of key/value pairs. The advantages of dictionary are it enables fast retrieval, deletion, and updating of the value by using the key. This chapter describes the basics of Dictionary. How to create dictionaries and common operations that used frequently are explained with examples. Traversing keys in a dictionary using a **for** loop, comparing whether two dictionaries have the same content or not and commonly used methods are also described with examples. The concepts of sets are also illustrate with examples.

9.1 DEFINITION

In Python, *A dictionary is defined as a collection of key and value pairs*. A dictionary is like a list, but it is more general. In a list, the indices have to be "integers"; in a dictionary they can be (almost) any type. Mapping

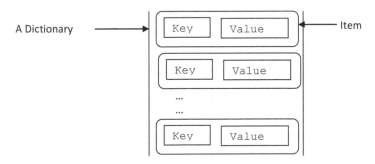

Fig. 9.1 A dictionary's item is a key/value pair.

between a set of indices (which are called keys) and a set of values is the defining things about dictionary. In a dictionary, each key maps to a value. The association of a key and a value is called a "key-value pair" or sometimes an "ITEM" as shown in Fig. 9.1.

9.2 CREATING A DICTIONARY

We can create a dictionary by enclosing the items inside a pair of curly braces ({ }). Each item consists of a key, followed by a colon, followed by a value. The items are separated by commas. For example, the following statement:

```
eng2hin = {'one' : 'aek'}
```

creates a dictionary with one item. The item is in the form **key : value**. The key is **one**, and its corresponding value is **aek**.

For example, let us build a dictionary that map from English to Hindi words, so the keys and the values are all *strings*. The function dict() creates a new empty dictionary. Dictionaries are like lists except that the "indices" need not be integers—they can be values of any immutable type. Since they are not ordered, we call them **keys** rather than indices. Literals of type dict() are enclosed in curly braces, and each element is written as a key followed by a colon followed by a value. Because dict() is the name of a built-in function, we should avoid using it as a variable name.

```
>>> eng2hin = dict()
>>> eng2hin
{}
```

Another way to create an empty dictionary can be done as follows, without using the dict( ) method:

eng2hin = { }

There are different ways for creating dictionaries. One of the examples of nested dictionaries are as follows:

```
>>> nestDict = {'first': { 42: 1, type(' '): 2 },
'second': []}
```

Here nestDict is a nested dictionary. The first key has a dictionary value. Another interesting property of Python is that we can use the type() function as a key in the dictionary as shown in the above inner dictionary. Let us see how to access the key a value pair of the nested directory.

```
>>> print nestDict # or >>> nestDict
{'second': [], 'first': {42: 1, <type 'str'>: 2}}
>>> nestDict['first'][42] # will print
1
```

```
>>> nestDict['first'] [type(' ')]
2
>>> nestDict['second']
[]
```

Some of the important ways to create dictionaries using the constructor dict ( ) are as follows:

```
>>> Dict2 = dict(name='Bob', age=45, job=('mgr',
'dev'))
>>> Dict2 # This will print in the following way:
{'job': ('mgr', 'dev'), 'age': 45, 'name': 'Bob'}
```

The point to be noted in the above example is that when we assign to a variable *i.e.*, age = 45, age becomes **key** and 45 is its **value**.

We can also use the zip( ) method to create a dictionary: type constructor.

```
>>> Dict3 = dict(zip('abc', [1, 2, 3]))
>>> Dict3
{'a': 1, 'c': 3, 'b': 2}
```

We may create a dictionary by passing key/value pair with the dict( ) method:

```
>>> Dict4 = dict([['a', 1], ['b', 2], ['c', 3]])
>>> Dict4
{'a': 1, 'c': 3, 'b': 2}
```

ord( ) method returns the corresponding ASCII(American Standard Code for Information Interchange) value of the character. For example, ASCII value for A is 65 and a is 97. We may use this method in creating dictionary as follows:

```
>>> Dict5 = {c: ord(c) for c in 'apple'}
>>> Dict5
{'a': 97, 'p': 112, 'e': 101, 'l': 108}
```

9.3 ADDING, MODIFYING, AND RETRIEVING VALUES

The curly-brackets, { }, represent an empty dictionary. Using square brackets (on the left hand side) we can add items, as follows:

```
>>> eng2hin['one'] = 'eak'
>>> eng2hin
{'one': 'eak'}
```

If the key is already in the dictionary, the following statement replaces the value for the key.

```
>>> eng2hin['one'] = 'aek'
>>> eng2hin
{'one': 'aek'}
```

In general, the order of items in a dictionary is unpredictable. But that's not a problem because the elements of a dictionary are never indexed with integer indices. For example,

```
>>> eng2hin = {'one' : 'aek', 'two' : 'do', 'three'
: 'teen'}
>>> eng2hin
{'three': 'teen', 'two': 'do', 'one': 'aek'}
```

Again, we can use the keys to look up the corresponding values:

```
>>> eng2hin['two']
do                 # no quotes
>>> eng2hin['three']
teen               # not eak as we think.
```

If the key isn't in the dictionary, you get an exception:

```
>>> eng2hin['five']
KeyError: 'five'
```

Dictionary enables fast retrieval, deletion, and updating of the value by using the key. The values in a dictionary don not have any particular order but are stored under a key, which may be a number, a string, or even a tuple (we will discuss tuple in the next chapter).

We can use the method keys() to return a list containing the keys of a dictionary. For example,

```
>>> eng2hin.keys()
```

will print a list of the keys of the dictionary eng2hin, as follows.

```
['three', 'two', 'one']
```

A dictionary is more appropriate than a list in many situations. Here are some examples of uses of Python dictionaries:

- Representing the state of a game board, with each key being a tuple of coordinates
- Storing file modification times, with file names as keys
- A digital telephone/address book

Note: *The key* can be any immutable type; strings and numbers can always be keys. Tuples can be used as keys if they contain only strings, numbers, or tuples; if a tuple contains any mutable object either directly or indirectly, it cannot be used as a key. We can't use lists as keys, since lists can be modified in place using index assignments, slice assignments, or methods like append() and extend().

9.4 THE DICTIONARY METHODS

Some of the more useful methods on dictionaries are given in the following Table 9.1.

Table 9.1

Methods	Descriptions
len(d)	returns the number of items (length) in d.
d.keys()	returns a list containing the keys in d.
d.values()	returns a list containing the values in d.
d.get(k, v)	returns d[k] if k in d, and v otherwise.
k in d	returns True if key k is in d.
d.items()	returns a sequence of tuples. Each tuple is (key, value) for an item.
del d[k]	remove the key k from d.
d.clear()	Deletes all entries.
d.pop(k)	Removes the item for the key k from d and returns its value.
d.popitem()	Returns a randomly selected key/value pair as a tuple from d and removes the selected item.
d.copy()	Returns a shallow copy of d.
d.setdefault(k, v1)	Same as d.get(k, v), but also assigns key to default if it is not found in d.
dict.fromkeys()	

Let us take up a few examples to show the use of the above methods in dictionaries. Let us recall the above dictionary eng2hin

```
>>> eng2hin = {'one' : 'aek', 'two' : 'do', 'three' : 'teen'}
```

To get the number of items (length)of the dictionary,

```
>>> len(eng2hin) # or print len(eng2hin)
3
```

The len() method returns the number of key-value pairs.

To get the values of a dictionary we can use the method `values()` as follows:

```
>>> vals = eng2hin.values() # No arguments in the
function call
>>> print vals
['teen', 'do', 'aek']
```

One of the important methods of using in dictionary is the `get()` method. It returns the corresponding value of the key, if the key is present (first argument). Otherwise, it will show a message (from the second argument), as follows:

```
>>> eng2hin.get('one', 'Not found')
aek
>>> eng2hin.get('four', 'Not found')
Not found
```

We can omit the second argument. If we omit this, the `get()` method returns None. For example:

```
>>> eng2hin.get('one')
aek
>>> eng2hin.get('four')
None
```

The advantage of "in" operator is that it tells you whether something appears as a "key" in the dictionary (NOT values). For example:

```
>>> 'one' in eng2hin
True
>>> 'eak' in eng2hin
False
```

> **Note :** The "in operator" uses different algorithms for lists and dictionaries. For lists, it uses a search algorithm, as the list gets longer, the search time gets longer in direct proportion. For dictionaries, Python uses an algorithm called a "hash-table" that has a remarkable property.

The `items()` method returns the list of tuples. We can use this method in the following way:

```
>>> eng2hin = {'one' : 'aek', 'two' : 'do', 'three'
: 'teen'}
>>> eng2hin
{'three': 'teen', 'two': 'do', 'one': 'aek'}
>>> eng2hin.items()
[('three', 'teen'), ('two', 'do'), ('one', 'aek')]
```

Note: Can you see the difference in the above example?

Again, if we want to clear the content of the directory, we can use the clear ()
method. It removes all items from the dictionary.

```
>>> eng2hin = {'one' : 'aek', 'two' : 'do', 'three'
: 'teen'}
>>> eng2hin.clear()
{}
```

Again invoking pop () method removes the item in the dictionary with the
corresponding key. The advantage of this method is that we can assign the
deleted value to a variable and can be reused again afterwards, if required.

```
>>> eng2hin = {'one' : 'aek', 'two' : 'do', 'three'
: 'teen'}
>>> x = eng2hin.pop('one')
>>> eng2hin
{'three': 'teen', 'two': 'do'}
>>> x
aek
```

Another method popitem() randomly returns a selected key/value pair as a
tuple and removes the selected item from the dictionary.

```
>>> eng2hin = {'one' : 'aek', 'two' : 'do', 'three'
: 'teen'}
>>> y = eng2hin.popitem()
>>> eng2hin
{'two': 'do', 'one': 'aek'}
>>> y
('three', 'teen')
```

To copy a dictionary to another dictionary, we can use the copy ( ) method
as follows:

```
>>> eng2hin = {'one' : 'aek', 'two' : 'do', 'three'
: 'teen'}
>>> Dict7= eng2hin.copy()
>>> Dict7
{'one': 'aek', 'three': 'teen', 'two': 'do'}
```

The getdefault ( ) method is same as get( ) method. The advantage is
that it will also assign a key if it is not found in the dictionary.

```
>>> eng2hin = {'one' : 'aek', 'two' : 'do', 'three':
'teen'}
```

```
>>> Dict8 = eng2hin.setdefault('one', 'test')
aek
>>> Dict8 = eng2hin.setdefault('four', 'test')
test
```

In the above example, the key 'one' has its value 'aek'. So it returns the corresponding value. In the second run, the key 'four' does not have its value so, it assign 'test' as its value.

9.5 DELETING ITEMS

Another important method that can be used in dictionaries is the del() method. It is used to remove the corresponding key value pair. For example:

```
>>> del eng2hin['one']
>>> eng2hin
{'three': 'teen', 'two': 'do'}
```

Here the deleted item can't be assigned to a variable as we have done in pop() method.

9.6 LOOPING ITEMS

If we want to iterate over the keys in a dictionary, we can use a **for loop** as follows:

```
>>> eng2hin = {'one' : 'aek', 'two' : 'do', 'three'
: 'teen'}
>>> for key in eng2hin:
...        print key
...
three
two
one
```

9.7 EQUALITY TEST

We can use the == and != operators to test whether two dictionaries contain the same items. For example:

```
>>> d1 = {"Monday":1, "Wednesday":3}
>>> d2 = {"Wednesday":3, "Monday":1}
>>> d1 == d2
True
```

```
>>> d1 != d2
False
```

In this example, **d1** and **d2** contain the same items regardless of the order of the items in a dictionary.

Note : We cannot use the relational operators (>, >=, <=, and <) to compare dictionaries because the items are not ordered as other sequences.

9.8 DICTIONARIES OF DICTIONARIES

We can use a dictionary of dictionaries - the outer dictionary acts as a database, and the inner nested dictionaries are the records within it. Instead of a simple list of records, a dictionary-based database allows us to store and retrieve records by symbolic key, as follows:

```
>>> person1 = dict(name='Singh', age=42, sex='M',
salary = 50000)
>>> person2 = dict(name='Devi', age=50, sex='F',
salary = 60000)
>>> database1 = {} # empty Dictionary
>>> database1['person1'] = person1 # passing reference
>>> database1['person2'] = person2
>>> database1
{'person2': {'salary': 60000, 'age': 50, 'name':
'Devi', 'sex': 'F'}, 'person1': {'salary': 50000,
'age': 42, 'name': 'Singh', 'sex': 'M'}}
```

This output shows us that the by-passing as a reference, we can access in easier way.

9.9 SETS

Sets are use for storing a collection of elements. We can create a set of elements by enclosing the elements inside a pair of curly braces ({ }) as we used in dictionaries. The elements are also separated by commas. Unlike lists and dictionaries, the elements in a set are non-duplicates and are not placed in any particular order. When our application does not require about the order of the elements, using a set to store elements is more efficient than using lists due to Python's implementations.

Now let us see how to use sets in the following examples.

We can create an empty set using the set() method

```
>>> s1 = set()
```

```
>>> print s1
set([])
```

Again we can create a set with four elements using the curly bracket, as follows:

```
>>> s2 = {1, 2, 3, 4}
>>> print s2
set([1, 2, 3, 4])
```

We also can create a set from a tuple:

```
>>> s3 = set((1, 2, 3, 4))
>>> print s3
set([1, 2, 3, 4])
```

In the same way, we can create a set from a given list:

```
>>> s4 = set([1, 2, 3, 4])
>>> print s4
set([1, 2, 3, 4])
# Another way to create a set from a list generated using a loop
>>> s5 = set([x * 2 for x in range(1, 10)])
>>> print s5
set([2, 4, 6, 8, 10, 12, 14, 16, 18])
```

One of the important properties of a set is that it is non-duplicate.

```
>>> s6 = set([1, 3, 3, 5, 5])
>>> print s6
set([1, 3, 5])
```

On the other hand, we can create a list or a tuple from a set by using the syntax **list(set)** or **tuple(set)** respectively. For example,

```
>>> s7 = {1, 4, 7, 9} # not [1, 4, 7, 9]
>>> s8 = list(set(s7))
>>> print s8
[9, 7, 4, 1]
>>> s9 = (1, 4, 7, 9)
>>> s10 = tuple(set(s9))
>>> print s10
(1, 4, 9, 7)
```

We have seen that there are different ways for creating sets. We can also create a set from a string. Each character in the string becomes an element in the set(if no duplicate characters are there). For example:

```
>>> s11 = set("abcabcd")
>>> s11
set(['a', 'c', 'b', 'd'])
```

Note that although the character **a b** and **c** appears twice in the string, it appears only once in the set because a set does not store duplicate elements.

A set can also contain the elements of mixed data types. For example,

```
>>> s12 = {1, 2, 3, 'a', 'b', 'c'}
>>> print s12
set(['a', 1, 'c', 3, 2, 'b'])
```

9.10 ACCESSING SETS WITH COMMON FUNCTIONS

For manipulating sets, we can use the common functions like, **len, min, max,** and **sum** on sets, as in lists and dictionaries, and a **for** loop to traverse all elements in a set. We can add an element to a set or remove an element by using the **add(e)** or **remove(e)** method respectively. Let us see some examples:

```
>>> s1 = {14, 2, 46, 89, 5, 55}
>>> s1.add(6) # to add an element in a set
>>> print s1
set([2, 5, 6, 14, 46, 55, 89])
>>> print len(s1) # to get the length of a set
7
>>> print max(s1) # to get the largest element in a
set
89
>>> print min(s1) # to get the smallest element in a
set
2
>>> print sum(s1) # to find the sum of the elements
in a set.
217
>>> s1.remove(46) # to remove an element from a set
>>> print s1
set([2, 5, 6, 14, 55, 89])
```

Note: If the element is not in the set, the **remove(e)** method will throw a **KeyError** exception.

9.11 SUBSET AND SUPERSET IN SETS

Subset: A set **s1** is a subset of **s2** if every element in **s1** is also in **s2**. In Python, we can use the **issubset( )** method to determine whether **s1** is a subset of **s2**, as shown in the following example:

```
>>> s1 = {1, 2, 3, 4}
>>> s2 = {1, 4, 5, 2, 6, 4}
>>> print s1.issubset(s2) # Is s1 a subset of s2 ?
True
```

Superset: A set **s1** is said to be a superset of set **s2** if every element in **s2** is also in **s1**. We can use the **issuperset( )** method to determine whether **s1** is a superset of **s2**, as shown in the following example:

```
>>> s1 = {1, 5, 8, 2, 4, 6, 3}
>>> s2 = {1, 2, 3, 4}
>>> print s1.issuperset(s2) # Is s1 a superset of s2?
True
>>> print s2.issuperset(s1) # Is s2 a superset of s1?
False
```

9.12 RELATIONAL OPERATORS IN SETS

As we have seen that the elements in a set is not necessarily in proper order. Thus, it makes no sense to compare the sets using the conventional relational operators(>, >=, <=, and <) except the == and !=. However, the == and != operators can be used to test if two sets contain the same elements, regardless of the order of the elements. The following examples show the usages of these operators.

```
>>> s1 = {2, 3, 4, 5}
>>> s2 = {5, 4, 2, 3}  # with different order
>>> s1 == s2# No  space  is  allowed  in  between  the
operators
True
>>> s1 != s2
False
```

Now, Let us consider two sets, **s1** and **s2**. If **s1** is a *proper subset* of **s2**, every element in **s1** is also in **s2**, and at least one element in **s2** is not in **s1**.

If **s1** is a proper subset of **s2**, then **s1 < s2** returns `True`, as shown below:

```
>>> s1 = {1, 2, 3, 4}
>>> s2 = {1, 4, 5, 2, 6, 3}
>>> print s1 < s2
True
```

Note: the set attribute has no `sort()` method and `indexing` is also not allowed in sets.

Again, if we want to use the less than or equal to operator (<=) in set, then

```
>>> s1 = {1, 2, 3, 4}
>>> s2 = {1, 2, 3, 4, 5, 6}
>>> print s1 <= s2 # Actually, the print keyword is
not needed
True
>>> s3 = {1, 2, 3, 4}
>>> s1 <= s3
False
```

In the above example, s1 <= s2 returns `True` because **s1** is a subset of **s2**. However, in the second example it returns `False` because **s1** is not less than **s3**.

If **s1** is a proper superset of **s2**, the **s1> s2** returns `True`, as follows:

```
>>> s1 = {1, 4, 5, 2, 6, 3}
>>> s2 = {1, 2, 3, 4}
>>> print s1 > s2
True
>>> print s1 >= s2
True
```

The statement **s1 >= s2** also returns `True` because **s1** is also a superset of **s2**.

9.13 SET OPERATIONS

Python provides a few methods for performing set union, intersection, difference, and symmetric difference operations. They are summarized in Table 9.2.

Table 9.2: Set Methods

Methods	Meaning
union (or |)	Return all the elements from both sets
intersection (or &)	Return the elements that appear in both sets
difference (or –)	Return the elements from first set only
symmetric difference (or ^)	Return the elements contained in either set, but not in both sets

The *union* of two sets is a set that contains all the elements from both sets. We can use the **union** method or the | operator to perform this operation. For example:

```
>>>s1 = {1, 2, 3, 4}
>>> s2 = {1, 5, 6, 7}
>>> print s1.union(s2)
set([1, 2, 3, 4, 5, 6, 7]) # same as {1, 2, 3, 4, 5, 6, 7}
>>> print s1 | s2    # Another way to use set union
{1, 2, 3, 4, 5, 6, 7}
```

The *intersection* of two sets is a set that contains the elements that appear in both sets. We can use the **intersection** method or the **&** operator to perform this operation. For example:

```
>>> s1 = {1, 2, 3, 4}
>>> s2 = {1, 5, 6, 7}
>>> print s1.intersection(s2) # set([1]) = {1}
{1}
>>> print s1 & s2  # Another way to use set intersection
{1}
```

The *difference* between **set1** and **set2** is a set that contains the elements in **set1** but not in **set2**. We can use the **difference** method or the minus (–) operator to perform this operation. For example:

```
>>> s1 = {1, 2, 3, 4}
>>> s2 = {1, 5, 6, 7}
>>> print s1.difference(s2)
set([2, 3, 4])      #same as {2, 3, 4}
>>> print s1 - s2   # Another way to call difference
method
set([2, 3, 4])
```

The *symmetric difference* (or *exclusive- or*) of two sets is a set that contains the elements in either set, but not in both sets. You can use the **symmetric_ difference** method or the ^ operator to perform this operation. For example:

```
>>> s1 = {1, 4, 5, 2, 6, 3}
>>> s2 = {1, 2, 3, 4}
>>> print s1.symmetric_difference(s2)
set([5, 6])
>>> print s1 ^ s2
set([5, 6])# {5, 6}
```

Note that these set methods return a resulting set, but they do not change the elements in the sets. For example:

```
>>> print s1
{1, 4, 5, 2, 6, 3}
>>> print s2
{1, 2, 3, 4}
```

Example 9.1: Illustrating the uses of Set

The following program illustrate the details of set in Python

```
set1 = {"Programming", "Python"} # Create a set from
a string
print 'set1=', set1

set2 = set([11,6,89,43,90,3,8]) # Create a set from
a list
print 'set2=', set2

print "Length of Set2 = ", len(set2) # Use function
len
print "Sum of set2 = ", sum(set2) # Use function sum
print "Maximum element in set2 = ", max(set2) # Use
max function
print "Minimum element in set2 = ", min(set2) # Use
min

set3 = set2 | {1, 2, 11, 90} # Set union
print 'set3 (union) = ', set3
set4 = set2 - {3, 33, 44, 55} # Set difference
print 'set4 (difference) = ', set4
```

```
set5 = set2 & {1, 4, 6, 11, 43} # Set intersection
print 'set5 (intersection) =', set5
set6 = {2, 4, 6,8}
set7 = set2 ^ set6 # Set exclusive or
print 'set7 (exclusive) = ', set7

list1 = list(set2) # Obtain a list from a set
print 'list1 = ', list1
set1.add("in" )
print 'New set1 = ', set1
set1.remove("in")
print 'Final set1 = ', set1
```

The output of the above program is:

```
set1= set(['Python', 'Programming'])
set2= set([3, 6, 8, 11, 43, 89, 90])
Length of Set2 =   7
Sum of set2 =   250
Maximum element in set2 =   90
Minimum element in set2 =   3
set3 (union) =   set([1, 2, 3, 6, 8, 43, 11, 89, 90])
set4 (difference) =   set([11, 6, 8, 43, 89, 90])
set5 (intersection) = set([43, 11, 6])
set7 (exclusive) =   set([2, 43, 4, 11, 3, 89, 90])
list1 =   [3, 6, 8, 11, 43, 89, 90]
New set1 =   set(['Python', 'Programming', 'in'])
Final set1 = set(['Python', 'Programming'])
```

In this chapter, we have studied the common operations on dictionaries and sets. The **len()** function can be used to return the number of items in dictionary and sets. Some of the commonly used methods for Dictionary and sets are also discussed.

EXERCISES

9.1. State the following are true or false.

(*a*) A *dictionary* can be used to store *key/value pairs*.

(*b*) The value in a dictionary can be retrieved using a *key*.

(*c*) The keys are like an index operator. In a list, the indexes are integers only.

(*d*) In a dictionary, the keys can be any hashable objects such as numbers and strings.

(*e*) `del ()` method can be used to delete an item for the given key.

(*f*) A `while` loop can be use to traverse all keys in a dictionary.

(*g*) The `len()` function returns the number of items in a dictionary.

(*h*) We can not use the **in** and **not** in operators to test if a key is in a dictionary.

(*i*) The operators `==` and `!=` are used to test if two dictionaries are the same.

(*j*) *Sets* are like lists and use them for storing a collection of elements.

(*k*) The elements in a set are non-duplicates and are not placed in any particular order.

(*l*) The `add()` method can be used to add an element to a set.

(*m*) The `remove()` method cannot use to remove an element from the list.

(*n*) The `len, min, max,` and `sum` functions can be applied to a set.

(*o*) A for loop can use to traverse the elements in a set.

9.2. Which of the following dictionaries are created correctly?

```
d = {1:[10, 20], 3:[30, 40]}
d = {[10, 20]:1, [30, 40]:3}
d = {(10, 20):1, (30, 40):3}
d = {1:"apple", 3:"egg"}
d = {"apple":1, "egg":3}
```

9.3. Suppose a dictionary named **mixed** is {"apple":3, "egg":2}. What do the following statements do?

```
(a)  mixed["tomato"] = 5
(b)  mixed["apple"] = 5
(c)  mixed["apple"] += 5
(d)  del students["apple"]
```

9.4. Suppose a dictionary named students is {"john":3, "peter":2}. What do the following statements do?

```
(a)  print(len(students))
(b)  print(students.keys())
(c)  print(students.values())
(d)  print(students.items())
```

9.5. How to create an empty dictionary?

9.6. Each item in a dictionary has two parts. What are they called?

9.7. How do you create an empty set?

9.8. Can a list, set, or tuple have elements of different types?

9.9. Which of the following sets are created correctly?

```
s = {1, 3, 4, 6}
s = {{1, 2, 3}, {4, 5, 6}}
s = {[1, 2, 3], [4, 5, 6]}
s = {(1, 2, 3), (4, 5,6)}
```

9.10. What are the differences between a list and a set? How do you create a set from a list?

9.11. How do you create a list from a set? How do you create a tuple from a set?

9.12. Show the printout of the following code:

```
students = {"peter", "john"}
print(students)
students.add("john")
print(students)
students.add("peterson")
print(students)
students.remove("peter")
print(students)
```

9.13. Will the following code have a runtime error?

```
students = {"peter", "john"}
students.remove("johnson")
print(students)
```

9.14. Show the printout of the following code:

```
student1 = {"peter", "john", "tim"}
student2 = {"peter", "johnson", "tim"}
print(student1.issuperset({"john"}))
print(student1.issubset(student2))
print({1, 2, 3} > {1, 2, 4})
print({1, 2, 3} < {1, 2, 4})
print({1, 2} < {1, 2, 4})
print({1, 2} <= {1, 2, 4})
```

9.15. Show the printout of the following code:

```
numbers = {1, 4, 5, 6}
print(len(numbers))
print(max(numbers))
print(min(numbers))
print(sum(numbers))
```

9.16. Show the printout of the following code:

```
s1 = {1, 4, 5, 6}
s2 = {1, 3, 6, 7}
print(s1.union(s2))
print(s1 | s2)
print(s1.intersection(s2))
 print(s1 & s2)
print(s1.difference(s2))
print(s1 - s2)
print(s1.symmetric_difference(s2))
print(s1 ^ s2)
```

9.17. Show the printout of the following code:

```
set1 = {5, 8, 7, 12, 40}
print(5 in set1)
print(4 in set1)
print(len(set1))
print(max(set1))
print(min(set1))
print(sum(set1))
print(set1.issubset({5, 8, 9, 7, 12}))
print(set1.issuperset({5,8, 7, 40}))
```

9.18. What is the output of the following code segment?

```
Dict6 = {'a': 1, 'c': 36, 'b': 2, 'a': 10, 'a': 109}
print Dict6
```

9.19. What is the output of the following code segment?

```
names = ['name', 'age', 'pay', 'job']
values = ['Sue Jones', 45, 40000, 'hdw']
list1 = list(zip(names, values))
dict1 = dict(zip(names, values))
print list1
print dict1
```

9.20. Write a Python program to store the pairs of states and capitals in a dictionary and display the pairs randomly.

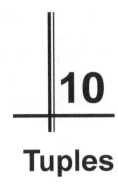

10

Tuples

10.1 DEFINITION

In Python, A tuple is a sequence of immutable values. Tuples are sequences, just like lists. The differences between tuples and lists are, the tuples cannot be changed unlike lists and tuples use parentheses, whereas lists use square brackets. Once a tuple is created, we cannot add new elements, delete elements, or reorder the elements in the tuple.

Hence if there is no need to change the contents of a list, it is better to use a tuple to prevent elements from being added, deleted, or replaced accidentally. A tuple is very much like a list, except that its elements are fixed. Furthermore, tuples are more efficient than lists due to Python's implementations.

Syntactically, a tuple is a comma-separated list of values. For example:

```
>>> t1 = 'a', 'b', 'c','d'
```

Although it is not necessary, it is common to enclose tuples in parentheses:

```
>>> t = ('a', 'b', 'c', 'd', 'e')
```

To create a tuple with a single element, we have to include a final comma:

```
>>> t1 = 'x',
>>> type(t1)
<type 'tuple'>
```

If we omit comma, then a value in parentheses is not a tuple:

```
>>> t2 = ('x')
>>> type(t2)
<type 'str'>
```

Like strings, tuples are ordered sequences of elements. The difference is that the elements of a tuple need not be characters. The individual elements can be of any type, and need not be of the same type. For example:

```
>>> t3 = (1, 'two', 3, 'four')
```

We can use either single or double quotes for representing strings in tuples. For example:

```
>>> t4 = 'a','b','c'
>>> print t4
('a', 'b', 'c')
>>> t5 = "a","b","c"
>>> print t5
('a', 'b', 'c')
```

Another way to create a tuple is to use the built-in function `tuple`, known as Python objects. With no argument, we can create an empty tuple:

```
>>> t6 = tuple()
>>> print t6
()
```

If the argument is a sequence (string, list or tuple), the result is a tuple with the elements of the sequence:

```
>>> t7 = tuple('Python') # using strings as elements
>>> print t7
('P', 'y', 't', 'h', 'o', 'n')
>>>t8 = tuple(['P','y','t','h','o','n'])#using list
as arguments
>>> print t8
t9 = tuple([1,2,3,4,5]) # using list of numbers as
arguments
>>> print t9
>>> t10 = tuple(('T','e','s','t'))# tuple as arguments
>>> print t10
('T', 'e', 's', 't')
```

Tuple is the name of a built-in function, so we should avoid using it as a variable name, though this is not an error. For example:

```
>>> tuple = 123 # must be avoided
```

Most of the list operators also work on tuples. Like list indices, tuple indices start at 0, and they can be sliced, concatenated, and so on. For example:

```
>>> t11 = (1, 'two', 3, 'four')
>>> t12 = (t11, 5.75)
>>> print t12
((1, 'two', 3, 'four'), 5.75)
```

In the above example, the second assignment statement binds the name t12 to a tuple that contains the tuple, t11 and the float 5.75. This is possible because a tuple, like everything else in Python, is an object, so tuples can contain tuples.

```
>>> t13 = (t11 + t12)
>>> print t13
(1, 'two', 3, 'four', (1, 'two', 3, 'four'), 5.75)
```

The above statement prints the expression generated by concatenating the values bound to t11 and t12, which is a tuple with six elements (not nine elements).

```
>>> print t13[3]
four
>>> print t13[4]
(1, 'two', 3, 'four')
```

The statement t13[3] prints the fourth element (as always in Python, indexing starts at 0), and t13[4] prints the fifth elements, here it is a tuple, of the concatenated tuple.

The following statement creates and prints a slice of that tuple:

```
>>> print t13[2:5]
(3, 'four', (1, 'two', 3, 'four'))
```

Note: The main difference between lists and tuples is that the elements in a list can be changed but not in a tuple. This means a list might be more useful when elements are to be added or removed. But a tuple can be useful when there is no need for a change the sequence. Reasons for the latter are usually rather technical, because, some built-in functions return tuples. Tuples are used as dictionary keys but not lists, because the keys cannot be modified.

If we try to modify one of the elements of the tuple, we get an error:

```
>>> t14 = ('a', 'b', 'c', 'd')
>>> t14[0] = 'A'
TypeError: object doesn't support item assignment
```

While the elements of a tuple cannot be modified but the elements of one tuple can be replaced with the elements of another. For example:

```
>>> t14 = ('A',) + t14[1:]
>>> print t14
('A', 'b', 'c', 'd')
```

Note: Sometimes nested tuples may be confusing. So to get rid of nested tuples, we can use as follows:

```
>>> t11 = (1, 'two', 3,'four')
>>> t12 = t11 + (5.75,)
>>> print t12
(1, 'two', 3, 'four', 5.75)
```

The + sign can only concatenate tuple (not "float") to tuple. So we have to convert the float value to a tuple.

10.2 TUPLE ASSIGNMENT

Tuples aren't very complicated and there are many things we really can do with them except create them and access their elements. Sometimes it is often useful to swap the values of two variables. With conventional assignments, you has to use a temporary variable. For example, to swap *a* and *b*, using a third variable:

```
>>> a = 10
>>> b = 20
>>> temp = a
>>> a = b
>>> b = temp
>>> print 'a =', a,
>>> print 'b =', b
```

And without using a third variable, mathematically we can do as follows:

```
>>> a = a + b
>>> b = a - b
>>> a = a - b
>>> print 'a =', a,
>>> print 'b =', b
```

This solution may be written in one line with tuple assignment:

```
>>> a, b = b, a
```

The left side represents a tuple of variables and the right side is a tuple of expressions. Each value is assigned to its respective variable. All the expressions on the right side are evaluated before any of the assignments. The following is a valid expression:

```
>> a, b = b, a - b
```

The number of variables on the left and the number of values on the right must be same:

```
>>> a, b = 10, 20, 50
```

```
ValueError: too many values to unpack
```

In general, the right side can be any kind of sequence (string, list or tuple). For example, to split an email address into a user name and a domain name, we may write:

```
>>> address = 'mss@yahoo.co.in'  # as a string
```

```
>>> user_name, domain_name = address.split('@')  #
split by '@'
```

The first element is assigned to user_name, the second to domain_name.

```
>>> print user_name
```

```
mss
```

```
>>> print domain_name
```

```
yahoo.co.in
```

Thus, if we know the length of a sequence (*e.g.*, *a* tuple, *a* list or *a* string), it is convenient to use Python's multiple assignment statement to extract the individual elements. One more example, the statement:

```
>>> a, b, c = 'PQR'
```

will bind a to 'P', b to 'Q', and c to 'R'.

10.3 TUPLES AS RETURN VALUES

Normally, a function returns only one value, but if the returned value is a tuple, the effect is the same as returning multiple values. For example, if we want to divide two integers and compute the quotient and remainder, it is inefficient to compute x/y and then $x\%y$. It is better to compute them both at the same time.

The built-in function divmod takes two arguments and returns a tuple of two values, the quotient and remainder. We can store the result as a tuple:

```
>>> t = divmod(14, 3) # using built-in-function
>>> print t
(4, 2)
```

Tuple assignment can also be used to store the elements separately:

```
>>> quotient, remainder = divmod(14, 3)
>>> print quotient
4
>>> print remainder
2
```

On the other hand, user defined function may also be used to return a tuple. Let us consider a function:

```
def MinMaxDivisors(no1, no2):
    divisors = () #the empty tuple
    minVal, maxVal = None, None
    for i in range(2, min(no1, no2) + 1):
        if no1%i == 0 and no2%i == 0:
            if minVal == None or i < minVal:
                minVal = i
            if maxVal == None or i > maxVal:
                maxVal = i
    return (minVal, maxVal)


minDivisor, maxDivisor = MinMaxDivisors(150, 300)
print 'minDivisor = ', minDivisor
print 'maxDivisor = ',maxDivisor
```

```
Output of the above program:
minDivisor = 2
maxDivisor = 150
```

10.4 THE BASIC TUPLE OPERATIONS

The common operations for sequences shown in Table 10.1 can be used for tuples. We can use the functions **len**, **min**, **max**, and **sum** on a tuple. And also we can use a **for** loop to traverse all elements in a tuple, and can access the elements or slices of the elements using an index operator. We can use the **in** and **not in** operators to determine whether an element is in a tuple, and can also compare the elements in tuples using the comparison operators.

Table 10.1: Common Operations for Tuple

Operation	Description
x **in** tuple, t	True if element x is in tuple, t.
x **not in** tuple, t	True if element x is NOT in tuple, t.
t1 + t2	Concatenates two tuples t1 and t2
t * n or n * t	n copies of tuples t are concatenated.
t[i]	ith element in tuple, t
t[i : j]	slices of tuple, t from index i to j–1.
len(t)	returns the length of the tuple, t.
min(t)	returns the smallest element in tuple, t.
max(t)	returns the largest element in tuple, t.
sum(t)	returns the sum of all numbers in tuple, t.
for loop	Traverse elements from left to right in a for loop.
Relational operators: <, <=, >, >=, ==, !=	Compares two tuples
cmp(t1, t2)	Compares two tuples (or objects) t1 and t2

The following examples explained the use of these common operations in tuples.

```
# Creates two tuples t1 and t2
t1 = (1,2,3,4,5)
t2 = ('a', 'b', 'c')
# Using in operator in t1 and t2
print 5 in t1
print 'a' in t2
# Using not in operator in t2
print 'b' not in t2
# Combines the two tuple t1 and t2 and assign the
value to t3
t3 = t1 + t2
print 't3 = ', t3
#Duplicate the tuple t1 two times
t4 = 2*t1
print "t4 =", t4
# Using index operator
print "The First element in t1[0] is:", t1[0]
# Using slicing operator
print "Slicing elements : ", t1[2:5]
# To find the length of the tuple, t3
print "Length of tuple t3 is :", len(t3)
```

```
# To find the minimum value in tuple, t1
print "Minimum value in tuple, t1 = ", min(t1)
# To find the maximum value in tuple, t1
print "Maximum value in tuple, t1 = ", max(t1)
# To find the sum of the elements in tuple, t1
print "Sum of the elements in tuple, t1 = ", sum(t1)
# Traversing the elements in a tuple with for loop
for i in t3:
    print i,
# Comparing two tuples
print t1 == t2
print t1 != t2
'''
```

When comparing two tuples, it starts from the first element. If they are equal, it goes on to the next elements, and so on, until it finds elements that differ. Subsequent elements are not considered (even if they are really large).
'''

```
print (0, 10, 2) < (0, 30, 4)
print (1, 6, 800000) < (1, 9, 400)
print cmp(t1, t1) # returns +ve or 0 or -ve
```

Output of the above program:
```
True
True
False
t3 = (1, 2, 3, 4, 5, 'a', 'b', 'c')
t4 = (1, 2, 3, 4, 5, 1, 2, 3, 4, 5)
The First element in t1[0] is: 1
Slicing elements :  (3, 4, 5)
Length of tuple t3 is : 8
Minimum value in tuple, t1 = 1
Maximum value in tuple, t1 = 5
Sum of the elements in tuple, t1 = 15
1 2 3 4 5 a b c
False
True
True
True
0
```

Note: We can create a list from a tuple using the list() method:
```
>>> list1 = list(t3)
>>> print list1
[1, 2, 3, 4, 5, 'a', 'b', 'c']
We can use the sort() function in a list, but not
in a tuple :
>>> list1.sort()
```

Tuples have fixed elements which mean that we cannot add new elements, delete elements, replace the elements, or shuffle the elements in a tuple.
Some special cases:
As we mentioned that a tuple contains a fixed list of elements. An individual element in a tuple may be mutable.
For example, the following code creates a tuple of circles, and changes the first circle's radius to **15**.
```
>>> from CircleFromGeometricObject import Circle
>>> circles = (Circle(5), Circle(8), Circle(10))
>>> circles[0].setRadius(15) # change to 15
>>> circles[0].getRadius() # show the radius
15
```
Again cmp(t1, t2) compares two tuples and return an integer according to the outcome. The return value is positive if t1 > t2, zero if t1 == t2 and negative if t1 < t2.

10.5 VARIABLE-LENGTH ARGUMENT TUPLES

Most of the functions can accept a variable number of arguments. A parameter name that begins with * *gathers* arguments into a tuple. Let us write a user defined function called Print_All() takes any number of arguments and prints them, as follows:
```
def Print_All( *args):
    print args
```
The gather parameter can have any name, but args is conventional. Let us see how the function works:
```
>>> Print_All('one', 2.0, 3, 4.0)
('one', 2.0, 3, 4.0)
```
In the above program, when we call the function Print_All() with 4 arguments, the function works without any errors. This can be achieved by the gather parameter.

On the other hand, the complement of gather is *scatter*. When we want to pass multiple arguments to a function from a sequence of values, we can use the

* operator. For example, the built-in function `divmod()` takes exactly two arguments and returns a tuple of two values, the quotient and remainder; it doesn't work with a tuple:

```
>>> t1 = (14, 3) # t1 contains two arguments
>>> divmod(t1) # divmod needs two arguments
TypeError: divmod expected 2 arguments, got 1
```

But if we scatter the tuple, with the help of *scatter* parameter, it works:

```
>>> divmod(*t) # Scattered the arguments
(4, 2)
```

Note: Most of the built-in functions use variable-length argument tuples. For example, `max()` and `min()` can take any number of arguments whereas the `sum()` function can take only 2 arguments:

```
>>> max(10,20,3)
20
>>> min(10,20,3)
3
```

But sum does not.

```
>>> sum(1,2,3)
TypeError: sum expected at most 2 arguments, got 3
```

10.6 RELATIONSHIP BETWEEN LISTS AND TUPLES

zip is a Python built-in function that takes two or more sequences and "zips" them into a list of tuples where each tuple contains one element from each sequence.

For example, this example zips a string and a list:

```
>>> str1 = 'Python'
>>> list1 = [0, 1, 2, 3, 4]
>>> t2 = zip(str1, list1)
>>> print t2
[('P', 0), ('y', 1), ('t', 2), ('h', 3), ('o', 4), ('n', 5)]
```

The result is a *list of tuples* where each tuple contains a character from the string, `str1` and the corresponding element from the list, `list1`.

If the sequences are not of the same length, then the zip function will result the length of the shorter one.

```
>>> str1 = 'Python'
>>> list2 = [1, 2, 3]
```

```
>>> lt2 = zip(str1, list2)
>>> print lt2
[('P', 1), ('y', 2), ('t', 3)]
```

We can use tuple assignment in a for loop to traverse a list of tuples:

```
t3 =[('P', 0), ('y', 1), ('t', 2), ('h', 3), ('o',
4), ('n', 5)]
for letter, number in t3:
    print number, letter
```

The output of the above program segment is:

```
0 P
1 y
2 t
3 h
4 o
5 n
```

If we combine **zip, for** and **tuple assignment**, we get a powerful tool for traversing two (or more) sequences at the same time. For example, is_ match takes two sequences, t1 and t2, and returns True if there is an index i such that t1[i] == t2[i]:

```
def is_match(t1, t2):
    for x, y in zip(t1, t2):
        if x == y:
            return True
    return False
```

When we execute the above function with the following sequences:

```
>>> t1 = ["python"]
>>> t2 = ["python"]
>>> print is_match(t1, t2)
True
>>> t1 = ["python"]
>>> t2 = ("python")
>>> print is_match(t1, t2)
False
```

```
>>> t1 = ["python"]
>>> t2 = ["high"]
>>> print is_match(t1, t2)
False
```

10.7 RELATIONSHIPS BETWEEN DICTIONARIES AND TUPLES

The relationship between dictionaries and tuples can be achieved using a method called *items* (a dictionary method) that returns a list of tuples, where each tuple is a key-value pair. For example:

```
>>> d1 = {'a':1, 'b':2, 'c':3, 'd':4}
>>> t1 = d1.items()
>>> print t1
[('a', 1), ('c', 3), ('b', 2), ('d', 4)]
```

On the other hand, we can use a list of tuples to initialize a new dictionary with the help of the `dict()` method, as follows:

```
>>> t2 = [('a', 1), ('c', 3), ('b', 2), ('d', 4)]
>>> d2 = dict(t2)
>>> print d2
{'a': 1, 'c': 3, 'b': 2, 'd': 4}
```

Combining `dict()` with `zip()` yields a concise way to create a dictionary:

```
>>> d3 = dict(zip('abc', '123'))
>>> print d3
{'a': '1', 'c': '3', 'b': '2'}
```

The dictionary method `update()` also takes a list of tuples and adds them, as key-value pairs, to an existing dictionary. For example:

```
>>> d={}
>>> t2 = [('a', 1), ('c', 3), ('b', 2), ('d', 4)]
>>> d.update(t2)
>>> print d
{'a': 1, 'c': 3, 'b': 2, 'd': 4}
```

Again, combining items, tuple assignment and for loop, we get the idiom for traversing the keys and values of a dictionary:

```
for key, val in d.items():
    print val, key
```

The output of this loop is:

```
1 a
3 c
2 b
4 d
```

Note: It is common to use tuples as keys in dictionaries because it is not changeable (immutable) whereas we cannot use lists because they can be changed easily (mutable). For example, a telephone directory might map from first-name, last-name pairs to telephone numbers. For example:

```
first_name = ['Shubha', 'Elton', 'Salman']
last_name = ['singh', 'John' , 'Khan']
name = tuple(zip(first_name, last_name))
print name
number = [12345, 23456, 34567]
directory={}
for i in range(len(number)):
    directory[first_name[i], last_name[i]] = number[i]
print directory
```

Output of the above program:
```
(('Shubha', 'singh'), ('Elton', 'John'), ('Salman',
'Khan'))
{('Salman',    'Khan'):    34567,    ('Elton',    'John'):
23456, ('Shubha', 'singh'): 12345}
```

In the above example, we are using lists for the first_name and last_name because updating the names afterwards will be easier. Combining the zip and tuple methods we convert the lists into tuples.

Example 10.3: To sort a list of words from longest to shortest:

The sort function works the same way in tuples. It sorts primarily by first element, but in the case of a tie, it sorts by second element, and so on.

```
def sort_by_length(words):
    t = []
    for word in words:
        t.append((len(word), word))
    print t
    t.sort(reverse=True)
```

```
    result = []
    for length, word in t:
        result.append(word)
    return result
#  First Run
words = [ 'abcd', 'pqr', 'ijklmnop', 'a', 'university']
r = sort_by_length(words)
print r
# Second Run : To show the tie break condition
words1 = [ 'abcd', 'pqrs','a', 'g']
r1 = sort_by_length(words1)
print r1
```

Output of the above program:
 # Output of the first run
```
[(4, 'abcd'), (3, 'pqr'), (8, 'ijklmnop'), (1,
'a'), (10, 'university')]
['university', 'ijklmnop', 'abcd', 'pqr', 'a']
```

 # Output of the second run
```
[(4, 'abcd'), (4, 'pqrs'), (1, 'a'), (1, 'g')]
['pqrs', 'abcd', 'g', 'a']
```

In the above program, the first loop builds a list of tuples, where each tuple is a word preceded by its length. A sample output is shown below:

```
[(4, 'abcd'), (3, 'pqr'), (8, 'ijklmnop'),…]
```

After creating a list of tuples, `sort()` method compares the first element, length, first, and only considers the second element to break ties. The keyword argument `reverse=True` tells sort to go in decreasing order.

Lastly, the second loop traverses the list of tuples and builds a list of words in descending order of length.

EXERCISES

10.1. State whether the following are **true** or **false**.

    (*a*) A *tuple* is like a fixed list. We cannot add, delete, or replace elements in a tuple.

    (*b*) Since a tuple is a sequence, the common operations for sequences can be used for tuples.

(*c*) Though we cannot add, delete, or replace elements in a tuple, we can change the content of individual elements if the elements are mutable.

(*d*) A tuple is *immutable* if all its elements are immutable.

(*e*) We can add an element to a tuple using the **add** method and remove an element with **remove** method.

(*f*) The **min, max,** and **sum** functions can be applied to tuples

(*g*) We can use a **for** loop to traverse the elements in a tuple.

(*h*) Tuples are more efficient than lists for testing whether an element is in a tuple or a list.

(*i*) The **len** function cannot use to return the number of elements in a tuple.

(*j*) The **in** and **not in** operators cannot apply to tuples.

10.2. Show the printout of the following code:

```
t = (11, 22, 13, 17, 79, 80, 51, 9)
print(t)
print(t[0])
print(t[1: 3])
print(t[-1])
print(t[ : -1])
print(t[1 : -1])
```

10.3. Show the printout of the following code:

```
t = (11, 22, 13, 17, 79, 80, 51, 9)
print(max(t))
print(min(t))
print(sum(t))
print(len(t))
```

10.4. What will be the output of the following code segments?

```
t1 = (11, 22, 13, 17, 79, 80, 51, 9)
t2 = (2, 5, 78, 55, 10, 45, 45, 78)
print(t1 > t2)
print(t1 < t2)
print(t1 == t2)
print(t1 != t2)
```

10.5. What is wrong in the following code?

```
t = (10, 11, 12, 13)
t.append(4)
t.remove(0)
t[0] = 1
print t[0]
```

10.6. Is the following code correct?

```
t1 = (11, 22, 13, 17)
t2 = (79, 80, 51, 9)
t1 = t2
print t1
```

10.7. What will be the output of the following code segments?

```
t = ('a', 'b', 'c', 'd', 'e')
print t[0]
print t[-1]
print t[1:4]
```

10.8. Is the following code correct?

```
t1 = (1, 'two', 3, 'four')
t2 = t11 + ('5.75',) # instead of (t11, 5.75)
print t12
```

10.9. Is the following code correct?

```
t = (123, 456,'hello')
a, b, c = t
print 'a =', a
print 'b =', b
print 'c =', c
```

10.10. What is wrong in the following code segment?

```
t1 = ("Physics", "Chem", "Maths", "Biology")
print t1
del t1
print t1
```

10.11. Analyze the outputs in the following code segment.

```
t1 = (1,2,3,4)
t2 = t1 + t1
t3 = "test" * 3
t4 = 3*"test"
print t1
print t2
print t3
print t4
print 5 in t1
```

10.12. Find out errors (if any) in the following code segment?

```
t1= (1,2,3)
print sum(t1)
print sum(1,2,3)
print sum((1,2,3))
```

10.13. Write a program that reads a list of words and prints all the sets of words that are anagrams.

Here is an example of what the output might look like:

```
['deltas','desalt', 'lasted', 'salted', 'slated',
'staled']
```

```
['retainers', 'ternaries']
```

```
['generating', 'greatening']
```

```
['resmelts', 'smelters', 'termless']
```

Hint: you might want to build a dictionary that maps from a set of letters to a list of words that can be spelled with those letters. The question is, how can you represent the set of letters in a way that can be used as a key?

10.14. Modify the previous program so that it prints the largest set of anagrams first, followed by the second largest set, and so on.

10.15. What are the differences between a list and a tuple? How do you create a tuple from a list? How do you create a list from a tuple?

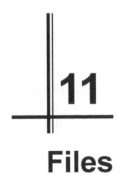

11

Files

11.1 INTRODUCTION

This chapter will describe how to read and write data from and to a file. Data used in a program is temporary and it is lost when the program terminates unless the data is specifically saved. To permanently store the data created in a program, we need to save it in a file on a disk or some other permanent storage devices. The file can be transported and read later by other programs.

In Chapter Four, we read values from the input device using `input()`, `raw_input()`, and printing with `print()` methods. In this chapter, we go one step further and let our programs catch a glimpse of the world of files and streams.

Other programs are *persistent* means they run for most of the time; they keep at least some of their data in permanent storage and when they shut down and restart, they pick up where they left off. Examples of persistent programs are operating systems, which run pretty much whenever a computer is on, and web servers, which run all the time, waiting for requests to come in on the network. One of the simplest ways for programs to maintain their data is by reading and writing text files.

11.2 TEXT FILES AND BINARY FILES

Files can be classified into text or binary files. A file that can be processed (that is, read, created, or modified) using a text editor such as Notepad on Windows or vi/vim on UNIX is called a *text file*. All the other files are called *binary files*. For example, Python source programs are stored in text files and can be processed by a text editor, but Microsoft Word files are stored in binary files and are processed by the Microsoft Word program.

Although it is not technically precise and correct, we can envision a text file as consisting of a sequence of characters and a binary file as consisting of a sequence of bits. Characters in a text file are encoded using a character encoding scheme such as ASCII and Unicode. For example, the decimal integer **123** is stored as the sequence of the three characters **1**, **2**, and **3**, in a text file, and the same integer is stored as a byte-type value **7B** in a binary file, because decimal **123** equals hex **7B** ($7 \times 16 + 11$) The advantage of binary files is that they are more efficient to process than text files. However, Computers do not differentiate between binary files and text files. All files are stored in binary format, and thus all files are essentially binary files. Text IO (input and output) is built upon binary IO to provide a level of abstraction for character encoding and decoding.

11.3 ABSOLUTE AND RELATIVE FILENAME

A file is placed in a directory (also called "folder") in the file system. An *absolute filename* contains a filename with its complete path and drive letter. For example, C:\Documents and Settings\Python\Output.txt is the absolute filename for the file Output.txt on the Windows operating system. Here, C:\ Documents and Settings\Python is referred to as the *directory path* to the file. Absolute filenames are machine dependent. On the UNIX or Linux platform, the absolute filename may be /home/ Python/Output.txt, where /home/ Python/ is the directory path to the file Output.txt.

A *relative filename* is relative to its current working directory. The complete directory path for a relative file name is omitted. For example, File1.py is a relative filename. If its current working directory is C:\Documents and Settings\Python, the absolute filename would be C:\Documents and Settings\ Python\File1.py.

Every running program has a "current directory," which is the default directory for most operations. For example, when you open a file for reading, Python looks for it in the current directory.

The os module provides functions for working with files and directories ("os" stands for "operating system"). `os.getcwd` returns the name of the current working directory. For example:

```
>>> import os
>>> cwd = os.getcwd()
>>> print cwd
/home/Python
```

`cwd` stands for "current working directory." The result in this example is / `home/Python`, which is the home directory of a user named Python. A string like `cwd` that identifies a file is called a path.

To find the absolute path to a file, we can use `os.path.abspath`:

```
>>> os.path.abspath('Output.txt')
'/home/Python/Output.txt'
```

`os.path.exists` checks whether a file or directory exists:

```
>>> os.path.exists('Output.txt')
True
```

If it exists, `os.path.isdir` checks whether it's a directory:

```
>>> os.path.isdir('Output.txt')
False
```

because `Output.txt` is a file not a directory.

```
>>> os.path.isdir('Video')
True
```

Similarly, `os.path.isfile` checks whether it's a file or not.

`os.listdir` returns a list of the files (and other directories) in the given directory:

```
>>> os.listdir(cwd)
['Music', 'Python', 'Photos', 'Output.txt']
```

To demonstrate these functions, the following example "walks" through a directory, prints the names of all the files, and calls itself recursively on all the directories.

```
def walk(dirname):
    for name in os.listdir(dirname):
        path = os.path.join(dirname, name)
    if os.path.isfile(path):
        print path
    else:
        walk(path)
```

In the above example, `os.path.join` takes a directory and a file name and joins them into a complete path.

11.4 OPENING A FILE

The syntax for opening a file is:

```
fileVariable = open(filename, mode)
```

The `open` function returns a file object for `filename`. The `mode` parameter is a string that specifies how the file will be used (for reading or writing), as shown in Table 11.1.

Table 11.1: File Mode

Mode	Description
r	Opens a file for reading
w	Opens a file for writing. If the file is already exits, its old contents are clears out.
a	Opens a file for appending data from the end of the file.
rb	Opens a file for reading binary data
wb	Opens a file for writing binary data
+	Opens a file for read and write mode

For example, to write a file, we have to open it with mode 'w' as a second parameter:

```
>>> fout = open('Output.txt', 'w')
>>> print fout
<open file 'Output.txt', mode 'w' at 0x04050288>
```

If the file already exists, opening it in write mode clears out the old data and starts fresh, so we should be careful. If the file doesn't exist, a new one is created.

To read a file in the current directory, the following statement opens a file named Output.txt:

```
>>> fin = open("Output.txt", "r")
```

we can also use the absolute filename to open the file in Windows, as follows:

```
input=open(r" C:\Documents and Settings\Python\
         ↑ Output.txt ", "r")
```

The statement opens the file 'Output.txt' that is in the C:\Documents and Settings\Python directory for reading. The **r** prefix before the absolute filename specifies that the string is a *raw string*, which causes the Python interpreter to treat backslash characters as literal backslashes. Without the **r** prefix, we would have to write the statement using an escape sequence as follows:

```
input=open("C:\\Documents   and   Settings\\Python\\
Output.txt","r")
```

The '+' can be added to any of the other modes to indicate that both reading and writing is allowed. So, for example, 'r+' can be used when opening a text file for reading and writing.

11.5 WRITING DATA

The write method puts data into the file. We can use the `write()` method as follows:

```
>>> fout = open ("Output.txt", "w")
>>> line1 = "Programming in Python \n"
>>> fout.write(line1)
```

Again, the file pointer keeps track of where it is, so when we call the `write()` method again, it adds the new data to the end.

```
>>> line2 = "is just like playing games.\n"
>>> fout.write(line2)
```

After writing into the file, we must close the file with the `close()` method.

```
>>> fout.close()
```

The following program writes three lines of strings to the file Test1.txt.

```
#Open file for output
p = open ("Test1.txt", "w")
#Write data to the file
p.write(" Most of the innocent people \n")
p.write(" in this world are small children \n")
p.write(" and drunk people. \n")
# Close the output file
p.close()
```

Output of the above program:

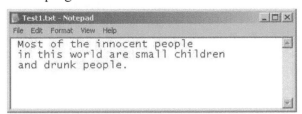

The program opens a file named `Test1.txt` using the **w** mode for writing data. If the file does not exist, the `open()` methods creates a new file. If the file already exists, the contents of the file will be overwritten with new data. When a file is opened for writing or reading, a special marker called a *file pointer* is positioned internally in the file. A read or write operation takes place at the pointer's location.

When a file is opened, the file pointer is set at the beginning of the file. When we read or write data to the file, the file pointer moves forward.

Figure 11.1 shows the position of the file pointer after each write.

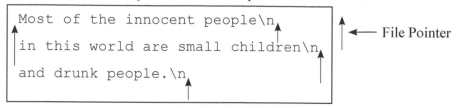

Fig. 11.1 Showing the position of the file pointer when writing to the file.

When we invoke `print(str)`, the function automatically inserts the newline character `\n` after displaying the string. However, the `write ()` method does not automatically insert the newline character. So we have to explicitly write the newline character to the file.

11.6 SOME COMMONLY USED METHODS FOR FILE HANDLING

Once we make a file object with open, we can call its methods to read from or write to the associated external file. In all cases, file text takes the form of strings in Python programs; reading a file returns its text in strings, and text is passed on to the write methods as strings.

Some of the commonly used methods for accessing file is summarized below:

Methods	Description
`read(N)`	Returns the specified number of *characters*, N (int) from the file. If the argument is omitted, the entire remaining contents in the file are read.
`readline()`	Returns the next line of the file as a *string*.
`readlines()`	Returns *a list* of the remaining lines in the file.
`write(S)`	Writes the string, S to the file.
`writelines(S1):`	Write each element of sequence, S1 to the file.
`open()`	To open a file
`seek(N)`	Change file position to offset N for next operation
`close():`	Closes the file.
Examples :	
`p = open(r'C:\Test.txt', 'w')`	Create output file called Test.txt. Either single or double quotes can be used ('w' means write).
`p = open('Test1.txt', 'r')`	Open Test1.txt for reading ('r' means read)
`p = open('Test1.txt')`	Open Test1.txt for reading ('r' is the default). Omitting the file mode means the file is in read mode.
`Str1 = p.read()`	Read entire file into a single string, `Str1`
`Str1 = p.read(N)`	Read up to next N characters (or bytes) into a string, `Str1`

Contd...

`Str1 = p.readline()`	Read next line (including \n newline) into a string, `Str1`
`List1 = input.readlines()`	Read entire file into list of line strings (with \n)
`p.write(S)`	Write a string of characters, S (or bytes) into file
`p.writelines(L)`	Write all line strings in a list, L into file
`p.flush()`	Flush output buffer to disk without closing

The best way to read a text file line by line is to *not read it at all*—instead, allow the for loop to automatically advance to the next line on each iteration. The file object's iterator will do the work of automatically loading lines as we go. The following example reads a file line by line and printing the uppercase version of each line along the way, without ever explicitly reading from the file at all:

```
for line in open('test4.txt'):
    print line.upper(),
    #print(line.upper(), sep = ',', end =' ')
```

Notice that the print uses end =' ' here to suppress adding a newline, \n, because line strings already have one (without this, our output would be double-spaced). However, these sep = ',' and end =' ' are not supported in Python 2.7. The easiest way to solve this problem in Python 2.7 is to use the comma operator. The best way to read text files is line by line since: it's the simplest way to code, it might be the fastest to run, and is the most efficient of memory usage.

On the other hand, the older, original way to achieve the same effect with a for loop is to call the file `readlines()` method to load the file's content into memory as a list of line strings:

```
for line in open('test4.txt').readlines():
    print(line.upper())
```

Note: When we run the following program segment, we get the output with newlines, as follows:
```
>>> for i in range(5):
... print i
...
0
1
2
3
4
```

To remove unwanted newlines, we can proceed in two ways:
```
>>> for i in range(5): # based on Python 2.7
... print i,      # using comma operator
0 1 2 3 4 >>>
>>> for i in range(5): # based on Python 3
... print(i, end=' ')
...
0 1 2 3 4 >>>
```

This `readlines()` technique still works, but it is not considered the best practice nowadays because it performs poorly in terms of memory usage. In fact, because this version really loads the entire file into memory all at once and it will not even work for files too big to fit into the memory space available on computer.

On the other hand, the iterator-based version reads one line at a time and it is immune to such memory-explosion issues it.

11.7 WRITING AND READING NUMERIC DATA

To write numbers to a file, we must first convert them into strings because the **write ()** method accepts only strings. On the other hand, in order to read the numbers back correctly, we separate them with whitespace characters, such as " " **or \t** or **\n.**

As an example let us write one to thirty to a file and reads them back properly again from the file.

Example 11.1: To Write the numbers 1 to 30 in a file

```
# Open file for writing data
file1 = open("Numbers.txt", "w") # Using double quotes
for i in range(30):
    file1.write(str(i) + " ")
# Close the file
file1.close()
# Open file for reading data
file2 = open('Numbers.txt', 'r') # Using Single quotes
list1 = file2.read()
numbers = [eval(x) for x in list1.split()]
for no in numbers:
    print no,
# Close the file
file2.close()
```

Output of the above program:
```
0  1  2  3  4  5  6  7  8  9  10  11  12  13  14  15  16  17  18  19
20  21  22  23  24  25  26  27  28  29
```

Explanation: The program opens a file named **Numbers.txt** using the **w** mode for writing data using the file object **file1**. The **for** loop writes thirty numbers into the file, separated by spaces. Note that the numbers are converted to strings before being written to the file.

The program closes the output file and reopens it using the **r** mode for reading data through the file object **file2**. (Suppose the file is not closed, what will happen? Then the file pointer will be at the last position of the file. When we reopen it again, the file pointer will be at the beginning of the file so that we can read the data in that file. We can use seek () method to manipulate the file pointer.) The **read()** method reads all data as a *string*. Since the numbers are separated by spaces, the string's **split**() method splits the string into a list. The numbers are obtained from the list and displayed.

Example 11.2: To write the numbers 1 to 30 randomly in a file
```python
import random
# Open file for writing data
file1 = open("Numbers1.txt", "w") # Using double quotes
for i in range(30):
    file1.write(str(random.randint(1, 30)) + " ")
# Close the file
file1.close()
# Open file for reading data
file2 = open('Numbers1.txt', 'r') # Using Single quotes
list1 = file2.read()
numbers = [eval(x) for x in list1.split()]
for no in numbers:
    print no,
# Close the file
file2.close()
```

The output of the above program:
```
25  10  26  15  28  22  18  19  18  20  18  29  10  13  7  18  29
19  21  23  2  4  5  4  26  23  24  27  2  17
```

The basic difference with Example 11.1 and Example 11.2 is that we are using randint() method from the random module to generate numbers between 1 and 30.

Example 11.3: A Python program to open a file called '**datafile.txt**' and the contents of that file will be at least a (*i*) Tuple, (*ii*) String, (*iii*) Dictionary and (*iv*) list.

```
X, Y, Z = 43, 44, 45 # Native Python objects, Tuples
S = 'String' # Must be strings to store in file
D = {'a': 1, 'b': 2} # a dictionary
L = [1, 2, 3]  # a list

F = open('datafile.txt', 'w') # Create output file
F.write(S + '\n') # Terminate lines with \n
F.write('%s,%s,%s\n' % (X, Y, Z)) # Convert numbers
to strings
F.write(str(L) + ' ' + str(D) + '\n') # Convert and
separate with blankspace
F.close()
```

The important point to be noted here is that when we write something in a file using write() method, we should convert it to strings whether it may be numbers or any sequence.

Note: In Python 3.0 we can redirect the output of the print() function to a file:

```
        with open('datafile.txt', 'rt') as f:
            print('Hello World!', file = f)
```

Example 11.4: A Python program that counts the occurrences of words in a text file and displays ten most frequently used words in decreasing order of their occurrence counts.

```
def main():
    # Prompt the user to enter a file
    filename = input("Enter a filename: ").strip()
    infile = open(filename, "r") # Open the file
    # Open a test file
    #infile   =   open("C:\Documents   and   Settings\
    Shubhakanta\ words.txt", "r")
    # Create an empty dictionary to count words
    wordCounts = { }
    for line in infile:
        processLine(line.lower(), wordCounts)
```

```python
    # Get pairs from the dictionary
    pairs = list(wordCounts.items())
    # Reverse pairs in the list
    items = [[x, y] for (y, x) in pairs]
    # Sort pairs in items
    items.sort()

    for i in range(len(items) - 1, len(items) - 11, -1):
        print(items[i][1] + "\t" + str(items[i][0]))


# Count each word in the line
def processLine(line, wordCounts):
    # Replace punctuation with space

    # Get words from each line

    line = replacePunctuations(line)
    words = line.split()
    for word in words:
        if word in wordCounts:
            wordCounts[word] += 1
        else:
            wordCounts[word] = 1


# Replace punctuation in the line with a space
def replacePunctuations(line):
    for ch in line:
        if ch in "~@#$%^&*()_-+=~<>?/,.;:!{}[]|'\"":
            line = line.replace(ch, " ")
    return line


main() # Call the main function
```

```
Output of the above program:
to         3
of         3
the        2
physics 2
is         2
a          2
when       1
we         1
us         1
understanding    1
```

The above program uses a dictionary, wordCounts, to store an item consisting of a word and its count. The program determines whether each word is already a key in the dictionary. If not, the program adds a dictionary item with the word as the key and the value 1. Otherwise, the program increases the value for the word by **1** in the dictionary. We assume the words are case-insensitive with lower()method,(for example, **Copy** is treated the same as **copy**). The program displays the ten most frequently used words in the file in decreasing order of their count.

EXERCISES

11.1. State whether the following are **true** or **false**:

(*a*) A file must be opened before it can be used.

(*b*) All files must be explicitly closed.

(*c*) Using **seek()** method we can start reading the file from the beginning.

(*d*) When an existing file is open using **w** mode, the contents of the file are deleted.

(*e*) It is an error to open a file for reading when it does not exist.

(*f*) The **read()** and **readline()** methods can be used to read data from a file.

(*g*) The **write()** method is used to write only strings to a file.

(*h*) The **readlines()** methods can not used in reading integer values from a file

11.2. What is the output of the following program segment?
```
q = open('Names.txt', 'a')
q.write('John\n')
```

```
q.write('Khan\n')
q.write('Singh')
q.close()
q = open('Names.txt', 'r')
for line in q:
     print line[:-1]
q.close()
```

11.3. Using the file 'Names.txt' opened in **ex.11.1**, write the outputs of the following program segments:

(a) ```
     p = open('Names.txt', "r")
     str1= p.read(3)
     print str1
     ```

(b)  ```
     p = open('Names.txt', "r")
     str1= p.read()
     print str1
     ```

(c) ```
     p = open('Names.txt', "r")
     str1= p.readline()
     print str1
     ```

(d)  ```
     p = open('Names.txt', "r")
     str1= p.readlines()
     print str1
     ```

11.4. What is output of the following program:

```
p1 = open("test4.txt","w")
st2 = [' Most of the innocent people.... \n', ' in
this world are small children \n']
p1.writelines(st2)
p1 = open("test4.txt")#,"w")
st5= p1.read()
print st5
```

11.5. Using the file 'test4.txt' opened in **ex.11.3**, justify the outputs of the following program segments:

(a) ```
    for line in open('test4.txt'):
          print line.upper() # No Comma
    ```

(b) ```
    for line in open('test4.txt'):
          print line.upper(), # with Comma
    ```

11.6. The following program open a file called `myfile.txt`. Then we write only two lines of strings in the file. And we want to see the contents of the file using `readline()` method. By calling `readline()` method 3 times, can we see the output correctly? Justify your answer.

```
file1 = open('myfile.txt', 'w')
file1.write('Welcome to File\n')
file1.write('handling in Python\n')
file1.close()


file1 = open('myfile.txt')
file1.readline()
file1.readline()
file1.readline()
```

11.7. What is the output of the following program? Assume that the file `datafile.txt` is already exists in the directory `'C:\Python`.

```
import pprint
pprint.pprint(open(r'C:\Python\somefile.txt').
readlines())
```

11.8. How do you open a file for reading, for writing, and for appending, respectively?

11.9. What is wrong about creating a file object using the following statement?

```
File1 = open("c:\python\test.txt", "r")
```

11.10. When you open a file for reading, what happens if the file does not exist?

11.11. What happens when you open a file for writing, if the file already exists?

11.12. What method do you use to read all data from a file into a string?

11.13. What method do you use to read a line?

11.14. What method do you use to read all lines from a file into a list?

11.15. What function do you use to write data to a file?

11.16. How do you determine whether a file exists or not?

11.17. How do you write and read numeric data?

11.18. How do you denote a raw string literal in the program?

11.19. When reading data, how do you know if it is the end of the file?

11.20. Will your program have a runtime error if you invoke **read()** or **readline()** at the end of the file?

11.21. Write a Python program to copy the contents of one file to another file.

11.22. Write a Python program that compares two files and return True if they are equal and False if they are not equal. Do not use built in function **cmp()**.

11.23. Write a Python program that appends one file at the end of the another file.

11.24. Write a Python program that reads a file containing integers and appends at its end the sum of all the integers.

11.25. Write a program that removes all the occurrences of a specified string from a text file. The program should prompt the user to enter a filename and a string to be removed.

11.26. Write a program that will count the number of characters, words, and lines in a file. Words are separated by a white space character.

Computational Physics–
Application in Physical Systems

12.1 INTRODUCTION

Physics is a corner-stone of every technological field. When we have a solid understanding of physics, and the computational know-how to calculate solutions to complex problems, success is sure to follow us in the high-tech environment of this century. In this chapter we give a brief introduction to Computational Physics and how it can be used in solving simple to complex physical systems with specific Python implementation. A brief idea on how to use Monte Carlo Technique and Runge-Kutta fourth order method to solve physical problems with Python is also given.

12.2 WHAT IS COMPUTATIONAL PHYSICS?

Computational physics provides a means to solve complex numerical problems.

We can apply it in many ways. For example, a typical introductory physics problem is to calculate the motion of a cannon ball in two dimensions. This problem is always treated without air resistance. One of the difficulties of physics is that the moment one goes away from such an idealized system, the task rapidly becomes rather complicated. If we want to calculate the solution with real-world elements (*e.g.*, drag), things become rather difficult. A way out of this mess is to use the methods of computational physics to solve this linear differential equation.

One important aspect of computational physics is modeling large complex systems. For example, how a meteorologist would try to predict changes in climate? These problems can be solved by employing Monte Carlo techniques. This technique is simply impossible without computers and, as just noted, has applications which reach far beyond physics.

Another class of physics problems are phenomena which are represented by nonlinear differential equations, like the chaotic pendulum. Again, computational physics and numerical methods are a perfect tool to study such systems. If these systems were purely confined to physics, one might argue that this does not deserve an extended treatment in an undergraduate course. However, there is an increasing list of fields which use these equations; for example, meteorology, epidemiology, neurology, astronomy and System Biology to name just a few.

An advantage of computational physics is that one can start with a simple problem which is easily solvable analytically. The analytical solution illustrates the underlying physics and allows one the possibility to compare the computer program with the analytical solution. Once a program has been written which can handle the case with the typical physicist's approximation, then we add more and more complex real-world factors.

This brief introduction shows how interesting and important computational physics is in studying real -life complex systems. Starting with simple examples, following sections explain the steps for solving a problem and then how it can be implemented in Python.

12.3 OSCILLATORY MOTION

12.3.1 Ideal Simple Harmonic Oscillator

The best example of a near ideal simple harmonic oscillator (S.H.O.) from real life situations is a loaded horizontal spring shown in Fig. 12.1. Within elastic limits, the spring follows Hooke's law and has a force constant k. As long as the spring is stretched by a small amount, the restoring force F is directly proportional to the extension (or compression) in a direct ion opposite to it. By placing a block of mass m on an air-track or carbon-puck, it can slide on a smooth frictionless surface. Stable position of the block is when it is neither compressed nor elongated. Let this position be $x = 0$.

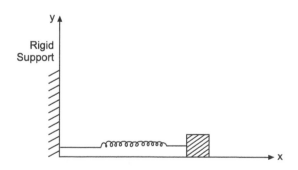

Fig. 12.1 A SMO of a mass spring system

When the mass reaches the equilibrium position it overshoots i.e., it keeps on going and stops at some point in the opposite direction. Once again it proceeds for its return trip. This to and fro motion is called oscillation.

An interesting aspect of this motion is that this system oscillates with a fixed frequency whatever amplitude you may give to it.

The force law for this motion is

$$F = -kx \tag{1}$$

where F represents the **restoring force** (implied by negative sign), and k is the intrinsic property of the spring. The equation of motion of the mass can be obtained by applying Newton's law of motion as

$$ma = -kx \tag{2}$$

We define $\omega_0 = \left(\dfrac{k}{m}\right)^{1/2}$ which is called the **natural angular frequency** of the system.

Solving with Numerical Method:

If we know the initial conditions, *i.e.*, displacement and velocity at some instant t, we can find these quantities at all the times. Given the eq. (2), the velocity can be written as

$$v(t) = -\omega_0^2 \int x(t)\,dt$$

And displacement then can be calculated as

$$x(t) = \int v(t)\,dt = \omega_0^2 \int \left[\int x(t)\,dt \right] dt$$

which has an integrand we don't know as yet. So what are we to solve?

For the case of the loaded spring, we can guess what would be the solution *i.e.*

either $x(t) = \cos(\omega_0 t)$ or $x(t) = \sin(\omega_0 t)$

or more generally

$$x(t) = A\cos(\omega_0 t) + B\omega_0 \tag{3}$$

where A and B are two unknown parameters. Obviously, this is not the unique solution and initial conditions are needed to fix the parameters. Let the initial conditions be:

$$\boxed{x(t) = x_0 \text{ and } v(t) = v_0 \text{ at } t = 0} \tag{4}$$

This yields,

$$A = x_0,\ B = \frac{v_0}{\omega_0} \qquad \because v(t) = \frac{dx(t)}{dt} \text{ using eq. (3)}$$

Another form of the solution may be written as

$$x(t) = A\cos(\omega_0 t + \varphi)$$

where A and φ are constants called amplitude and phase respectively. These can also be fixed by the initial conditions of eq. (4).

To solve it numerically using computational tool, the equation can be written as a second order differential equations

$$\frac{d^2(v)}{dt^2} = -\omega_0^2 x = -\frac{k}{m} x \quad \because \omega_0 = \sqrt{\frac{k}{m}} \tag{5}$$

or as a set of two coupled first order differential equations,

$$\frac{dv}{dt} = f(x, v, t) \quad \text{and} \quad \frac{dx}{dt} = v \tag{6}$$

where $f(x,v,t) = -(k/m)x(t)$ for the mass on the spring system. In general, the function $f(x, v, t)$ need not be a simple function of x only. These equations can be easily converted into two coupled difference equations using **Euler method**,

$$v(t + h) = v(t) + hf(x, v, t) \tag{7}$$

and $\qquad\qquad x(t + h) = x(t) + hv(t) \tag{8}$

where h is the time step. An algorithm for the horizontally loaded spring is given below.

Algorithm : Simple Harmonic Motion of a Loaded Spring (using Euler Method)

Step 1 : Choose spring constant and mass of the object attached: k, m.

Step 2 : Choose initial position X_0 and initial velocity V_0.

Step 3 : Choose maximum time t_{max} for which motion is to be studied.

Step 4 : Choose time step h.

Step 5 : Find number of time steps $N = t_{max}/h$.

Step 6 : Initialize the time, displacement and velocity variables.

Step 7 : Begin a loop, over time steps.

Step 8 :   Find current time instant t.

Step 9 :   Find acceleration using $a = -kx/m$.

Step 10 :   Print or plot t, x, v.

Step 11 :   Update velocity: $v \leftarrow v + a h$.

Step 12 :   Update position: $x \leftarrow x + v h$.

Step 13 : Loop started at step 7 ends.

Python Implementation

We can write a simple Python program using the above algorithm as follows:

```
import pylab as pl
k = input("Enter the value of Spring constant :")
x = input("Enter the initial position :")
```

```
v = input ("Enter the initial velocity of the particle:")
m = input ("Enter the mass of the particle :")
tmax = input ("Enter the maximum time :")
h = input ("Enter the time step :")
t = 0
a = 0
X = []
T = []
while (t <= tmax) :
    a = -(k*x)/m
    X.append(x)
    T.append(t)
    v = v + a*h
    x = x + v*h
    t = t + h
pl.plot(T,X)
pl.xlabel("Time")
pl.ylabel("Distance")
pl.title("Time vs Distance")
pl.show()
```

The program can be run with the required inputs. Here is the sample data that we entered of our choice.

Spring constant	= 1 Nm^{-1}	Mass of the object	= 1 kg
Initial position	= 0 m	Initial velocity	= 1 m s^{-1}
Time step	= 0.01 s	Maximum time	= 10 s

Output of the above program:

FIRST RUN:	SECOND RUN:
Enter the value of Spring constant: 2	Enter the value of Spring constant:1
Enter the initial position:0	Enter the initial position:0
Enter the initial velocity of the particle:3	Enter the initial velocity of the particle:1
Enter the mass of the particle:1	Enter the mass of the particle:1
Enter the maximum time:20	Enter the maximum time:10
Enter the time step:0.01	Enter the time step:0.01

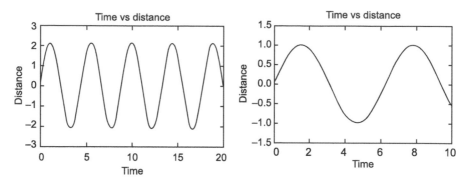

Accuracy of Algorithm and Numerical Method:

Always keep in mind that numerical solutions are approximate. To say that an obtained solution is correct depends upon the chosen tolerance *i.e.*, desirable accuracy. In the pictorial output graph, you might find that the amplitude is increasing (or decreasing) with each cycle.

Verification of the results: Conservation of Energy

Reliability of the results and the numerical method can be tested effectively using conservation of energy as a guide at each stage of the computation. In fact, it is an important ingredient of the numerical analysis usually performed for dynamical problems. In the case of a loaded spring, the sum of kinetic and potential energies,

$$E = \frac{1}{2} mv^2 + \frac{1}{2} kx^2 \tag{9}$$

must remain constant. We can verify this in the above program by implementing a line inside the loop.

12.3.2 Motion of a Damped Oscillator

The ideal loaded spring system is very difficult to encounter in nature. Due to dissipative forces which are always present, amplitude of the oscillations starts decreasing with time and the oscillations die out after sometime. This is called *damping*. Damping is desirable at times. Situations do occur in nature when we would like the oscillations to get damped as soon as these are produced. Consider for instance, a ride on a bumpy road. To make the ride smooth, vehicles are provided with shock absorbers. The good absorber dampens the oscillations the moment they are produced. If these oscillations continue for a long distance, it would make the journey a torture.

Generally, for small velocities, the damping force is taken to be directly proportional to the velocity. The force law then becomes

$$ma = -kx - cv \tag{10}$$

where c denotes the *damping coefficient* which decides the nature of the damping. Thus, the force depends on position as well as velocity.

There are three distinct situations which can be identified for a damped oscillator:

undamped (when $c = 0$)

over-damped (*when* $\left(\dfrac{c^2}{4m^2} > \dfrac{k}{m} \right)$) and

critically damped when $\left(\dfrac{c^2}{4m^2} = \dfrac{k}{m} \right)$

Critical damping is deliberately introduced in measuring instruments to obtain a quick reading. For example, this would avoid waiting for the needle of an ammeter or an indicator arm of a balance to settle down to its final reading.

In the following, we give the algorithm based on the Feynman-Newton method to describe the motion of a damped oscillator.

Algorithm: Motion of Damped Oscillator (using Feynman-Newton method)

Step 1 : Choose spring constant and mass of the object attached; k, m.

Step 2 : Choose initial position x_0 and initial velocity v_0.

Step 3 : Choose maximum time t_{max}, for which motion is to be studied.

Step 4 : Choose time step h.

Step 5 : Find number of time steps $N = t_{max}/h$.

Step 6 : Initialize the time, displacement and velocity variables.

Step 7 : Calculate velocity at the half-step: $v_{1/2} = v_0 + \dfrac{1}{2}ha_0$

Step 8 : Begin a loop over time steps.

Step 9 :   Find current time instant t.

Step 10 :   Find acceleration using eq. 10.

Step 11 :   Calculate total energy E (Kinetic + Potential).

Step 12 :   Print t, a, x, v.

Step 13 :   Find new velocity: $v \leftarrow v + at$.

Step 14 :   Find new position: $x \leftarrow x + vt$.

Step 15 : Loop started at step 8 ends.

Step 16 : Program ends.

Python Implementation

Next step is to implement a Python program using this algorithm. Most of the codes are almost same with the Simple Harmonic Oscillator as we have done earlier except the damping coefficient. In our program we used a new function `subplot()` to draw the graph in to rows.

The complete Python program is shown below:

```python
import pylab as pl
k = input("Enter the value of Spring constant :")
x = input("Enter the initial position :")
v = input("Enter the initial velocity of the particle:")
m = input("Enter the mass of the particle :")
tmax = input("Enter the maximum time :")
h = input("Enter the time step :")
c = input("Enter the damping constant :")

t = 0
a = 0
X = []
T = []
V = []
while (t <= tmax) :
    a = -(k*x)/m - (c*v)
    X.append(x)
    T.append(t)
    V.append(v)
    v = v + a*h
    x = x + v*h
    t = t + h
pl.subplot(2,1,1)
pl.plot(T,X)
pl.xlabel("Time")
pl.ylabel("Distance")
pl.title("Time vs Distance")
pl.axhline(0, 0, 1)
pl.subplot(2,1,2)
```

```
pl.plot(X, V, 'r')
pl.xlabel("Distance")
pl.ylabel("Velocity")
pl.title("Distance vs Velocity")
pl.axhline(0, 0, 1)
pl.axvline(0, 0, 1)
pl.show()
```

The above program have executed with the parameters which are shown below:

Spring constant	$= 1 \text{Nm}^{-1}$	Mass of the object	$= 1$ kg
Damping coefficient	$= 0.5$ N m^{-1}s	Initial position	$= 0$ m
Initial velocity	$= 1$ m s^{-1}	Time step h	$= 0.01$s
Maximum time	$= 20$ s		

Output of the above program is shown below. The second graph shows the Phase space trajectory.

```
Enter the value of Spring constant :1
Enter the initial position :0
Enter the initial velocity of the particle:1
Enter the mass of the particle :1
Enter the maximum time :20
Enter the time step :.01
Enter the damping constant :.5
```

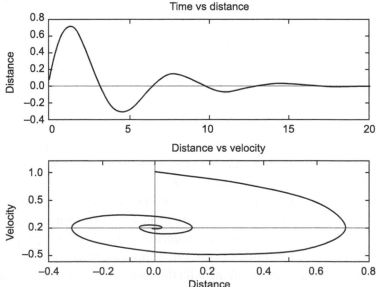

Note: Two basic plot types which you will find are used very often are (x, y) line and scatter plots. Some code for making these two types of plots is as follows:

A. For Line Plot

1. `import numpy as np`

2. `import pylab as pl`

3. `# Make an array of x values`

4. `x = [1, 2, 3, 4, 5]`

5. `# Make an array of y values`

6. `y = [1, 4, 9, 16, 25]`

7. `# use pylab to plot x and y`

8. `pl.plot(x, y)`

9. `# show the plot on the screen`

10. `pl.show()`

B. For Scattered Plots

By changing the line number 8 with the following code, we can get scattered graph very easily.

`pl.plot(x, y, 'ro')`

This will plot x and y as red circles

12.4 STATIONARY STATES AND TIME INDEPENDENT SCHRÖDINGER EQUATION

12.4.1 Introduction

In 1926, Schrödinger presented a phenomenological wave theory to describe the microscopic world and laid the foundation of wave mechanics. According to this theory, the wave equation is defined as,

$$-\frac{\hbar^2}{2m}\nabla\psi\,(x, t) = [E - V(x, t)] - \psi(x, t) \qquad (1)$$

This second order differential equation in essence describes the one dimensional non-relativistic motion of a particle of mass m and energy E in a potential $V(x, t)$. *Without $V(x, t)$ this equation describes free particle motion quantum mechanically.* Inclusion of $V(x, t)$ indirectly accounts for the interaction among particles in a force field in which the particle is moving. The function $y(x, t)$ denotes the *wavefunction* of the particle, properties of which are described completely by the Schrodinger equation only when suitable boundary conditions along with the continuity condition are imposed.

If V is independent of time, the solution of eq. (1) gives

$$\psi(x, t) = \varphi(x) \exp\left(\frac{-iEt}{h}\right) \tag{2}$$

$\psi(x, t)$ describes the **stationary state** of well-defined energy E. *However, if the particle is scattered by the potential $V(x)$,* the energy E can have any **positive** value corresponding to **unbound states.** If the particle is **bound** by the potential $V(x)$, E becomes **negative** and can only take *discrete* values, with E replaced by E_n. First, we solve eq. (1) for a bound state in one dimensional case. The Schrödinger equation for the bound states then reduces to

$$-\frac{\hbar^2}{2m}\frac{d^2\varphi_n(x)}{dx^2} = [E_n - V(x)]\,\varphi_n(x) \tag{3}$$

Its solutions $\varphi_n(x)$ satisfy the following properties:

(*i*) $\varphi_n(x)$ and $\dfrac{d\varphi_n(x)}{dx}$ are continuous, finite and single valued for all x, for finite $V(x)$

(*ii*) $\varphi_n(x) \to 0$ as $|x| \to \infty$ for bound states

(*iii*) $\varphi_n(x) \to 0$ as $V(x) \to \infty$

(*iv*) Further

$$\int_{-\infty}^{\infty} dx\,\varphi_n^*(x)\varphi_n(x) = 1$$

i.e., Net probability of finding a particle somewhere is unity. If

$$\int_{-\infty}^{\infty} dx\,\varphi_n^*(x)\varphi_n(x) \neq 1$$

it can be normalized to unity by a suitable choice of the normalization constant.

These properties provide the two boundary conditions required to solve the second order differential eq. (3).

12.4.2 Form of Potential

In our presentation, we are interested in potentials which are *symmetric*. In one dimension, this means

$$V(-x) = V(x) \tag{4}$$

It has some interesting consequences related to the symmetry for eq. (3). If we make a symmetry transformation, $x \to -x$, then if $\varphi(x)$ is a solution so is $\varphi(-x)$. These are related as

$$\varphi(-x) = P\,\varphi(x)$$

Also
$$\varphi(x) = P\,\varphi(-x) = P^2\,\varphi(x) \tag{5}$$

Thus $P^2 = 1$ or $P = \pm 1$ gives parity of the solution.

$$\text{If } \varphi(-x) = + \varphi(x), \text{ parity is even,}$$
$$\text{If } \varphi(-x) = - \varphi(x), \text{ parity is odd,}$$

Thus the wavefunction obtained as solution of eq. (3) must possess either odd or even parity.

Some well-known symmetric potentials, shown in Fig. 1, are

(a) Parabolic Potential: $V(x) = \dfrac{1}{2} kx^2$

(b) Square Well potential: $V(x) = \begin{cases} 0 \text{ for } |x| \le a \\ V_0 \text{ for } |x| > a \end{cases}$

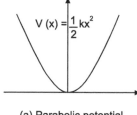

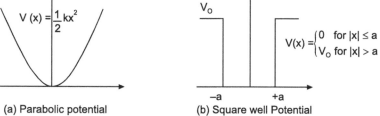

(a) Parabolic potential   (b) Square well Potential

(c) Hard Sphere Potential: $V(x) = \begin{cases} 0 \text{ for } |x| \le a \\ \infty \text{ for } |x| > a \end{cases}$

(d) Linear Potential: $V(x) = 1$

(e) Lennard-Jones Potential: $V(x) = \left(\dfrac{a}{x}\right)^{12} - \left(\dfrac{b}{x}\right)^{6}$

(f) Power law Potential: $V(x) = |x|^n$ for $n > 0$

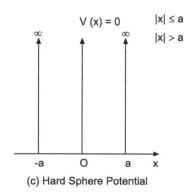

(c) Hard Sphere Potential

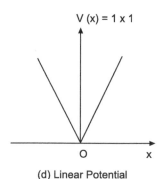

(d) Linear Potential

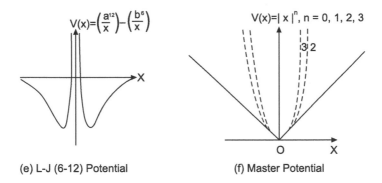

(e) L-J (6-12) Potential   (f) Master Potential

12.4.3 Eigen Value Problem

Primary work in describing a non-relativistic quantum system in one dimension is to solve the eq. (3) which in atomic units ($\hbar = 1$, $m = 1$), can be written as

$$\frac{d^2\varphi_n(x)}{dx^2} = -2[E_n - V(x)]\,\varphi_n(x) \tag{6}$$

For $V(x) = 0$, its solution is given by a linear combination of the sine and cosine functions. For $V(x) \neq 0$, we may use any of the computational methods available to solve a second order differential equation. It may keep in mind that for bound states the energy eigenvalues E_n, of eq. (6) are discrete. Each of the solutions corresponding to the eigenvalues describes some physical stationary state.

The simplest numerical method is to start with a energy eigenvalue and keep on changing it in steps till one arrives at the right energy value. Solution obtained for that value gives us the wavefunction of the quantum system. One of the basic questions is to decide on the trial energy eigenvalue. The boundary condition, $\varphi_n(x) \to 0$ as $|x| \to \infty$ helps us to achieve this. Unless the energy parameter is just right, numerical integration yields $\varphi_n(x)$ $\to +\infty$ or $-\infty$ as $|x| \to \infty$.

Runge-Kutta Method

A better method to integrate a second order differential equation is the Runge–Kutta method. In this method, we start with some trial energy value and find the wave-function starting from the initial value to some final value of x. We note that the wave-function diverges for large x for any of the energy values. We keep incrementing the trial energy value and look at the behaviour of the wave-function at large distance. At a particular energy value, the divergent part changes its direction i.e., goes from upward to downward direction or vice versa. When this takes place, we identify the energy range, formed by the present value and the previous value, in which the true energy eigenvalue lies. Once this range is determined, we repeat the run with smaller energy increment and narrow down the energy interval in which the true eigenvalue lies.

The Algorithm employing this method is given below:

Step 1 : Define potential $V(x) = -\dfrac{1}{2}x^2$

Step 2 : Choose maximum range for x.

Step 3 : Choose parity of the wavefunction: odd/even.

Step 4 : Guess energy eigenvalue.

Step 5 : Choose step size, h.

Step 6 : Choose initial value of the wavefunction and its first derivative according to the choice of parity of the wavefunction.

Step 7 : Begin loop over x.

Step 8 : Let φ and φ' denote the wavefunction and its derivative at some position, say x. Determine fourth-order Runge-Kutta coefficients:

$$k_1 = \varphi'$$
$$p_1 = -2[E - V(x)]\varphi$$
$$k_2 = \varphi' + \frac{1}{2}p_1 h$$
$$p_2 = -\left[E - V\left(x + \frac{1}{2}h\right)\right]\left(\varphi + \frac{1}{2}k_1 h\right)$$
$$k_3 = \varphi' + \frac{1}{2}p_2 h$$
$$p_3 = -2\left[E - V\left(x + \frac{1}{2}h\right)\right]\left(\varphi + \frac{1}{2}k_2 h\right)$$
$$k_4 = \varphi' + p_3 h$$
$$p_4 = -2[E - V(x + h)](\varphi + k_3 h)$$

Step 9 : Use these coefficients to determine wavefunction and its derivative at the next point $x + h$,

$$\varphi \leftarrow \varphi + \frac{h}{6}(k_1 + 2k_2 + 2k_3 + k_4)$$
$$\varphi' \leftarrow \varphi' + \frac{h}{6}(p_1 + 2p_2 + 2p_3 + p_4)$$

Step 10 : End of loop if range ends.

Step 11 : Check direction in which wavefunction j diverge for large x.

Step 12 : For another run, go to step 4.

Step 13 : Program ends.

Python Implementation

A program based on this algorithm is given below, which plots the eigenfunction vs. x for the harmonic oscillator potential (To be Verify again)

```python
# using 4th order Runge-Kutta method
import pylab as pl
SIZE = 5000
FLAG = 0
def POTFN(x):
    return (0.5*x*x)
while(1):
    parity = raw_input("Choose parity of state
desired: ODD/EVEN := ")
    parity = parity.lower()
    n=len(parity)
    if (parity != "odd" or parity != "even"):
        print 'parity= ',parity
        break
    else :
        print "Enter parity again :"
    if parity != "odd" :
        phi=1.0
        phi_prime=0.0
    else :
        phi=0.0
        phi_prime=1.0
phi=0.0 # The Odd parity condition
phi_prime=1.0
xmax = input("Enter maximum x:")
h = input("Enter the step size :")
E_Guess = input("Enter the Guess Energy of the State
:")
xmin=0.0
X=[]
E=E_Guess
```

```
phiold= []
Phi_prime = []
while E_Guess <=1.51:
    while xmin<xmax :
        k1=phi_prime
        p1=2.0*(POTFN(xmin)-E)*phi
        k2=phi_prime + 0.5*p1*h
        p2=2.0*(POTFN(xmin+0.5*h)-E)*(phi+0.5*k1*h)
        k3=phi_prime + 0.5*p2*h
        p3=2.0*(POTFN(xmin+0.5*h)-E)*(phi+0.5*k2*h)
        qk4=phi_prime + p3*h
        p4=2.0*(POTFN(xmin+h)-E)*(phi+k3*h)
        phi=phi+h*(k1+2*k2+2*k3+k4)/6.0
        phi_prime += h*(p1+2*p2+2*p3+p4)/6.0
        phiold.append(phi)
        Phi_prime.append(phi_prime)
        xmin=xmin+h;
        X.append(xmin)
        #print 'X=',X,
        #print 'length =', len(X)
        #print 'phiold =', phiold,
        #print 'length1=', len(phiold)
        print 'Energy = ', E_Guess
pl.plot(X, phiold)
pl.show()
E_Guess += .1
E = E_Guess
print 'Energy = ', E_Guess
```

We run the program again to find the energy eigenvalue of the harmonic oscillator. In Fig. 1, we show the graphs of the wavefunctions obtained for different trial energies. We determine the wavefunction at different lattice points. By suitable modification of the above program, numerical output can be obtained. These are displayed in Table 12.1 for the following choice of the parameters:

Parity of state   = even
Maximum x = 10

Table 12.1

E \ x	1.45	1.49	1.5	1.51	1.47	1.48	1.47	1.475	1.478	1.472	1.473
0.1	0.09952	0.0995	0.0995	0.0995	0.09951	0.09951	0.09951	0.09951	0.09951	0.09951	0.09951
0.2	0.19617	0.19606	0.19603	0.19601	0.19611	0.19609	0.19614	0.1961	0.19609	0.19611	0.19611
0.3	0.28721	0.28686	0.28677	0.28668	0.28703	0.28695	0.28712	0.28699	0.28696	0.28702	0.28701
0.4	0.37017	0.36936	0.36915	0.36895	0.36976	0.36956	0.36997	0.36966	0.3696	0.36972	0.3697
0.5	0.44296	0.44141	0.44102	0.44064	0.44218	0.4418	0.44257	0.44199	0.44187	0.44211	0.44207
0.6	0.50395	0.50135	0.5007	0.50006	0.50265	0.502	0.5033	0.50232	0.50213	0.50252	0.50245
0.7	0.55203	0.54806	0.54707	0.54608	0.55004	0.54905	0.55104	0.54955	0.54925	0.54985	0.54975
0.8	0.58667	0.58098	0.57956	0.57814	0.58382	0.5824	0.58525	0.58311	0.58269	0.58354	0.5834
0.9	0.60787	0.60012	0.59819	0.59627	0.60399	0.60205	0.60593	0.60302	0.60244	0.6036	0.60341
1	0.61613	0.60601	0.6035	0.60099	0.61106	0.60853	0.61359	0.6098	0.60904	0.61055	0.6103
2	0.30269	0.25526	0.24371	0.23229	0.27872	0.26693	0.29064	0.27281	0.26928	0.27635	0.27517
3	0.15856	-0.06084	-0.11251	-0.16295	0.04628	-0.00791	0.10177	0.01903	0.00282	0.03534	0.02989
4	2.04055	-1.54261	-2.36894	-3.1686	0.19227	-0.68906	1.10194	-0.25191	-0.51504	0.01375	-0.07509
5	110.914	-83.1044	-127.244	-169.722	10.3264	-37.2618	59.7031	-13.6887	-27.8853	0.66692	-4.1362
6	18143.6	-13485.3	-20606.1	-27429.7	1682.43	-6058.65	9746.73	-2227.99	-4535.9	108.61	-673.485
7	8.6E+06	-6.35E+06	-9.69E+06	-1.29E+07	794780	-2.86E+06	4.61E+06	-1.05E+06	2.14E+06	51290.6	317997
8	1.16E+10	8.50E+09	1.30E+10	1.72E+10	1.07E+09	3.83E+09	6.20E+09	1.41E+09	2.87E+09	6.89E+07	4.27E+08
9	4.38E+13	3.20E+13	4.87E+13	6.46E+13	4.03E+12	1.44E+13	2.34E+13	-5.32E+12	1.08E+13	2.60E+11	1.61E+12
10	4.62E+17	3.36E+17	5.11E+17	6.76E+17	4.24E+16	1.52E+17	2.47E+17	5.60E+16	-1.14E+17	2.73E+15	1.69E+16

Step size h $= 0.05$

Initial conditions: $\varphi(0) = 0,\ \varphi'(0) = 1$

Initial trial of energy values: E = 1.45 to 1.51.

At this particular energy E =1.47 and E =1.48, the divergent part changes its direction *i.e.* goes from upward to downward direction as we can see from the graph shown below. So, to get the true eigen energy value we narrow down the energy range further, *i.e.*, trial E = 1.471 to 1.479 which is shown in Fig. 12.2.

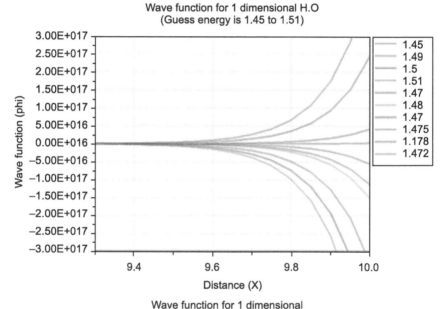

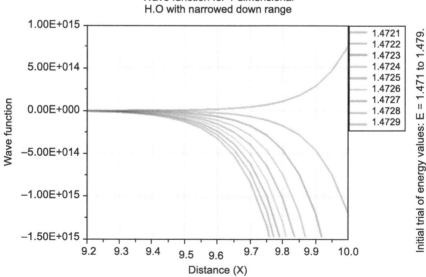

Fig. 12.2

12.5 FRACTALS

It is common in nature to notice objects, called fractals, that do not have well-defined geometric shapes, but nevertheless appear regular and pleasing to the eye. These objects have dimensions that are fractions, and occur in plants, sea shells, polymers, thin films, colloids, and aerosols. We will not study the scientific theories that lead to fractal geometry, but rather will look at how some simple models and rules produce fractals. To the extent that these models generate structures that look like those in nature, it is reasonable to assume that the natural processes must be following similar rules arising from the basic physics or biology that creates the objects.

12.5.1 Fractional Dimension (Math)

Benoit Mandelbrot, who first studied the fractional-dimension figures with the supercomputers at IBM Research, gave them the name *fractal*. Some geometric objects, such as the Koch curves, are exact fractals with the same dimension for all their parts. Other objects, such as bifurcation curves, are statistical fractals in which elements of randomness occur and the dimension can be defined only locally or on the average.

Consider an abstract "object" such as the density of charge within an atom. There are an infinite number of ways to measure the "size" of this object, for example; each moment of the distribution provides a measure of the size, and there are an infinite number of moments. Likewise, when we deal with complicated objects that have fractional dimensions, there are different definitions of dimension, and each may give a somewhat different dimension. In addition, the fractal dimension is often defined by using a measuring box whose size approaches zero. In realistic applications there may be numerical or conceptual difficulties in approaching such a limit, and for this reason a precise value of the fractional dimension may not be possible.

Our first definition of fractional dimension d_f (or Hausdorf–Besicovitch dimension) is based on our knowledge that a line has dimension 1; a triangle, dimension 2, and a cube, dimension 3. It seems perfectly reasonable to ask if there is some mathematical formula, which agrees with our experience for regular objects, yet can also be used for determining fractional dimensions. For simplicity, let us consider objects that have the same length L on each side, as do equilateral triangles and squares, and which have uniform density.

The dimension of an object is determined by the dependence of its total mass upon its length:

$$M(L) \propto L^{d_f} \tag{1}$$

where the power d_f is the *fractal dimension*. As you may verify, this rule works with the 1D, 2D, and 3D regular figures of our experience, so it is a reasonable hypothesis. When we apply (1) to fractal objects, we end up with fractional values for d_f. Actually, we will find it easier to determine the fractal dimension not from an object's mass, which is *extensive* (depends on size), but rather from its density, which is *intensive*. The density is defined as mass/length for a linear object, as mass/area for a planar object, and mass/volume for a solid object. That being the case, for a planar object we hypothesize that

$$\rho = \frac{M(L)}{Area} \propto \frac{L^{d_f}}{L^2} \propto L^{d_f - 2} \tag{2}$$

12.5.2 The Sierpinski Gasket

To generate our first fractal, we play a game in which we pick points and place dots on them. Here are the rules (which you should try out now):

1. Draw an equilateral triangle with vertices and coordinates:

    vertex 1: (a_1, b_1) vertex 2: (a_2, b_2)
    vertex 3: (a_3, b_3)

2. Place a dot at an arbitrary point $P = (x_0, y_0)$ within this triangle.

3. Find the next point by selecting randomly the integer 1, 2, or 3:

    (*a*) If 1, place a dot halfway between P and vertex 1.

    (*b*) If 2, place a dot halfway between P and vertex 2.

    (*c*) If 3, place a dot halfway between P and vertex 3.

4. Repeat the process, using the last dot as the new P.

Fig. 12.3 (a) A sample of Sierpinsky gasket: (here it is not by points)

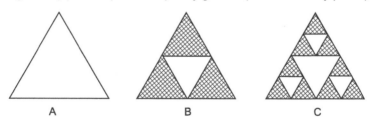

Fig. 12.3 (b) - A Sierpinski gasket constructed by successively connecting the midpoints of the sides of each equilateral triangle. A, B, and C show the first three steps in the process.

Mathematically, the coordinates of successive points are given by the formula

$$(x_{k+1}, y_{k+1}) = \frac{(x_k, y_k) + (a_n, b_n)}{2} \quad n = \text{integer } (1 + 3r_i) \tag{3}$$

where r_i is a random number between 0 and 1, and where the *integer* function outputs the closest integer smaller than, or equal to, the argument. After 15,000 points, you should obtain a collection of dots like Fig. 12.4.

Python Implementation of Sierpinsky Implementation :

```python
import pylab as pl
import random
max_iteration = 30000 # number of iterations
a1 = 20.0 # vertex 1
b1 = 20.0
a2 = 320.0 # vertex 2
b2 = 20.0
a3 = 170.0 # vertex 3
b3 = 280.0

x0 = 180.0; # starting point
y0 = 150.0;
x = []
y = []
x.append(x0)
y.append(y0)
for i in range(max_iteration) :
    r = random.random()
    if r <= 0.3333:
        x1 = 0.5*(x[i] + a1)
        y1 = 0.5*(y[i] + b1)
    elif (r > 0.3333 and r <= 0.6666):
        x1 = 0.5*(x[i] + a2)
        y1 = 0.5*(y[i] + b2)
    else:
        x1 = 0.5*(x[i] + a3)
        y1 = 0.5*(y[i] + b3)
    x.append(x1)
    y.append(y1)

pl.plot(x,y,'.')
pl.title('Sierpinski Gasket for 30000 points')
pl.show()
```

Output of the above program

We run the program for two different points, *i.e.*, 15000 and 30000 points. The following two figures are shown below.

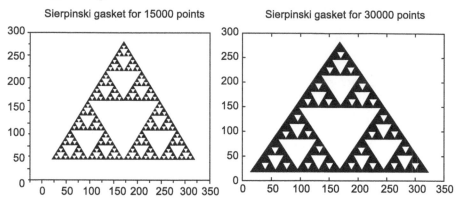

Fig. 12.4 Sierpinski gasket for different points

12.5.3 Assessing Fractal Dimension

The topology of Fig. 12(0)b was first analyzed by the Polish mathematician Sierpinski. Observe that there is the same structure in a small region as there is in the entire figure. In other words, if the figure had infinite resolution, any part of the figure could be scaled up in size and will be similar to the whole. This property is called *self-similarity*.

We construct a regular form of the Sierpinsky gasket by removing an inverted equilateral triangle from the center of all filled equilateral triangles to create the next figure (Fig. 1). We then repeat the process *ad infinitum*, scaling up the triangles so each one has side $r = 1$ after each step. To see what is unusual about this type of object, we look at how its density (mass/area) changes with size, and then apply Eqn. (2) to determine its fractal dimension.

Assume that each triangle has mass m, and assign unit density to the single triangle:

$$\rho(L = r) \propto \frac{M}{r^2} = \frac{m}{r^2} = \rho_0 \ \text{Fig. } 12.3(b)\,\text{A}$$

Next, for the equilateral triangle with side $L = 2$, the density

$$\rho(L = 2r) \propto \frac{(M = 3m)}{(2r)^2} = 34mr^2 = \frac{3}{4}\rho_0 \ \text{Fig. } 12.3(b)\,\text{B}$$

We see that the extra white space in Fig. 1b.B leads to a density that is 34 that of the previous stage. For the structure in Fig. 1b.C, we obtain

$$\rho(L = 4r) \propto \frac{(M = 9m)}{(4r)^2} = (34)\frac{m}{r^2} = \left(\frac{3}{4}\right)^2 \rho_0 \ \text{Fig. } 12.3(b)\,\text{C}$$

We see that as we continue the construction process, the density of each new structure is ¾ that of the previous one. This is unusual. Yet in eqn. (2) we have derived that

$$\rho \propto CL^{d_f-2} \tag{4}$$

Equation (2) implies that a plot of the logarithm of the density ρ the logarithm of the length for successive structures, yields a straight line of slope:

$$d_f - 2 = \frac{\Delta \log \rho}{\Delta \log L}$$

As applied to our problem:

$$d_f = 2 + \frac{\Delta \log \rho\, (L)}{\Delta \log L} = 2 + \frac{\log 1 - \log\left(\dfrac{3}{4}\right)}{\log 1 - \log 2}$$

$$= 1.58494$$

As is evident in Fig. 1b, as the gasket gets larger and larger (and consequently more massive), it contains more and more open space. So even though its mass approaches infinity as $L \to \infty$, its density approaches zero! And since a two-dimensional figure like a solid triangle has a constant density as its length increases, a 2D figure would have a slope equal to 0. Since the Sierpinski gasket has a slope $d_f - 2 \cong -0.41504$, it fills space to a lesser extend than a 2D object, but more than does a 1D object; it is a fractal.

12.5.4 Beautiful Plants

It seems paradoxical that natural processes subject to change can produce objects of high regularity and symmetry. For example, it is hard to believe that something as beautiful and symmetric as a fern (Fig. 12.5) has random elements in it. Nonetheless, there is a clue here in that much of the fern's beauty arises from the similarity of each part to the whole (self-similarity), with different ferns similar, but not identical, to each other. These are characteristics of fractals. Our **problem** is to discover if a simple algorithm including some randomness can draw regular ferns. If the algorithm produces objects that resemble ferns, then presumably you have uncovered mathematics similar to that responsible for the shape of ferns.

Self-Affine Connection (Theory)

In Equation (3), which defines mathematically how a Sierpinski gasket is constructed, a scaling factor of ½ is part of the relation of one point to the next. A more general transformation of a point $P = (x, y)$ into another point $P' = (x', y')$ via scaling is

$$(x', y') = s(x, y) = (sx, sy) \quad \textbf{(scaling)} \tag{5}$$

If the scale factor $s > 0$, an amplification occurs, whereas if $s < 0$, a reduction occurs.

Fig. 12.5

In our definition eqn. (3) of the Sierpinski gasket, we also added in a constant. This is a , which has the general form

$$(x', y') = (x, y) + (a_x, a_y) \text{ (translation)} \tag{6}$$

Another operation, not used in the Sierpinski gasket, is a by angle θ:

$$x' = x \cos \theta - y \sin \theta \quad y' = x \sin \theta + y \cos \theta \text{ (rotation)} \tag{7}$$

The entire set of transformations, scalings, rotations, and translations, define an *affine transformation* ("affine" denotes a close relation between successive points). The transformation is still considered affine even if it is a more general linear transformation with the coefficients not all related to one θ (in that case, we can have contractions and reflections). What is important is that the object created with these rules turn out to be self-similar; each step leads to new parts of the object that bear the same relation to the ancestor parts as did the ancestors to theirs. This is what makes the object look similar at all scales.

Barnsley's Fern Implementation

We obtain a Barnsley's Fern by extending the dots game to one in which new points are selected using an affine connection with some elements of chance mixed in

$$(x, y)_{n+1} = \begin{cases} (0.5, 0.27y_n) & \text{with 2\% probability} \\ (-0.139x_n + 0.263y_n + 0.57, \\ 0.246x_n + 0.224y_n - 0.036) & \text{with 15\% probability} \\ (0.17x_n - 0.215y_n + 0.408 , \\ 0.222x_n + 0.176 + 0.0893) & \text{with 13\% probability} \\ (0.781x_n + 0.034y_n + 0.1075, \\ -0.032x_n + 0.739y_n + 0.27) & \text{with 70\% probability} \end{cases} \quad \text{(A)}$$

To select a transformation with probability P, we select a uniform random number r, in the interval $[0, 1]$ and perform the transformation if r is in a range proportional to P :

$$P = \begin{cases} 2\% & r < 0.02 \\ 15\% & 0.02 \le r \le 0.17 \\ 13\% & 0.17 < r \le 0.3 \\ 70\% & 0.3 < r < 1 \end{cases} \quad \text{(B)}$$

The above two equations (A) and (B) can be combined into one as follows:

$$(x, y)_{n+1} = \begin{cases} 0.5, 0.27y_n) & r < 0.02 \\ (-0.139x_n + 0.263y_n + 0.57, \\ 0.246x_n + 0.224y_n - 0.036) & 0.02 \le r \le 0.17 \\ (0.17x_n - 0.215y_n + 0.408, \\ 0.222 x_n + 0.176 + 0.0893) & 0.17 < r \le 0.3 \\ (0.781x_n + 0.034 y_n + 0.1075, \\ -0.032x_n + 0.739 y_n + 0.27) & 0.3 < r < 1 \end{cases} \quad \text{(C)}$$

Although Eqn. (A) makes the basic idea clearer, Eqn. (C) is easier to program. The starting point in Barnsley's fern (Fig. 12.5) is $(x_1, y_1) = (0.5, 0.0)$, and the points are generated by repeated iterations. An important property of this fern is that it is not completely self-similar, as you can see by noting how different are the stems and the fronds. Nevertheless, the stem can be viewed as a compressed copy of a frond, and the fractal obtained with (A) is still *self-affine*, yet with a dimension that varies in different parts of the figure.

Python Implementation

The Python program may be implemented as follows:

```python
import pylab as pl

import random

max_iteration = 30000 # number of iterations

x0 = 0.5; # starting point

y0 = 0.0;

x = []

y = []

x.append(x0)

y.append(y0)


for i in range(max_iteration) :
    # r = random.uniform(0,1)
    r = random.random()
    if r < 0.02:
        x1 = 0.5
        y1 = 0.27*y[i]
    elif (r >= 0.02 and r <= 0.17):
        x1 = -0.139*x[i] + 0.263*y[i] + 0.57
        y1 = 0.246*x[i] + 0.224*y[i] - 0.036
    elif (r >0.17 and r <= 0.3):
        x1 = 0.17*x[i] - 0.215*y[i] +0.408
        y1 = 0.222*x[i] + 0.176*y[i] + 0.0893
    else:
        x1 = 0.781*x[i] + 0.034*y[i] + 0.1075
```

```
        y1 = -0.032*x[i] + 0.739*y[i] + 0.27

   x.append(x1)

   y.append(y1)

pl.plot(x,y,'.')

pl.title("Barnsley's Ferm for 30000 points")

pl.show()
```

OUTPUT of the above Program:

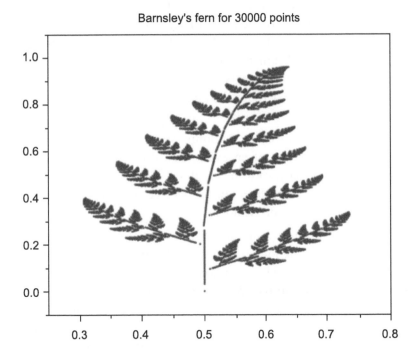

Barnsley's fern for 30000 points

12.6 RANDOM NUMBERS IN COMPUTER SIMULATION

12.6.1 Introduction

Nature has an abundance of random phenomena. Among the most familiar examples from physics are radioactivity, diffusion and percolation. Despite the randomness involved these phenomena follow well defined laws, which look very startling when seen superficially. However, computer simulation of these processes has been an interesting field and has helped us to gain an in-depth understanding. In some instances these simulations have resulted in simpler approaches to understand many outstanding and insurmountable problems.

These phenomena are stochastic Realization of a scheme on a computer which is stochastic for such phenomena requires the knowledge of random numbers and their generation. The accuracy of simulation experiments depends much on the quality of the random numbers generated by the computer. In this chapter, we concern ourselves with the study of random number generators usually employed in computer simulations.

12.6.2 Randomness: Some Intuitive Concepts

In order to make some sense about random physical processes, it is important to comprehend the meaning of *randomness*. In a particular process it needs to be interpreted according to the context. For example, in diffusion process , the randomness lies in the random (Brownian) motion of molecules in a liquid. For percolation phenomena, randomness appears to remain frozen and is the property of the medium in which something *e.g.* a liquid, has to flow. In radioactivity, the randomness lies in the process of decay of the nucleus.

Another important feature of the randomness is the *statistical independence* involved in the occurrence of an event. In diffusion, taking a step in any direction (forward or backward in one dimensional case) is independent of how the previous steps were taken. In radioactive decay, a nucleus in a sample of uranium, has nothing to do with its past.

Once we have an intuitive understanding of the randomness, the next task is to understand the phenomenon involved. To do this we introduce the concept of *probability*. The probability for an event to occur always lies between zero and unity. We use this concept intuitively in a day-to-day conversation. When one talks of tossing a coin or rolling a dice one is talking about the probability of occurrence of an event. Event in the case of a coin is either head or tail. In the case of an unbiased flipping of a coin, the probability of getting head or tail is 1/2. For a perfect cubical dice, probability of getting any number from 1 to 6 is 1/6. These considerations laid the foundation of all the phenomena based on the statistical processes in science and can be used to simulate a natural random process on the computer.

12.6.3 Random Number Generators

In principle, a random number is simply a particular value taken on by a random variable. Random numbers are of two types: truly random and pseudo random. A sequence of truly random numbers is unpredictable and therefore cannot be reproduced. Such a sequence can only be generated by an actual physical process. We can also generate a random number by randomly interrupting any uniform process. Shaking a dice in a box and throwing it involves interrupting the process of shaking and letting the dice roll, which is an entirely random process. If the dice is unbiased, it will produce an integer between 1 and 6. If it is not so, a biasing may appear in the generation of this sequence of numbers. One number out of these six numbers may appear more often than the others.

Random numbers were generated by known random physical processes such as radioactivity. A sample of radioactive isotopes through a detector may be used to open and close an electronic gate between an oscillator and a counter. Between successive openings which are completely random, number of pulses reactivating the counter may vary. Record of the pulses is a record of random numbers. Another way of generating the random numbers has been through measurement of the noise level generated in an electronic valve. Using these physical processes, Rand corporation (1955) published large tables of pre-calculated random sequences which were used till the recent past by workers in many fields, from statistics to physics. Such generated random numbers were termed as true random numbers. With the availability of computers the generation of these random numbers is accomplished via some known algorithm. However, the random numbers so generated are not truly random, for they can be reproduced with ease unlike random numbers generated in a natural process. Such random numbers are called pseudorandom numbers. In practice, however, it is very difficult to have fast continuous physical generator of truly random numbers. Moreover, attaching physical devices to generate random numbers with today's multipurpose computers can be a costly affair.

12.6.4 Pseudo-Random Number Generators

As computers became available for statistical work or simulations, it was felt that the tables of true random numbers be stored in the memory of the computer, from which one could draw random numbers to do computations.

As a result, utilizing physical or mechanical processes to generate random numbers, went out of fashion. However, many present day problems which are being simulated on computers require millions of such random numbers and storing them would utilise a good chunk of computer memory for data storage alone, thereby making the main computation job extremely slow. However, these random numbers so generated are not easily reproducible. The method itself is fraught with some inherent shortcomings which may arise rise because of errors during the experiments themselves. Furthermore, these random number generators were needed only for specialized purposes, as in Monte Carlo methods.

The other choice left was to develop algorithms to produce random number generators, though pseudo. For the first time in 1951, Von Neumann, father of modern computers, suggested to produce random numbers purely by an arithmetic algorithm run on a computer provided it satisfies certain criteria. If such an algorithm passed the laid down criteria, it can be taken as true random number generator. Such algorithms have many advantages. These are generated according to a strict mathematical formula and hence reproducible. By performing a few operations, we can get the desired result. The rate at which these numbers are thus generated match the speed of the computers and are therefore convenient to use. Unlike the random numbers generated through physical processes, which needed to be stored, utilizing a large storage space, these require a few memory storage locations to generate random numbers. Also, no periodic checks are needed to test the quality of the random numbers generated. These checks are necessary for random numbers generated through physical processes, as these processes can get halted or errors may creep in because of malfunctioning of the apparatus itself. It needs to be emphasized again that, in strict mathematical sense, these numbers are not at all truly random, but are seemingly random *i.e.* indistinguishable from a truly generated sequence of random numbers. In developing these algorithms, an effort is always made to generate random numbers with the properties of true random numbers.

However, the algorithmic generation of random numbers is deterministic in nature. In fact, the deterministic nature of the generated sequence of pseudo-random numbers has its own advantage. One of the desirable features of any computer simulation is its reproducibility. So the pseudo random-number generators fulfill this basic requirement, which allows repetition of a simulation under the same conditions. The algorithms available for this purpose can produce random numbers which are distributed uniformly or according to some specific distribution, which could be normal or exponential. Here we shall limit ourselves only to the uniform distribution in the interval [0, 1].

12.6.5 Basic Strategy

Most of the algorithms for generating pseudo random numbers are recursive in nature. This may be expressed as

$$x_{i+1} = f(x_i)$$

where x_i is a number lying between 0 and 1. The innovation lies in choosing the form of the function $f(x)$. For a uniform distribution on [0, 1], the function should be such that it should fill the square of unit length uniformly and densely.

Suppose we choose a function $f(x_i) = x_i$, all the numbers will lie on a parabolic arc, as in Fig. 12.6(*a*), hence, unfit to produce uniform pseudo—random numbers. Another choice may be

$$x_{i+1} = mx_i$$

where m is a large number and the square bracket stands for keeping fractional part of the product of m and x_i. Now the square will be filled densely. You may check this feature for any number m. For $m = 10$, the graph is shown in Fig. 12.6(b). However, one can easily note that some correlation exists amongst the successive numbers. The basic choice of $f(x_i)$ is the key to a good pseudorandom number generator.

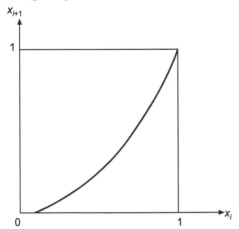

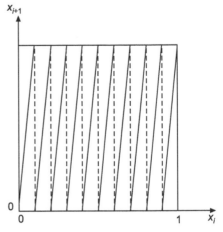

Fig. 12.6 (a) Function for Choosing random number generator f(x) = x *x

Fig. 12.6 (b) Function for another random number generator

12.6.6 Mid-Square Generator

This was the first algorithm used to generate pseudo-random numbers and was built on a suggestion from Von Neumann in 1951. It starts with a seed number having four digits. The seed is then squared, and the first two and the last two digits of the produced number are chopped off. The resulting number is used as a new seed. A random number lying in the interval [0, 1] is obtained by dividing it by 10000. Stepwise algorithm is given which can be easily run on a PC.

Algorithm: Random Number Generator (Mid Square Method)

Step 1 : Choose total number of random numbers, you want to generate.

Step 2 : Give four digit seed, SD (in double precision).

Step 3 : Start a loop over iterations.

Step 4 : Square the seed: $x = SD^2$

Step 5 : Chop off the last two digits of the obtained number x.

Step 6 : Chop off the first two digits of the number resulted in step 5.

Step 7 : Get the random number by dividing the number obtained in step 6 by 10000 and print it.

Step 8 : Replace the seed by the number resulted in step 6.

Step 9 : Loop started at step 3 ends.

Step 10 :   Program ends.

Python Implementation

Now we can implement the above algorithm into its equivalent python program as follows:

```
#Mid Square Random Generator
import pylab as pl
number = input("Enter the total number of Random
numbers to be generated :")
SD = input(" Enter a four digit Seed :")
x = []
rn = []
print "Random numbers are = ",
for i in range(1, number+1) :
    X = SD ** 2
    #print "New X =", X,
    X = X/100 # To chop off the last two digits
    L = len(str(X)) # To get the length of the number
    X = X%(10 ** (L-2)) # To chop off the first two
digits
    #print "X=",X,
    ran_no = X/10000.0
    print ran_no,
    SD = X
    #print "New Seed = ", SD,
    rn.append(ran_no)
    x.append(i)
pl.plot(x,rn,'.')
pl.show()
```

Output of the above program:

```
Enter the total number of Random numbers to be
generated :10
Enter a four digit Seed :6998
```

```
Random numbers are =  0.972 0.4784 0.8866 0.6059
0.7114 0.6089 0.0759 0.006 0.0 0.0
```

The corresponding graph can be drawn as follows:

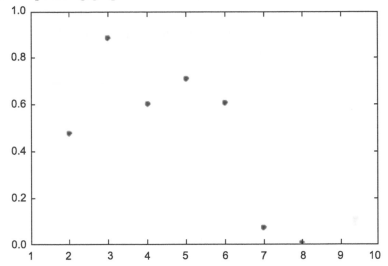

12.6.7 Multiplicative Congruential Generator

This is the most commonly employed generator of pseudorandom numbers. This method is also known as the *method of power residues*. It was suggested by D. Lehmer. It employs the following recursion relation.

$$x_{j+1} = (a\,x_i) \bmod m \qquad\qquad (A)$$

where '*a*' and '*m*' are termed as *magic numbers*. The sequence begins with a seed x_0, and '*a*' and '*m*' are preferably chosen to be large positive prime numbers. Number $x_{j+1,1}$ resulting in eq. (A) is called the *residue, i.e.,* remainder, in the division of *(ax$_j$)* by m. This is also known as modulo operation. It can be any number lying between 0 and $m-1$. The desired random number in the interval 0, 11 is then obtained by dividing each x_{j+1} by in.

The choice of '*a*' and '*m*' is of crucial importance. The choice of '*a*' decides whether full cycle of $m-1$ pseudo-random numbers will be generated or not. The choice of *m* (*an integer*) also decides the maximum period of the generator.

Note: If *l* is the word length of the computer register in bits, the longest integer which can be stored in it is 2^l. If *m* is equal to 2^l, then the maximum period of a simple multiplicative generator is *m*/4. This number is sensitive to the choice of the seed. *If one starts with an even seed, no odd numbers would be generated*, thereby the period reduces to *m*/8. If one starts with an odd seed, no even numbers are produced and thus the period is again reduced to *m*/4. Such considerations lead to partially periodic multiplicative congruential generators.

Crucial conditions for multiplicative congruential generators:

(*i*) '*m*' should be prime,

(*ii*) '*a*' should be a positive primitive root of *m*. It is indeed difficult to guess.

Some of the magic numbers (m, a) used in the literature are given below.

(*i*) $m = 2^{35} + 1$ (34, 359, 738, 369), a = 23;

(*ii*) $m = 2^{35} - 31$ (34, 359, 738, 337), a = 3125 (used on a 36 bit mainframe computer – DEC 10);

(*iii*) $m = 2^{31} - 1$(2, 147, 483, 647), $a = 16806$

(used on a 32 - bit mainframe computer – IBM 370);

(*iv*) $m = 2^{59}$ and $a = 13^{13}$

(used on a 60-bit mainframe computer - CDC 7600).

12.6.8 Mixed Multiplicative Congruential Generator

It is an improvement over the above method. In this method, besides the seed x_0, it has three magic numbers '*m*', '*a*' and '*c*'. The eq. (A) is modified as

$$x_{i+1} = (ax_i + c) \bmod m \qquad\qquad (B)$$

The algorithm for implementing this method is given below.

Algorithm for Random Number Generator (Mixed Multiplicative Congruential Generator):

Step 1 : Choose total number of random numbers, NRAN, you want to generate.

Step 2 : Enter the magic numbers **a** (multiplicative factor), **c** (constant to be add), and **m** (for modulo operation).

Step 3 : Give a seed **x1**.

Step 4 : Start a loop over *i* from 1 to NRAN iterations.

Step 5 :   Calculate the new number as

$$x_{i+1} = (ax_i + c)$$

Step 6 :   Replace x_i by x_{i+1}.

Step 7 :   Get the random number as remainder of the numbers obtained in step 5 on division by *m* and print it.

Step 8 : Loop started at step 4 ends.

Step 9 : Program ends.

Python Implementation

The Python code is implemented below:

```
#Mid Square Random Generator
import pylab as pl
```

```
import random
number = input("Enter the total number of Random
numbers to be generated :")
a = input("Enter the magic Number :")
c = input("Constant to be added, c :")
m = input("An Integer for modulo operation preferably
large prime no., m :")
x = input("Enter a Seed :")
X = [] # For drawing graph -X Axis
Y = [] # For drawing graph -Y Axis
for i in range(1, number+1):
    x1 = (a*x + c) % float(m)
    x = x1
    ran_no = x1 /float(m)
    print ran_no,
    Y.append(ran_no)
    X.append(random.uniform(0,1))
    #X.append(i)
pl.plot(X,Y,'.')
pl.show()
```

We run the program using the following input parameters:

Magic numbers : a = 1317, c = 3917, m = 713   Seed = 7361

Output of the above program:

```
Enter the total number of Random numbers to be
generated :100
Enter the magic Number : 1317
Constant to be added, c :3917
An Integer for modulo operation preferably large
prime no., m :713
Enter a Seed :7361
```

0.179523141655	0.925666199158	0.596072931276
0.521739130435	0.62412342216	0.464235624123
0.892005610098	0.26507713885	0.600280504909
0.0631136044881	0.614305750351	0.534361851332

0.24824684432	0.434782608696	0.102384291725
0.333800841515	0.109396914446	0.569424964937
0.426367461431	0.0196353436185	0.353436185133
0.969144460028	0.856942496494	0.0869565217391
0.015427769986	0.81206171108	0.978962131837
0.786816269285	0.730715287518	0.84572230014
0.309957924264	0.708274894811	0.291725105189
0.695652173913	0.667601683029	0.725105189341
0.457223001403	0.656381486676	0.948106591865
0.150070126227	0.136044880785	0.664796633941
0.0308555399719	0.130434782609	0.276297335203
0.377279102384	0.370266479663	0.134642356241
0.817671809257	0.367461430575	0.440392706872
0.490883590463	0.987377279102	0.869565217391
0.711079943899	0.985974754558	0.0224403927069
0.0476858345021 ...		

The following graph shows the distribution of the random numbers generated using this mixed multiplicative method.

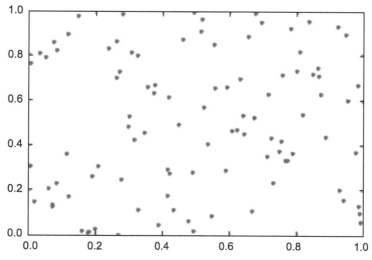

12.6.9 Tests For Randomness

Quality of simulation depends very much on the quality of random number generator employed, whether it is Brownian motion, *Monte Carlo method* or dynamics of a waiting queue. Among the desirable qualities are: (*i*) *long period,* (*ii*) *efficiency,* (*iii*) *reproducibility and* (*iv*) *passing out certain statistical tests.* All of which are impossible to be found in a set of pseudo-random numbers. We shall discuss important statistical tests which can be employed to test the randomness of the set of random numbers produced. The tests are:

   (*i*) Uniformity Test,

   (*ii*) Auto-correlation Test,

   (*iii*) Periodicity Test, and

   (*iv*) Serial-Correlation Test.

Uniformity Test

This is a well known statistical test to divide a given data into classes of equal sizes. The data is scanned and put in different classes. By plotting a bar chart, one can visualize whether each class has the same number of random numbers or not. Numerically, one can calculate chi-square (χ^2), a quantitative measure of the agreement between the observed and expected distribution, as

$$\chi^2 = \frac{1}{\text{No. of Classes}} \sum_{1}^{\text{Classes}} \frac{(\text{Observed}_i - \text{Exp}_i)^2}{(\text{Exp}_i)^2} \qquad (C)$$

If $\chi^2 = 0$, the obtained random numbers are perfectly distributed, If $\chi^2 < 1$, the numbers are distributed according to normal distribution.

The expected value of chi-square for a given test depends upon the number of classes expressed in terms of degrees of freedom.

    No. of degrees of freedom = No. of classes − 1   (D)

For a 95% level of confidence, *i.e.* there is one chance in 20 that our results are wrong, the acceptance of χ^2 can be checked from statistical tables. An algorithm for performing uniformity test is given below.

Algorithm for Uniformity Test for a Generated Set of Random Numbers

Step 1 : Give number of classes.

Step 2 : Calculate expected number of random numbers in each class.

Step 3: Find Class size = 1 / (number of classes).

Step 4 : Initialize the number in each class.

Step 5 : Start a loop over NRAN (total number of random numbers).

Step 6 : Start a loop over the classes.

Step 7 : Count the number of random numbers falling in each class.

Step 8 : End of loop started at step 6.

Step 9 : End of the loop started at step 5.

Step 10 : Calculate χ^2.

Step 11 : Program ends.

For each set of the 100 random numbers generated with different methods, this test is performed for classes of 5, 10 and 25; and χ^2 is given in Table below.

Generator of Classes	5	10	15
Mid square method (with seed 3761)	1.04	0.96	0.86
Multiplicative congruential method Magic numbers: a = 1317, c = 3917, m =. 713, seed = 7361	0.12	0.24	0.28

Auto-correlation Test

Auto-correlation test checks the serial auto-correlation between two number; by calculating auto-correlation function which describes the correlation between the two random numbers at different places in the generated sequence. It is defined as

$$C(k)= \frac{< x_i x_{i+k} > - < x_i >< x_{i+k} >}{< x_i x_i > - < x_i >< x_i >}$$

where x_i is the ith term in the sequence and $< ... >$ represents the mean. If x_i and X_{i+k} are not correlated then

$$<x_i x_{i+k}> - <x_i> < x_{i+k}> = 0$$

and C (k) = 0. Here, we give an algorithm to find such correlations.

Algorithm for Auto-correlation Test :

Step 1 : Initialize the sum to find average and average square.

Step 2 : Start a loop over random number N.

Step 3 : Sum the numbers.

Step 4 : Sum the square of numbers.

Step 5 : Loop started at step 2 ends.

Step 6 : Find mean of squares.

Step 7 : Give the interval between two random numbers in the generator sequence with which auto-correlation is to be checked.

Step 8 : Initialize the sum of the products of consecutive random number in pairs step interval chosen.

Step 9 : Initialize the sum of the successive random numbers separated by the interval chosen for looking for correlation.

Step 10 : Calculate the no. of random numbers, NL, upto which pairs can be found.

Step 11 : Start a loop over NL.

Step 12 : Calculate sum of the product of the consecutive random number pairs separated by intervals.

Step 13 : Calculate sum of the consecutive random numbers separated by chosen interval.

Step 14 : End of loop begin at step 11.

Step 15 : Find average of the products initialized in step 8 and 9.

Step 16 : Calculate auto-correlation function and print it.

Step 17 : Program ends.

The auto-correlation function for each of the sets generated have been tabulated below.

Generators k =	2	8	16	32
Mid square method Seed 3761)	.0164166	.2040777	.212353	.0088573
Multiplicative Congruential method a =1317, c=3917, m=713, seed=7361	−0.1067474	−0.009735	−0.044173	0.1583768

12.7 MONTE CARLO METHOD

12.7.1 Introduction

Very often in physics problems, one has to evaluate integrals over definite intervals. Geometrically, this amounts to finding the area under the curve represented by the integrand within certain limits of integration. There are two ways to achieve it. One way is to employ the conventional polynomial method which has some limitations with respect to the dimensionality of the problem. The other is a statistical method based on random sampling, known as the Monte Carlo method. This is quite powerful and efficient in case of evaluation of multidimensional integrals. We discussed about the conventional numerical methods referred to as the Integro-difference techniques (*e.g.*, Trapezoidal method, Taylor Series Method, Simpson's 1/3 and 3/8 rules).

12.7.2 Multi-Dimensional Integrals:

Let us carefully look at the economics of our methods *vis-a-vis* the kinds of problems which are likely to be encountered in physics, where we seldom have to evaluate one dimensional integrals. If a system has N atoms, each having 3 degrees of freedom, the number of degrees of freedom of the system turns out to be 3N, resulting in 3N dimensional integrals. In any of the methods discussed earlier, we shall have to discretize each dimension into π intervals involving π sums. The 3N dimensions therefore require p3N sums. If there are 10 particles, we shall deal with 30 degrees of freedom and if each dimension has just 10 intervals we shall have to perform 1030 sums, a mind boggling work.

To appreciate what we are saying, let us perform a two-dimensional integral by rectangular rule. The basic strategy is in extending at a two— dimensional integral as a product of two one — dimensional integrals. For the sake of simplicity, let us assume that the limits of integration are [a, b] and [c, d] for x and y variables respectively. Then

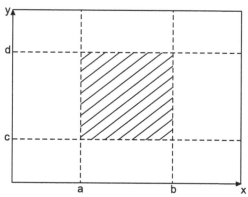

Fig. 12.7 Region for Two-dimensional numerical integration.

Here, we give an algorithm using the Simpson rule to determine the integral in the above equation.

Algorithm: Two-dimensional Integral (using Simpson Rule).

Step 1 : Input lower limit of $x = a$, lower limit of $y = c$, upper limit of $x = b$, upper limit of $y = d$, and number of intervals $= N_1, N_2$.

Step 2 : Find width of the x-interval $h_1 = (b - a)/N_1$, and width of the y interval $h_2 = (d - c)/N_2$.

Step 3 : Define integrand function $f(x, y)$.

Step 4 : Initialize sums: SUM1 = 0, SUM2 = 0.

Step 5 : Initialize x and y: $x = a, y = c$.

Step 6 : Begin loop over x from a to b.

Step 7 : Begin loop over y from c to d.

Step 8 : Replace SUM2 by SUM2 + fac * f(x, y), where fac is the appropriate factor appearing in the Simpson formula.

Note: It is not necessary that the region of integration be a rectangular one. It can be of any type determined by the lower and upper limits of y, say y_1 and y_2 depending on x, with x lying within the intervals x_1 and x_2. These limits may be constrained by some equation describing a closed curve.

We apply this in C program to integrate with

$$f(x, y) = xy$$

between the following limits and lattice points:

Lower and upper limits of variable $x = 0, 1$

Lower and upper limits of variable $y = 0, 1$

No. of lattice points in x and y directions $= 50, 50$.

Output is

Value of the integral $= 0.2499999$ (numerical)

Exact Value $= 0.25$ (analytical)

12.7.3 MONTE CARLO METHOD: Hitting The Bull's eye Blind-Folded

We have already observed how the computer starts getting breathless to perform double integration as the step size decreases, thereby increasing the number of sub-intervals. Is there a way out? Suppose you are asked to predict the results of a presidential poll, and if you don't have the resource to contact each of the voters how would you feel? Psychologists employ a simple method to predict these results based on the idea of random sampling. These are called opinion polls. Few voters are contacted and their opinion is gathered to predict the poll. Larger the sample, better is the prediction. This method, known as the Monte Carlo method is the most convenient method to calculate higher dimensional integrals. It would not be exaggerating to say that it is like hitting the bull's eye blind-folded.

To understand it explicitly, imagine you are to find the area of an irregularly shaped plane figure, Fig. 12.8. Enclose it within a square of known area. Hang it on a board and ask a blind-folded shooter to shoot at it randomly. Count the total number of shots and the number of shots lying within the irregular figure. Assuming the unbiased probability of hitting, we obtain the following relation:

$$\frac{\text{Area of the figure}}{\text{Area of the curve}} = \frac{\text{No. of shots falling in the figure}}{\text{Total number of shots}}$$

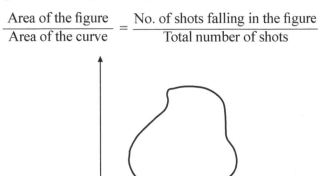

Fig. 12.8 Area of irregular shaped figure

The method being statistical in nature, we may calculate the statistical measure of error in our computation. One such measure of error is called standard deviation. The basic idea is to repeat the measurement many times keeping the number of shots fired fixed instead of measuring a value once. If m_i is the ith measurement and N is the number of times such measurements are made, calculate the mean of these measurements and the mean of their squares, is then given by

$$\sigma^2 = \left(\frac{\Sigma_i m_i^2}{N}\right) - \left(\frac{\Sigma_i m_i}{N}\right)^2$$

Square root of this quantity called **standard deviation**, σ, tells us that a given measurement can deviate for a fixed numbers of shots in an interval $(m - \sigma, m + \sigma)$, where m is the mean of the measurements

$$m = \frac{\Sigma_i m_i}{N}$$

We see that the standard deviation a varies with N as

$$\sigma \propto \frac{1}{\sqrt{N}}$$

i.e. greater the number of measurements, more precisely can we locate the true value.

12.7.4 Application of the Monte Carlo Method: Finding the Value of π

What is π? One can define it as the area of a unit circle. The following algorithm helps us to calculate the value of π. We shall exploit the symmetry of the problem and instead of finding area of the full unit circle, we calculate area of the first quadrant of the unit circle and multiply the result finally by four.

Step 1 :   Start a random number generator.

Step 2 :   Give the number of times hitting to be done, say N.

Step 3 :   Initialize counter, m, to count the random number lying within the unit circle.

Step 4 :   Begin a loop to shoot N times.

Step 5 :   Fetch two random numbers for x and y such that
            $0 \leq x \leq 1$ and $0 \leq y \leq 1$.

Step 6 :   If $(x^2 + y^2) \leq 1$ *i.e.*, the pair (x, y) lies within the quarter = circle, increment the counter $m = m + 1$.

Step 7 : Loop started at step 4 ends.

Step 8 : Calculate value or $\pi = 4$ (m / N) and print it.

Step 9 : Program ends.

Python Implementation

We can implement the above algorithm in the Python program as follows:

```python
#To find the value of pi using Monte Carlo Simulation
import random
N = input("Enter the number of times hitting to be
done:")
m = 0
for i in range(N):
    x = random.random()
    y = random.random()
    if (x**2 + y**2) <=1 :
        m += 1
PI = 4.0*(float(m)/float(N))
print PI
```

Output of the above program:

```
Enter the number of times hitting to be done:1000
3.232
Enter the number of times hitting to be done:2000
3.164
Enter the number of times hitting to be done:1500
3.14466666667
Enter the number of times hitting to be done:1200
3.15
Enter  the number of times hitting to be done:1100
3.12727272727
Enter the number of times hitting to be done:1300
3.17230769231
Enter the number of times hitting to be done:1200
3.13432
```

12.8 LORENZ EQUATION

The Lorenz equations for three dimensional systems from a drastically simplified model of convection rolls in the atmosphere are:

$$\frac{dx}{dt} = \sigma(y - x)$$

$$\frac{dy}{dt} = rx - y - xz$$

$$\frac{dz}{dt} = xy - bz$$

Now our aim is to solve these simultaneous non linear differential equations using Runge Kutta 4th order method. We store the values of x, y and z in a file. The program is implemented below:

Example 12.16.1: Python Implementation (File method)

```
sigma=10
r=28.
b=8/3.

def RK4(f,g,h ):
    fout = open("RK421.txt", "w")
    x=0
    y=1
    z=0
    n=1
    dt=0.005
    while(n<=20000):
            k1=dt*f(x,y,z)
             l1=dt*g(x,y,z)
            m1=dt*h(x,y,z)
            k2=dt*f(x+k1/2,y+k1/2,z+m1/2)
            l2=dt*g(x+k1/2,y+k1/2,z+m1/2)
            m2=dt*h(x+k1/2,y+k1/2,z+m1/2)
            k3=dt*f(x+k2/2,y+l2/2,z+m2/2)
            l3=dt*g(x+k2/2,y+l2/2,z+m2/2)
            m3=dt*h(x+k2/2,y+l2/2,z+m2/2)
            k4=dt*f(x+k3,y+l3,z+m3)
```

```
            l4=dt*g(x+k3,y+l3,z+m3)
            m4=dt*h(x+k3,y+l3,z+m3)
            x+=(k1+k2*2+k3*2+k4)/6
            y+=(l1+l2*2+l3*2+l4)/6
            z+=(m1+m2*2+m3*2+m4)/6
                n=n+1
            print x,y,z #correct answer
            if n>500 :
                        fout.write(str(x))
                        fout.write("\t")
                        fout.write(str(y))
                        fout.write("\t")
                        fout.write(str(z))
                        fout.write("\t")
                        fout.write("\n")

        return x,y,z
def f(x,y,z) :
    return sigma*(y-x)
def g(x,y,z) :
    return (r*x-y-x*z)
def h(x,y,z) :
    return (x*y-b*z)
x,y,z = RK4(f,g,h)
```

Output of the above Program:

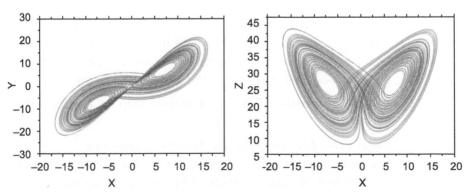

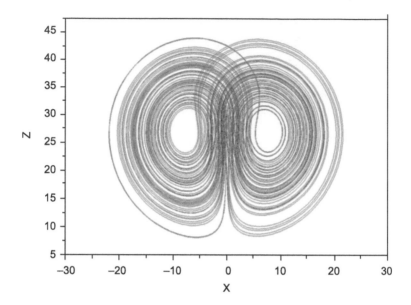

EXERCISES

12.1 The logistic map is a simple non-linear (see quadratic term) iterative mapping, often to study how complex, chaotic behaviour can arise in a deterministic system. The equation of the system is given

$$x_{n+1} = rx_n(1 - x_n) \text{ for } 0 \leq r \leq 4 \text{ and } 0 \leq r \leq 1$$

(a) Plot x_n vs. n for different values of r, $r = 1$, $r = 2.8$, $r = 3.4$ and $r = 4$ (make a subplots (2, 2) with appropriate labels). For a given value of r and $x_0 \in [0, 1]$, find the sequences $x_1, x_2, x_3 \ldots$. This process is called iteration.

(b) Plot the return map (x_n vs. x_{n+1}) for the above values of r.

(c) Plot the **cobweb diagram** for above values of r.

Note: Procedure of making cobweb diagram:
Given a map $x_{n+1} = f(x_n)$ and an initial condition x_0, draw a vertical line until it intersects the graph of f; that height is the output x_1. From x_1, draw a horizontal line until it intersect the diagonal line ($x_{n+1} = x_n$). Repeat the procedure to get the x_2 from x_1. Continue the process n times to generate the first n points in the orbit.

(d) Plot the **bifurcation diagram** of logistic map by varying r from 0 to 4.

Note: Procedure of making bifurcation diagram:
For each value of r, iterate the map 30 steps. Remove transients (discard first 20 points) and take 10 points to plot x_n vs. r.

(e) Plot the variation of **Lyapunov exponents** (λ) vs. r. Lyapunov exponent is a quantity that characterizes the rate of separation of infinitesimally close trajectories. For discrete time systems ($x_{n+1} = f(x_n)$), for an orbit starting with x_0, the Lyapunov exponents is given by

$$\lambda = \lim_{n\to\infty} \frac{1}{n} \sum_{i=0}^{n-1} \ln|f'(x_i)|.$$

12.2 Consider the following map

$$x_{n+1} = \begin{cases} rx_n & \text{for } 0 \le x_n < \dfrac{1}{2} \\[2mm] r - rx_n & \text{for } \dfrac{1}{2} \le x_n < n \end{cases} \quad \text{for } 0 \le r \le 2 \text{ and } 0 \le x \le 1$$

(a) Plot the return map (x_{n+1} vs. x_n) for different values of r, and see why this map is called the 'tent map'.

(b) Plot the corresponding cobweb diagrams and identify the nature of the orbits. Is it a steady state, periodic or chaotic?

(c) Plot the return map and cobweb diagram for $r = 2$.

(d) Plot the bifurcation diagram of tent map by varying r from 0 to 2.

(e) Plot the variation of Lyapunov exponents vs. r for tent map.

12.3. The baker's map of the square $0 \le x \le 1$, $0 \le y \le 1$ to itself is given by

$$(x_{n+1}, y_{n+1}) = \begin{cases} (2x_n, ay_n) & \text{for } 0 \le x_n < \dfrac{1}{2} \\[3mm] \left(2x_n - 1, ay_n + \dfrac{1}{2}\right) & \text{for } \dfrac{1}{2} \le x_n < n \end{cases}$$

where a is a parameter in the range $0 < a \le \dfrac{1}{2}$. The transformation is a product of two simpler transformations. A square is flattened into a $2 \times a$ rectangle. The rectangle is cut into half, yielding two $1 \times a$ rectangles, and the right half is stacked on the top of the left such that its base is at the level $y = 1/2$.

(a) Plot n vs. x_n and n vs. y_n for $a = 0.25$.

(b) Plot the attractors (x_n, y_n) of the baker's map for $a = 0.1$ and $a = 0.25$ respectively.

12.4. Henon map is the first two-dimensional dissipative quadratic map given by the coupled equations

$$x_{n+1} = 1 - ax_n^2 + y_n$$
$$y_{n+1} = \beta x_n$$

(a) Plot the attractors (y_n vs x_n) at ($\alpha = 1.4$, $\beta = 0.3$) and ($\alpha = 0.2$, $\beta = 1.01$).

(b) Plot the bifurcation diagram of the system. Fixed $\beta = 0.3$ and vary α from zero to 1.5.

12.5. Lorenz equations : Ed Lorenz (1963) derived the following set of equations for 3-dimensional system from a drastically simplified model of convection rolls in the atmosphere,

$$\frac{dx}{dt} = \sigma(y - x)$$

$$\frac{dy}{dt} = rx - x - xz$$

$$\frac{dz}{dt} = xy - bz$$

Simulate and visualize this system for $\sigma = 10$, $b = \dfrac{8}{3}$ and $r = 28$.

(a) Plot the 2D attractors $x(t)$ vs. $z(t)$ and $y(t)$ vs. $z(t)$

(b) Plot the 3D attractor $x(t)$, $y(t)$, $z(t)$.

(c) Plot the time series $x(t)$, $y(t)$, $z(t)$ vs. t.

(d) **Lorenz map:** To compare results to those obtained with for 1-D maps, Lorenz used a trick to obtained a map from a flow. Lets construct Lorenz map: Take $z(t)$ and find the successive local maxima z_n of $z(t)$. Plot the return map z_{n+1} vs. z_n.

Appendix I:
Objective Type Questions

OBJECTIVE TYPE QUESTIONS

1. What is the difference between an Algorithm and a Program?

    (a) An algorithm is a conceptual idea, a program is a concrete instantiation of an algorithm.

    (b) An algorithm is limited to mathematical operation, a program can specify all kinds of operations.

    (c) An algorithm makes a slow program run fast.

    (d) An algorithm deals with computer hardware, a program deals with computer software.

2. The output of the following program segment is:

```
>>> no = 5.0
>>> no == 5
>>> print no
```

    (a) 5   (b) 5.0   (c) True   (d) False

    (e) None

3. The output of the following program segment is:

```
>>> b = 10
>>> c = b > 9
>>> print c
```

    (a) 10   (b) error   (c) True   (d) False

    (e) None

4. Choose the correct answer.

A. "a" + "bc"
   (a)   abc (b) a+bc   (c) error   (d) can't say

B. 3* "bc"
   (a) 3bc (b) bcbcbc (c) error   (d) can't say

C. "3" * "bc"
   (a) 3bc (b) bcbcbc (c) error   (d) can't say

D. "abcd"[2]
   (a) abcdabcd   (b) c
   (c) a   (d) abcd2

E. "abcd"[:2]
   (a) abcdabcd   (b) abc   (c) cd
   (d)   ab

F. "abcd"[2:]
   (a) abcd2 (b) bc   (c) cd   (d) c

5. Assume that we've made the following assignments:

```
>>> str1 = 'hello'
>>> str2 = ','
>>> str3 = 'world'
```

Then answer the following questions:

A. str1[1] # same as print str1[1]
   (a) hello   (b) h
   (c) e   (d) world

B. str1[-1]
   (a) hello   (b) olleh
   (c) d   (d) o

C. len(str1)
   (a) 5   (b) 1
   (c) 6   (d) None of these

D. str1[len(str1)]
   (a) ,   (b) w   (c) o   (d) error

E. str1 + str2 + ' ' + str3
   (a) hello,world   (b) hello, world
   (c) hello   (d) None of these

F. str3 * 3
   (a) worldworldworld   (b) world world world
   (c) wor worl world   (d) worworlworld

```
G. 'hello' == str1
```
    (a) can't assign in this way
    (b) True
    (c) False   (d) error

```
H. 'a' in str3
```
    (a) True   (b) False
    (c) Can't say   (d) error

```
I. str4 = str1 + str3
   'low' in str4
```
    (a) True   (b) False
    (c) Can't say   (d) error

```
J. str3[:-1]
```
    (a) world   (b) worl
    (c) ello   (d) can't say

```
K. str4[1:9]
```
    (a) elloworl   (b) elloworld
    (c) error   (d) can't say

```
L. str4[1:9:2]
```
    (a) hlool   (b) hloo
    (c) elwr   (d) elwrd

```
M. str4[:: -1]
```
    (a) hellod   (b) worldh
    (c) helloworld   (d) dlrowolleh

6. For each of the following expressions, indicate the value that prints out when the expression is evaluated.

```
A. temp = '32'
   if temp > 85:
       print "Hot"
   elif temp > 62:
       print "Comfortable"
   else:
       print "Cold"
```
    (a) Cold   (b) Comfortable
    (c) Hot   (d) None of all

```
B. var ='Panda'
   if var == 'panda':
       print "Cute!"
   elif var == "Panda":
       print "Regal!"
   else:
       print "Ugly..."
```
    (a) Cute!   (b) Regal!
    (c) Ugly...   (d) None of all

```
C. temp = 120
   if temp > 85:
       print "Hot",
   elif temp > 100:
       print "REALLY HOT!",
   elif temp > 60:
       print "Comfortable",
   else:
       print "Cold"
```

    (a) REALLY HOT!   (b) Comfortable

    (c) Hot   (d) Hot REALLY HOT!

7. The values in a list are called _____

    (*a*) elements   (*b*) items

    (*c*) both (*i*) and (*ii*)   (*d*) None of the above

8. The output of the program segment is

```
numbers = [12, 34, 56]
numbers[1] = 78
print numbers
```

    (a) [12, 78, 56]   (b) [12, 34, 56]

    (c) [78, 34, 56]   (d) None of the above

9. The output of the program segment is

```
strings1 = ['Computer', 'Maths', 'Physics']
strings1[2] = 'Chem'
print strings1
```

    (*a*) ['Computer', 'Maths', 'Physics']

    (*b*) ['Computer', 'Maths', 'Chem']

    (*c*) Syntax error is expected

    (*d*) None of the above

10. The relationship between indices and elements of a list is called a _____

    (*a*) tapping   (*b*) grouping   (*c*) indexing   (*d*) mapping

11. Some of the properties of List indices are :

    A. Any integer expression can be used as an index.

    B. Any character expression can be used as an index.

    C. If you try to read or write an element that does not exist, you get an `IndexError`.

    D. If an index has a negative value, it counts backward from the end of the list.

    (*a*) All are correct

    (*b*) Only A, B and C are correct

    (*c*) Only A, C and D are correct

    (*d*) Only B, C and D are correct

12. The length of the following list is

```
List1= ['test', 12, [1,3,45], ['com', 'abc', 'ph']]
```
    (*a*) 8   (*b*) 18   (*c*) can't say   (*d*) four

13. The output of the following program segment is

```
a = [10, 20, 30]
b = [40, 50, 60]
c = a + b
print c
```
    (*a*) [10, 20, 30, 40, 50, 60]   (*b*) [50, 70, 90]
    (*c*) No output   (*d*) Syntax error

14. The output of the following program segment is

```
a1 =['a','b','c']
b1 =['x', 'y', 'z']
a1.extend(b1)
print a1
```
    (*a*) ['a', 'b', 'c', ['x', 'y', 'z']]   (*b*) ['a', 'b', 'c', 'x', 'y', 'z']
    (*c*) extend() can't be used with list   (*c*) extend() should be assign to a
                                              variable

15. The output of the following program segment is

```
def SUM(t):
      total = 0
      for x in t :
            total += x
      return total
t=[1, 2, 3, 4]
s=SUM(t)
print s
```
    (*a*) 10   (*b*) 1
    (*c*) No output   (*d*) Syntax error

16. Which of the following is NOT a built-in function in python?

    (*a*) exp ( )   (*b*) print ( ) (c) input ( ) (*d*) Sum ( )

17. The ability of calling one function from within another function in python is called _____

    (*a*) composition   (*b*) nesting of function
    (*c*) function nesting   (*d*) scaffolding

18. The built-in function isinstance ( ) is used to verify the

    (*a*) argument is of type integer   (*b*) return type of the function
    (*c*) type of the argument   (*d*) all of the above

19. The term `item` in python refers to

   (*a*) the keys in a dictionary   (*b*) the values in a dictionary
   (*c*) the values in a list   (*c*) the key value pair in a dictionary

20. Which of the following is correct

   (*a*) Lists can be values in a dictionary
   (*b*) Lists can be keys in a dictionary
   (*c*) Lists can be both values and keys in a dictionary
   (*d*) All are correct

21. A previously computed value that is stored for later use in a dictionary is called a

   (*a*) call graph   (*b*) memo   (*c*) hashable   (*d*) memorize

22. The output of the following program segment is

```
a = 'python'
b = [1, 2, 3, 4, 5]
c = zip (a, b)
print c
```

   (*a*) [(1, *p*), (2, *y*), (3, *t*), (4, *h*), (5, *o*)]
   (*b*) [(*p*, 1), (*y*, 2), (*t*, 3), (*h*, 4), (*o*, 5)]
   (*c*) ([1, *p*], [2, *y*], [3, *t*], [4, *h*], [5, *o*])
   (*d*) ([*p*, 1], [*y*, 2], [*t*, 3], [*h*, 4], [*o*, 5])

23. The output of the following program segment is

```
d = {'a':0, 'b':1, 'c':2}
t = d.items ()
print t
```

   (*a*) [('*a*', 0), ('*c*', 2), ('*b*', 1)]
   (*b*) {('*a*', 0), ('*c*', 2), ('*b*', 1)}
   (*c*) (['*a*', 0], ['*c*', 2], ['*b*', 1])
   (*d*) None of these

24. The output of the following program segment is

```
def sort_by_length(words):
    t = [ ]
    for word in words:
        t.append((len(word), word))
        t.sort(reverse=False)
        res = []
        for length, word in t:
        res.append(word)
    return res
first = ['moira', 'laishram', 'Naorem']
w= sort_by_length(first)
```

    (*a*) ['moira', 'laishram', 'Naorem']
    (*b*) ['moira', 'Naorem', 'laishram']
    (*c*) ['laishram', 'Naorem', 'moira']
    (*d*) ('laishram', 'Naorem', 'moira')

25. To interchange the three values say, x to y, y to z and z to x, which of the following code is most appropriate?

    (*a*) x , y, z = y, z, x   (*b*) x, y, z = z, x, y
    (*c*) x, y, z == z, x, y   (*c*) x , y, z == y, z, x

26. The output of the following code segment is, assume that there is no error:

```
>>> print type ('17')
```

    (*a*) <type str>   (*b*) <type tuple> (*c*) <type int> (*d*) <type string>

27. What will be the output when following statement is executed ?

```
>>>"abcd"[2:]
```

    (*a*) ab   (*b*) cd
    (*c*) ac   (*d*) None of these

28. The comment in python starts with:

    (*a*) #   (*b*) $ (*c*) """""   (*d*) both (*a*) and (*c*)

29. Which arithmetic operator/s cannot be used with strings?

    (*a*) +   (*b*) *   (*c*) **   (*d*) All of the above

30. What is the output when following code is executed ?

```
>>>print r"\nhello"
```

    (*a*) a new line and hello   (*b*) \nhello
    (*c*) the letter r and then hello   (*d*) Syntax Error

31. What is the output when following statement is executed ?

```
>>>print 'new' 'line'
```

    (*a*) new\nline   (*b*) newline
    (*c*) new line   (*d*) None of these

32. The value of the expression 0xA + 0xB + 0xC is :

    (*a*) 0xA0xB0xC (*b*) 33   (*c*) 36   (*d*) Error

33. What is the output of the following code segment?

```
number2=[2,3,4,5,6]
for i in range(len(number2)):
    number2[i] = number2[i] * 2
print number2
```

    (*a*) Syntax Error   (*b*) [2, 3, 4, 5, 6]
    (*c*) [4, 6, 8, 10, 12]   (*d*) [4, 8, 12, 16, 20]

34. What is the output of the following code segment?

```
for x in []:
    print x.
```

(*a*) No output   (*b*) Syntax error

(*c*) Loop will not execute   (*d*) Infinite loop

35. What is the output of the following code segment?

```
a2 = [1, 2,3,4]
b2 = a2.append(78)
print a2
print b2
c2 = a2 + [5,6]
print c2
```

(*a*) [1, 2, 3, 4, 78, 5, 6]   (*b*) [1, 2, 3, 4, 5, 6]

(*c*) [1, 2, 3, 4, 78, [5, 6]]   (*d*) None of these

36. What will be the value of **b2** in the above **Question 35**?

(*a*) [1, 2, 3, 4, 78]   (*b*) None

(*c*) [1, 2, 3, 4, 78, 5, 6]   (*d*) None of the above

37. The output of the following program segment is:

```
hour = 3
ones = hour%10
tens = hour // 10
print tens, ones, ":00"
print str(tens), str(ones), ":00"
print str(tens) + str(ones) + ":00"
```

(*a*) 03:00   03:00   03:00

(*b*) 03:00   03:00   03:00

(*c*) 03:00   03:00   03:00

(*d*) None of these

38. The output of the following program segment is:

```
nums = set([1,1,2,3,3,3,4,4])
print len(nums)
```

(*a*) 8   (*b*) 7   (*c*) 5   (*d*) 4

39. The output of the following program segment is:

```
x = True
y = False
z = False
if x or y and z:
    print "if block"
else:
    print "else block"
```

(*a*) True   (*b*) False
(*c*) if block   (*d*) else block

40. If the value of **y** is change to **True**, then the output will be:

(*a*) True   (*b*) False
(*c*) if block   (*d*) else block

41. What is the output of the following code segment?

```
a = [1,2,3,None,(),[],]
print len(a)
```

(*a*) 3   (*b*) 4   (*c*) 7   (*d*) 6

42. The output of the following code segment is:

```
counter = 1
def G_Counter():
    global counter
    for i in (1, 2, 3):
        counter += 1
G_Counter()
print counter
```

(*a*) 4   (*b*) 7   (*c*) 8   (*d*) 9

43. What gets printed?

```
dir1 = {"username", "code", "password", "name1"}
print dir1['password']
```

(*a*) username   (*b*) syntax error (*c*) password   (*d*) name1

44. The output of the following program segment is:

```
name = "Python Programming"
print "%s" % name[4:10]
```

(*a*) Python   (*b*) Programming
(*c*) on Prog   (*d*) on Progr

45. Which numbers are printed?

```
for i in  range(3):
    print i
for i in range(5,8):
    print i
```

(*a*) 1 2 5 6 7   (*b*) 0 1 2 5 6 7 8
(*c*) 0 1 2 3 5 6 7   (*d*) 0 1 2 5 6 7

46. What is the output of the following program segment?

```
values = [1, 2, 1, 3, 3]
numbers = set(values)
def checkthis(num):
    if num in numbers:
        return True
```

```
        else:
            return False
    for i in filter(checkthis, values):
        print i,
```
(*a*) 1 2 1 3 3   (*b*) 1 2 3
(*c*) True   (*d*) False

47. The above example 46 made a small changes inside the `for` loop. What will be the output ?

```
    values = [1, 2, 1, 3, 3]
    numbers = set(values)
    def checkthis(num):
        if num in numbers:
            return True
        else:
            return False
    for i in filter(checkthis, numbers):
        print i,
```
(*a*) 1 2 1 3 3   (*b*) 1 2 3
(*c*) True   (*d*) False

48. What sequence of numbers will be printed?

```
    no1 = [2, 3, 4, 5]
    def function1(num):
        return num ** 2
    for i in  map(function1, no1):
        print i
```
(*a*) 2 3 4 5   (*b*) 4 6 8 10
(*c*) 4 9 16 25   (*d*) Syntax Error

49. What gets printed by the code snippet below?

```
    import math
    print math.floor(5.5)
```
(*a*) 5   (*b*) 5.0
(*c*) 5.5   (*d*) 6.0

50. The output of the following program segment is:

```
    x = "test"
    y = 2
    print x + y
```
(*a*) test2   (*b*) test 2
(*c*) testtest   (*d*) Error is expected

51. What gets printed by the code snippet below?

```
    def Function2():
    "This is a test of __doc__ "
```

```
return 1
print Function2.__doc__[8:14]
```
(*a*) Function2   (*b*) This is
(*c*) a test   (*d*) Error is expected

52. What does the role of the following code?

```
sys.path.append('/root/test1')
```
(*a*) Changes the location that the python executable is run from.
(*b*) Changes the current working directory.
(*c*) Adds a new directory to search for python modules that are imported.
(*d*) Removes all directories for `test1`.

53. Which of the following `print` statements will print all the names in the list on a separate line?

```
names = ['Ramesh', 'Rajesh', 'Bob', 'Dilip', 'Mike']
(a) print "\n".join(names)
(b) print names.join("\n")
(c) print names.concatenate("\n")
(d) print names.append("\n")
```

54. What gets printed?

```
foo = (3, 4, 5)
print type(foo)
```
(*a*) int   (*b*) list   (*c*) tuple   (*d*) both (*a*) and (*c*)

55. The output of the following program is:

```
confusion = {}
confusion[1] = 5
confusion['1'] = 10
confusion[1] += 2
sum = 0
for k in confusion:
    sum += confusion[k]
print sum
```
(*a*) 7   (*b*) 9   (*c*) 15   (*d*) 17

56. What is the output of the following program segment?

```
dir1 = {1:'1', 2:'2', 3:'3'}
dir1 = {}
print len(dir1)
```
(*a*) 3   (*b*) 0   (*c*) 6   (*d*) Syntax Error

57. What is the output of the following program segment?

```
dir2 = {1:'1', 2:'2', 3:'3'}
del dir2[1]
```

```
dir2[1] = '10'
del dir2[2]
print len(dir2)
```

(*a*) 1   (*b*) 2

(*c*) 3   (*d*) Error is Expected

58. The output of the following program segment is :

```
names = ['Khan', 'Amir', 'Charles', 'Rajesh']
print names[-1][-1],
print names[1][1]
```

(*a*) Khan Rajesh   (*b*) A m

(*c*) s h   (*d*) h m

59. What gets printed?

```
numbers = [1, 2, 3, 4]
numbers.append([5,6,7])
print len(numbers)
```

(*a*) 5   (*b*) 4   (*c*) 7   (*d*) Syntax Error

60. If we change the last line in the above example , as follows, the output will be:

```
numbers = [1, 2, 3, 4]
numbers.append([5,6,7])
print numbers
```

(*a*) [1, 2, 3, 4, 5, 6, 7]   (*b*) [1, 2, 3, 4, [5, 6, 7]]

(*c*) {1, 2, 3, 4, [5, 6, 7]}   (*d*) (1, 2, 3, 4, [5, 6, 7])

61. The "in" operator can be used in:

(*a*) list   (*b*) set

(*c*) dictionary   (*d*) All of the above

62. The output of the following program segment is:

```
list1 = [1, 2, 3, 4]
list2 = [5, 6, 7, 8]
print len(list1 + list2)
```

(*a*) 5   (*b*) 8   (*c*) 36   (*d*) 4

63. The output of the following program segment is:

```
def addItem(New_list):
     New_list += [1]
list1 = [1, 2, 3, 4]
addItem(list1)
print len(list1)
```

(*a*) 5   (*b*) 8

(*c*) 4   (*d*) Error is expected

64. If we add `print New_list` the above example, Program 63, in the function definition, the output will be:

```
def addItem(New_list):
    New_list += [1]
    print New_list
list1 = [1, 2, 3, 4]
addItem(list1)
```

   (*a*) [1, 2, 3, 4]   (*b*) [2, 3, 4, 5]
   (*c*) [1, 2, 3, 4, 1]   (*d*) [1, 1, 2, 3, 4]

65. What gets printed?

```
tuple1 = (1, 2, 3, 4)
tuple1.append((5, 6, 7))
print len(tuple1)
```

   (*a*) 5   (*b*) 8
   (*c*) 4   (*d*) Syntax Error

66. What will be the return type of this function?

```
def function3(arg11, *arg2):
    print type(arg2)
function3('abc', 'defg', '123')
```

   (*a*) int   (*b*) list
   (*c*) tuple   (*d*) string

67. What is the return type of this function?

```
def function4(arg1, **arg2):
    print type(arg2)
function4('Title', a='123',b='456', c='789')
```

   (*a*) dictionary   (*b*) list
   (*c*) tuple   (*d*) string

68. What is the value of the agr1 in the above example, Program 67?

```
def function4(arg1, **arg2):
    print arg1
function4('Title', a='123',b='456', c='789')
```

   (*a*) Title   (*b*) 123
   (*c*) 456   (*d*) 789

69. What is the value of the agr1 in the above example, Program 67?

```
def function4(arg1, **arg2):
    print arg2
function4('Title', a='123',b='456', c='789')
```

   (*a*) { 'a' : 'Title', 'c' : '456', 'b' : '123' }
   (*b*) { 'a' : '123', 'c' : '789', 'b' : '456' }
   (*c*) { 'a' : '123', 'c' : '789', 'b' : '456', 'Title' : None}
   (*d*) None of these

70. What will be the output of the following program segment?
```
def myfunc(a, b, c, d):
    print b + c
nums = [1, 2, 3, 4]
myfunc(*nums)
```
(*a*) 1   (*b*) 3
(*c*) 5   (*d*) Syntax Error

71. By passing one more value in the **nums** list in example Program 70, what will be the output?
```
def myfunc(a, b, c, d):
    print b + c
nums = [1, 2, 3, 4, 5]
myfunc(*nums)
```
(*a*) 3   (*b*) 5   (*c*) 7   (*d*) Syntax Error

72. What gets printed?
```
one = chr(104)
two = chr(105)
print "%s%s" % (one, two)
```
(*a*) hi   (*b*) 104105
(*c*) '104105'   (*d*) None of these

73. The output of the following program segment is:
```
x = 1
y = 0
a = cmp(x,y)
if a < x:
    print "A"
elif a == x:
    print "B"
else:
    print "C"
```
(*a*) A   (*b*) B
(*c*) C   (*d*) None of these

74. What will be the output of the following program segment?
```
x = 10
y = "20"
z = 30
sum = 0
for i in (x,y,z):
    if isinstance(i, int):
        sum += i
print sum
```
(*a*) 60   (*b*) 20   (*c*) 30   (*d*) 40

75. What will be the output, assuming that the user enters the following at the prompt?

```
#: test
a = input ("#: ") # Type test
print a
```
(*a*) test   (*b*) #:test   (*c*) t   (*d*) Error

ANSWERS

1. (*a*)	**2.** (*b*)	**3.** (*c*)	**4.A.** (*a*)	**4.B.** (*b*)	**4.C.** (*c*)
4.D. (*b*)	**4.E.** (*d*)	**4.F.** (*c*)	**5.A.** (*c*)	**5.B.** (*d*)	**5.C.** (*a*)
5.D. (*d*)	**5.E.** (*b*)	**5.F.** (*a*)	**5.G.** (*b*)	**5.H.** (*b*)	**5.I.** (*a*)
5.J. (*b*)	**5.K.** (*a*)	**5.L.** (*c*)	**5.M.** (*d*)	**6.A.** (*c*)	**6.B.** (*b*)
6.C. (*c*)	**7.** (*c*)	**8.** (*a*)	**9.** (*b*)	**10.** (*d*)	**11.** (*c*)
12. (*d*)	**13.** (*a*)	**14.** (*b*)	**15.** (*b*)	**16.** (*d*)	**17.** (*a*)
18. (*c*)	**19.** (*d*)	**20.** (*a*)	**21.** (*b*)	**22.** (*b*)	**23.** (*a*)
24. (*b*)	**25.** (*b*)	**26.** (*a*)	**27.** (*b*)	**28.** (*d*)	**29.** (*c*)
30. (*b*)	**31.** (*b*)	**32.** (*c*)	**33.** (*c*)	**34.** (*a*)	**35.** (*c*)
36. (*b*)	**37.** (*a*)	**38.** (*d*)	**39.** (*c*)	**40.** (*c*)	**41.** (*d*)
42. (*a*)	**43.** (*b*)	**44.** (*c*)	**45.** (*d*)	**46.** (*a*)	**47.** (*b*)
48. (*c*)	**49.** (*b*)	**50.** (*d*)	**51.** (*c*)	**52.** (*c*)	**53.** (*a*)
54. (*c*)	**55.** (*d*)	**56.** (*b*)	**57.** (2)	**58.** (*d*)	**59.** (5)
60. (*b*)	**61.** (*d*)	**62.** (8)	**63.** (5)	**64.** (*c*)	**65.** (*d*)
66. (*c*)	**67.** (*a*)	**68.** (*a*)	**69.** (*b*)	**70.** (*c*)	**71.** (*d*)
72. (*a*)	**73.** (*b*)	**74.** (*d*)	**75.** (*d*)		

Appendix II:
Descriptive Type Questions

DESCRIPTIVE TYPE QUESTIONS

1. Write a python program to convert decimal numbers to binary numbers.

```python
def init(n) :
    print "\n The Decimal Number is :", n
def decimal_to_binary(no) :
    binary = 0
    i = 0
    while no != 0 :
        remender = no % 2
        no /= 2
        binary += pow(10, i) * remender
        i = i + 1
    return binary
x = decimal_to_binary(20)
init(20)
print "\n The Binary Number is : ", x
```

Output of the above program :
The Decimal Number is : 20
The Binary Number is : 10100

Alternative Method : Using Recursive Function

```
def dec_to_bin_rec(n) :
    """ using recurssive function"""
    if n < 0 :
        return 'Enter a Positive integer'
    elif n == 0 :
        return '0'
    else :
        return dec_to_bin_rec(n//2) + str(n%2)
y = dec_to_bin_rec(20)
init(20)
print "\n The Binary Number is (Recursive):", y
```

> **Output of the above program :**
> The Decimal Number is : 20
> Binary Number is (Recursive) : 010100

2. **Write a python program to reverse the digits of an integer**

   (a) without using recursive function

   (b) using recursive function

Ans: **(a)** We can write these programs in many different ways. In this example we are using a global variable.

```
no = 1234 # global variable
def init (no) :
    print " \n The Input Number is : ", no
def reverse( no) :
    rev = 0
    while no > 0 :
        remender = no % 10
        no = no // 10
        rev = remender + 10 * rev
    return rev
init(no)
result = reverse(no)
print 'The Reverse number is :',result
```

> **Output of the above program is :**
> The Input Number is : 234556
> The Reverse number is : 655432

Note: Instead of using our user defined function init(), we can use the built in function input() as follows:

```
def reverse ( no) :
    rev = 0
    while no > 0 :
        remender = no % 10
        no = no // 10
        rev = remender + 10 * rev
    return rev
no = input (" \n The Input Number is : ")
a = reverse (no)
print a
```

(b) Using Recursive function:

```
def reverse_rec(x, prod=0):
    if x < 10 :
        return prod + x
    else :
        prod = prod * 10 + x % 10 *10
        return reverse_rec(x/10, prod)
no = input ("\n Enter a Number :")
result = reverse_rec(no)
print 'The reverse number is = ',result
# Another way of calling the function is
print reverse_rec(34567)
```

```
Output of the above program is :
Enter a Number :45789
The reverse number is  =  98754
76543
```

Note: If you want to learn more about recursive function, run the following program and correct the output.

```
temp = 0 # Global variable
def reverse_rec(no, temp1) :
    global temp
    if no < 10 :
        return temp * 10 + no
    else :
        temp = (no % 10) + temp * 10
        no = no // 10
        reverse_rec(no, temp)
    return temp
```

3. Write a python program to find the Greatest common divisor(GCD) of two numbers

```
def GCD(a, b) :
    while b:
        a, b = b, a%b
    return a
a = input( "Enter the first number :")
b = input( "Enter the second number :")
gcd1 = GCD(a, b)
print gcd1
# Another way for calling the function is:
# print GCD(28,6) # output is 2
# print GCD(6,28) # same, output is 2
```

Second Method:

```
# This is the one in standard library
def GCD1(x, y) :
    while y != 0 :
        (x,y) = (y, x%y) # using tuples
    return x
a = input( "Enter the first number :")
b = input( "Enter the second number :")
```

```
gcd1 = GCD1(a, b)
print 'GCD is :', gcd1
```

Output of the above program :

Enter the first number :24

Enter the second number :56

GCD is : 8

Enter the first number :56

Enter the second number :24

GCD is : 8

Third Method : The traditional one

```
def gcd2(m, n) :
    if (n > m) :
        m = m + n
        n = m - n
        m = m - n
    while (m % n != 0 ) :
        temp = n
        n = m % n
        m = temp
    return n
a = input( "Enter the first number :")
b = input( "Enter the second number :")
gcd1 = gcd2(a, b)
#gcd1 = gcd2(24,56) # we can test in this way
#gcd1 = gcd2(56,24) # here first is greater than
second number.
print 'The GCD(HCF) is ', gcd1
```

The output of the above program is :

Enter the first number :56

Enter the second number :24

 The GCD(HCF) is 8

**Note: You can try for different numbers
including zeros and negative numbers.**

4. Write a python program to verify a given number is prime or not.

The minimum number of loop can be achieved by using the square root of the given number.

```python
import math
def is_prime(no) :
    test = True
for i in range( 2, int(math.sqrt(no) + 1)) :
    if no % i == 0 :
        test = False
        break # end of the loop
    if test :
        print "The Number is Prime Number."
    else :
        print "The Number is NOT a Prime Number."
n = input("Enter a number :")
is_prime(n)
```

Output of the above program :
Enter a number :55
The Number is NOT a Prime Number.
Enter a number :89
The Number is Prime Number.

Here are different ways for writing programs. Another way for writing the above program using nested function is as follows:

```python
import math
def main() :
    n = input("Enter a number :")
is_prime(n)
def is_prime(no) :
    test = True
    for i in range( 2, int(math.sqrt(no) + 1)) :
        if no % i == 0 :
            test = False
            break # end of the loop
```

```
        if test :
            print "The Number is Prime Number."
        else :
            print "The Number is NOT a Prime Number."
    main()
```

5. **Write a python program to generate prime numbers between 1 to 100.**

Check the indents in this program properly. For example the `if(counter == 2)` : will be outside the for loop and the increment of `i`, "`i += 1;`" will be outside the `if statement` as well as outside the `for loop`.

```
def generate_prime(no) :
    i = 1
    while i <=no :
        counter = 0
        for j in range(1,i+1) :
            if(i%j == 0) :
                counter += 1;
        if(counter == 2) :
            print "%4d\t" % i;
        i += 1;
n = input ("Enter the maximum value : ")
print "The Prime Numbers are: "
generate_prime(n)
```

```
Output of the above program :
Enter the maximum value : 20
The Prime Numbers are:
    2    3    5    7    11    13    17    19
```

We may write these programs in different ways, using list, tuples and dictionaries. Some of the different methods are shown below :

Method 1:

```
import math
def isPrime(n):
    for i in range(2, int(math.sqrt(n)+1)):
```

```
        if n % i == 0:
            return False
    return True
print 2
for n in range(3, 50):
    if isPrime(n):
        print n
```

```
Output of the above program :
 2   3   5   7   11   13   17   19   23   29   31   37
43   47
```

Method 2 : (output will be in the form of list)

```
def is_prime(num):
    """Returns True if the number is prime
        else False."""
    if num == 0 or num == 1:
        return False
    for x in range(2, num):
        if num % x == 0:
            return False
    else: # this else part is for 'for loop' not for if
          # statement
        return True
print filter(is_prime, range(1, 20))
```

```
Output of the above program :
    [2  3    5   7    11   13   17   19]
NOTE : if we put the else part for if state-
ment, output will be in this form :
    [3, 5, 7, 9, 11, 13, 15, 17, 19]
```

Method 3 : (generating prime numbers in one line)

```
print [x for x in range(2,100) if not [t for t
in range(2,x) if not x%t]]
```

```
Output of the above program :
[2, 3, 5, 7, 11, 13, 17, 19, 23, 29, 31, 37, 41,
43, 47, 53, 59, 61, 67, 71, 73, 79, 83, 89, 97]
```

Method 4 : (with built in functions)

```python
def gen_primes():
    #Generate an infinite sequence of prime numbers.
D = {}
q = 2
while True:
    if q not in D:
        yield q
        D[q * q] = [q]
    else:
        for p in D[q]:
            D.setdefault(p + q, []).append(p)
```

Method 5 :

```python
def primes_max(max):
    yield 2
    for n in range(3, max, 2):
        if is_prime(n):
            yield n
# the first 'count' primes
def primes_count(count):
    counter = 0
    num = 3
    yield 2
    while counter < count:
        if is_prime(num):
        yield num
        counter += 1
    num += 2
```

6. Write a python program to organize a given set of numbers in ascending order using

    A. Insertion sort

    B. Bubble sort

    C. Selection sort

A. Insertion sort :

Method 1:

```
def insertion_sort(a):
    if len(a) <= 1:
        return a
    key = 2
    while key < len(a):
        _key = key
        while a[_key] < a[_key-1] and _key > 0:
            tmp = a[_key]
            a[_key] = a[_key-1]
            a[_key-1] = tmp
            _key -= 1
            print a # To see the steps of sorting
        key += 1
    return a
a = [3, 5, 2, 1, 2]
print insertion_sort(a)
```

```
The output of the above program is :
[3, 2, 5, 1, 2]
[2, 3, 5, 1, 2]
[2, 3, 1, 5, 2]
[2, 1, 3, 5, 2]
[1, 2, 3, 5, 2]
[1, 2, 3, 2, 5]
[1, 2, 2, 3, 5]
[1, 2, 2, 3, 5]
```

NOTE : Just to see how the sorting technique works, we are using the 'print a' statement. If we remove this line, only the last line will be shown.

Method 2 : (input values using random numbers)

```
import random
Array = random.sample(range(30), 7)
```

```
print Array
First = 0
Last = len(Array) - 1
PositionOfNext = Last - 1
while PositionOfNext >= First:
    Next = Array[PositionOfNext]
    Current = PositionOfNext
    while (Current < Last) and (Array[Current]
    > Array[Current + 1]):
        Current = Current + 1
        Array[Current - 1], Array[Current] =
        Array[Current], Array[Current -1]
    #print Array
    Array[Current] = Next
    PositionOfNext = PositionOfNext - 1
print Array
```

```
Output of the above program :
(with Array = random.sample(range(30), 5))
[8, 24, 4, 10, 27]
[4, 8, 10, 24, 27]
(with Array = random.sample(range(30), 7))
[23, 24, 17, 25, 28, 18, 20]
[17, 18, 20, 23, 24, 25, 28]
```

NOTE : Just to see how the sorting technique works, we are using the 'print Array' statement inside the inner while loop. If we remove this line, the details of the sorting sequence will not be shown.

```
[17, 24, 10, 12, 28, 26, 27]
[17, 24, 10, 12, 26, 28, 27]
[17, 24, 10, 12, 26, 27, 28]
[17, 10, 24, 12, 26, 27, 28]
[17, 10, 12, 24, 26, 27, 28]
[10, 17, 12, 24, 26, 27, 28]
[10, 12, 17, 24, 26, 27, 28]
[10, 12, 17, 24, 26, 27, 28]
```

B. Bubble Sort :

Method 1(for beginners) : This method just shows the sorting technique of Bubble sort. Here we don't use any function :

```
list1 = [12, 5, 13, 8, 9, 65]
i=0
while i < len(list1)-1:
    if list1[i] > list1[i+1]:
        x = list1[i]
        list1[i] = list1[i+1]
        list1[i+1] = x
        print list1
        i=0
        continue
    else:
        i+=1
print(list1)
```

```
The output of the above program is :
[5, 12, 13, 8, 9, 65]
[5, 12, 8, 13, 9, 65]
[5, 8, 12, 13, 9, 65]
[5, 8, 12, 9, 13, 65]
[5, 8, 9, 12, 13, 65]
[5, 8, 9, 12, 13, 65]
```

Method 2 : In this Bubble Sorting method, the larger element shifts all the way to the end. And decrement the end counter, "n" so that we will not have to compare it again. The while loop will continue as long as there are possible exchanges are available.

```
def bubble_sort(list1):
    exchanged = True
    iteration = 0
    n = len(list1)
    while(exchanged):
        iteration += 1
        exchanged = False
```

```
            Move the largest element to the end
            of the list
            for i in range(n-1):
                if list1[i] > list1[i+1]:
                    exchanged = True
                    list1[i], list1[i+1] = list1[i+1],
                    list1[i]
            n -= 1 # Largest element already towards
            the end
            print list1
        print 'Iterations: %s' %(iteration)
        return list1
print ("\nBubble Sort : \n")
list1 = [12, 5, 13, 8, 9, 65]
print bubble_sort(list1)
```

```
Output of the above program :
Bubble Sort :
[5, 12, 8, 9, 13, 65]
[5, 8, 9, 12, 13, 65]
[5, 8, 9, 12, 13, 65]
Iterations: 3
[5, 8, 9, 12, 13, 65]
```

C. Selection Sort :

```
def selection_sort(list):
    for index in range(0, len(list)):
        iSmall = index
        for i in range(index,len(list)):
            if list[iSmall] > list[i]:
                iSmall = i
        list[index],list[iSmall]= list[iSmall],
        list[index]
        print list
    return list
```

```
# if __name__ == '__main__': # Another way in python
print selection_sort([5,2,4,6,1,3,])
```

```
Output of the above Program :
[1, 2, 4, 6, 5, 3]
[1, 2, 4, 6, 5, 3]
[1, 2, 3, 6, 5, 4]
[1, 2, 3, 4, 5, 6]
[1, 2, 3, 4, 5, 6]
[1, 2, 3, 4, 5, 6]
[1, 2, 3, 4, 5, 6]
```

Note: Just to see how this sorting technique works, we are using the 'print list' statement inside the outer for loop. If we remove this line, the details of the sorting sequence will not be shown, only the last line will be the output of the program.

6. Write a python program to find out the Prime numbers from a sequence of Fibonacci series.

Method 1: In this method, we generate Fibonacci number one by one and check the number is prime number or not.

The function `check_Fibonacci()` generates the Fibonacci numbers while the function `isPrime()` checks the number is prime or not.

```
from math import sqrt
def isPrime(no):
    n = abs(int(no))
    if n < 2:
        return False
    elif n == 2:
        return True
    elif not n and 1:
        return False
    else:
        for x in range(3, int(sqrt(n)+1)):
            if n % x == 0:
```

```
                     return False
                 return True
def check_Fibonacci(no):
    first_num = 1
    second_num = 1
    third_num = 0
    counter = 0
    while (1):
        third_num = first_num + second_num
        if (isPrime(third_num)== True):
            counter += 1
            print third_num
            if (counter == no):
                break
        first_num = second_num
        second_num = third_num
print" How many prime numbers you want from the
Fibonacci series:"
n = input("Enter the number :")
print("The prime numbers are : ")
check_Fibonacci(n)
```

```
Output of the above program segment is:
How many prime numbers you want from the Fi-
bonacci series:
Enter the number :15
The prime numbers are :
2  5  13  21  55  89  233  377  987  1597  4181  6765
17711  28657  75025
```

Method 2 : In this program we generate all the Fibonacci numbers using a list. And store in it using append() function. After that we call one by one the Fibonacci numbers from the list and check it whether the number is prime number or not.

```
from math import sqrt
def fibonacci(no)  :
```

```
        a=[0, 1]
        first_term = 0
        second_term = 1
        print "The Fibonacci Series is:\n"
        #print first_term, second_term
        for i in range(no) :
            third_term=first_term + second_term
            first_term=second_term
            second_term=third_term
            #print " %-6ld\t" %third_term;
            a.append(third_term);
        print a
print("\n\nThe Prime Numbers in the Fibonacci
Series are:\n")
        for j in range (3,n+1):
            for z in range (2, int(sqrt(a[j])+1)):
                if a[j] % z == 0 :
                    break
            else :
                print a[j],
n = input( "\nEnter a Number :")
fibonacci(n)
```

```
Output of the above program segment is :
Enter a Number :14
The Fibonacci Series is:
[0, 1, 1, 2, 3, 5, 8, 13, 21, 34, 55, 89, 144,
233, 377, 610]
The Prime Numbers in the Fibonacci Series are:
2 3 5 13 89 233
```

7. **Write a python program to accept a string and convert the given string into a dictionary. From that dictionary, using the concept of reverse lookup, print all the corresponding keys with its corresponding values.**

```
def histogram(s):
```

```
        d = dict() # d = {}
        for c in s:
            if c not in d:
                d[c] = 1
            else:
                d[c] += 1
        return d
def reverse_lookup(d, v):
    list1 =[]
    for k in d:
        if d[k] == v:
                list1.append(k)
    return list1
    raise ValueError, 'Value does not appear in
    the directory.'
s = raw_input(" Enter a String :")
s1 = histogram(s)
v = s1.values() # values
new_v =[]
for i in v :
    if i not in new_v :
        new_v.append(i)
for i in new_v :
    k = reverse_lookup( s1, i)
    print "\nThe keys and values are ", i, " -->"
    for i in k :
        print i,
```

Output of the above program is :

Enter a String :parrot

```
The keys and values are  1  -->
a p t o
The keys and values are  2  -->
r
```

References

1. https://www.python.org/
2. E Balagurusamy, *Programming in ANSI C*, The McGraw-Hill Companies,2008.
3. Danial Liang, Y, *Introduction to Programming using Python*, Pearson, 2013.
4. Allen Downey, *Think Python*, Green Tea Press, 2014.
5. Magnus Lie Hetland, *Beginning Python*, Apress, 2008.
6. http://www.mypythonquiz.com/question.php
7. http://stackoverflow.com/

Index